Praise for *Food Rebellions!*

In this very timely book, two of the world's global food system, Eric Holt-Giménez and of hunger and the food price crisis, locating of capitalist industrial production dominated by corporations and driven by the search for profits for the few instead of the welfare of the many. The picture that emerges is a political economy of global production that is failing badly in terms of feeding the world and is itself contributing to the spread of inequalities that promote hunger.

Walden Bello, president of the Freedom from Debt Coalition and professor of sociology at the University of the Philippines

---

The small-scale farming systems spread widely across Africa are a social and ecological asset. As Food Rebellions! *demonstrates, planting indigenous trees and using traditional farming methods enhances environmental conservation and preserves local biodiversity. At a time of economic crisis, sustainable agriculture and the economic empowerment it can generate will be key to the survival of the many African families headed by women.*

Professor Wangari Maathai, Nobel Peace Prize winner and author of *The Challenge for Africa* (Heinemann, 2009)

The 20th century was the century of technological revolutions. This century is that of the knowledge revolution, and Eric Holt-Giménez and Raj Patel are in its vanguard. At long last, a book which confronts the real issues: How do we reform our food systems to avoid environmental disaster? How do we recapture the production and distribution of food from the tyranny of unchecked markets? This book is vital reading for all concerned with the right to food.

Olivier De Schutter, UN Special Rapporteur on the Right to Food

---

Food Rebellions! *demonstrates the imperative to protect and enhance the multifaceted knowledges, practices, and lands of sustainable farmers. Contrary to some views, sustainable food systems are most helpful to the poor, especially the rural poor, who suffer the most from the dire social and ecological effects of industrial agriculture. Absent perverse subsidies to agrifood industries, what is good for farmers is also good for eaters and citizens. Holt-Giménez and Patel contribute to an urgent awakening—*

supported by practical experiments and expert reports — to the necessity and possibility for transforming food systems. "Like cracks in the asphalt," solutions to the global food crisis can restore resilient food systems across the world.

Harriet Friedmann, professor of sociology, University of Toronto

Food Rebellions! *is a tour de force! Not only does it describe the corporate assault on the human right to food in all of its political, economic, cultural and environmental dimensions, it also documents the many ways rural and urban people are actively building alternative food systems to defend their land, water, seeds and livelihoods. These social movements and this inspiring book could not have come at a better time. In the face of multiple global crises, the growing local and international trends toward food sovereignty provide us with the hope we need to build a just and sustainable future.*

Paul Nicholson, Ehne (Basque Farmers Union) and Via Campesina

Food Rebellions! *situates with accuracy and precision the true meaning, causes and dynamics of what is commonly referred to as the "global food crisis." It shows how skewed and dysfunctional the global food system is, and how the concentration of market power by a handful of transnational corporations translates to power over land, water, food and, indeed, life itself. In Part One, the authors trace with startling clarity the history of hunger and poverty to North–South politics of domination and gender and class inequalities. They compel us to confront the questions: Who is hungry, and why? But all is not gloom and doom. In Part Two, the authors inspire us with examples of creative and constructive resistance by food producers and workers against the capitalist driven food system and propose strategies for transforming the food system — strategies that are practical and well within the reach of anyone concerned with social and political justice. If* Food Rebellions! *does not make food rights activist of its readers, I don't know what will. This is a truly remarkable book.*

Shalmali Guttal, senior associate of Focus on the Global South, Bangkok, Thailand

Hunger is a global scandal. I would call it a global structure of sin! Claiming to solve world hunger with the industrial age's solutions the corporations of the world really only structure the world for more hunger, poverty and misery. Food Rebellions! *provides an analysis that is clear, documented and searing in its challenge to the powers that be. It provides solutions appropriate to our ecological age and to a new era of food democracy and food sovereignty. It reflects the vision of those most affected by the food crisis. I strongly endorse this book and I hope that it gets a wide readership. More importantly, though, I hope that it gets the support of the nations of the world suffering from hunger and poverty. It provides insights from those directly suffering from hunger and poverty, who have a right to be heard.*

Miguel d'Escoto Brockmann, president of the 63rd General Assembly of the United Nations

---

The high and mighty proponents of free trade speak for the interests of multinational corporations when they try to stifle the economic policies that empower peasants, family farmers, and farm workers to grow healthy supplies of food while protecting Mother Earth. Rather than continue down the path that led to today's economic, environmental, and social catastrophe, Food Rebellions! *calls on us to raise our voices in rebellion, join together, and place sustainable production and rural economic opportunity at the base of our recovery efforts.*

George Naylor, former president of the National Family Farm Coalition—USA

Pambazuka Press – www.pambazukapress.org

 Formerly known as Fahamu Books, we are a pan-African publisher of progressive books that aim to stimulate debate, discussion, analysis and engagement on human rights and social justice in Africa and the global South. We have published books and CD-ROMs on Africa, the African Union, capacity building for civil society organizations, China and Africa, conflict, human rights, media, trade, aid & development, and women's rights.

Pambazuka News – www.pambazuka.org

 With over 1,500 contributors and an estimated 500,000 readers, Pambazuka News is the authoritative pan-African electronic weekly newsletter and platform for social justice in Africa, providing cutting-edge commentary and in-depth analysis on politics and current affairs, development, human rights, refugees, gender issues and culture in Africa.

Food First – www.foodfirst.org

FOODFIRST Called one of the country's "most established food **B O O K S** think tanks" by the New York Times, the Institute for Food and Development Policy, also known as Food First, is a "people's" think tank. Our work informs and amplifies the voices of social movements fighting for food sovereignty: people's right to healthy and culturally appropriate food produced through ecologically sound and sustainable methods.

Grassroots International – www.grassrootsonline.org

Grassroots Grassroots International works to create a just and **INTERNATIONAL** sustainable world by building alliances with progressive movements. We provide grants to our global South partners and join them in advocating for social change. Our primary focus is on land, water and food as human rights and nourishing the political struggle necessary to achieve these rights.

Food Rebellions!

Crisis and the Hunger for Justice

Eric Holt-Giménez and Raj Patel

with Annie Shattuck

Pambazuka Press

A publication of Pambazuka Press, Food First Books
and Grassroots International

Published 2009 by Pambazuka Press
Cape Town, Dakar, Nairobi and Oxford
www.pambazukapress.org and www.pambazuka.org

Food First Books
Oakland CA
www.foodfirst.org

and Grassroots International
Boston MA
www.grassrootsonline.org

Pambazuka Press, Fahamu Ltd, 2nd floor, 51 Cornmarket Street,
Oxford OX1 3HA, UK
Pambazuka Press, c/o Fahamu Kenya, PO Box 47158, 00100 GPO, Nairobi,
Kenya
Pambazuka Press, c/o Fahamu Senegal, 9 Cité Sonatel 2, POB 25021, Dakar-Fann,
Dakar, Senegal
Pambazuka Press, c/o Fahamu South Africa, c/o 27A Esher St, Claremont, 7708,
Cape Town, South Africa

Food First Books, 398 60th Street, Oakland, CA 94618, USA

Grassroots International, 179 Boylston Street, 4th floor
Boston, MA 02130, USA

First published 2009

Copyright © 2009 Institute for Food and Development Policy

British Library Cataloguing in Publication Data
A catalogue record for this book is available from the British Library

US Library of Congress Cataloging-in-Publication Data on file
with Food First Books

UK ISBN: 978-1-906387-30-3 (paperback)
UK ISBN: 978-1-906387-42-6 (ebook)
US ISBN-13: 978-0-935028-34-8
US ISBN-10: 0-935028-34-X

Printed in Canada

Contents

Boxes

Foreword

By Walden Bello

The world is now plunged into a deep recession—indeed, into what many are beginning to call a depression. In the North, the current crisis initially took the form of a financial collapse that then brought down the real economy. The financial crisis in the North, however, was preceded by the food price crisis which rolled through the South beginning in 2006.

In 2006–08, food shortages became a global reality, with the prices of commodities spiraling beyond the reach of vast numbers of people. International agencies were caught flatfooted, with the World Food Program warning that its rapidly diminishing food stocks might not be able to deal with the emergency.

Owing to surging prices of rice, wheat and vegetable oils, the food import bills of the least developed countries (LDCs) climbed by 37% in 2008, from $17.9 million in 2007 to $24.6 million in 2008, after having risen by 30% in 2006. By the end of 2008, the United Nations reported, "the annual food import basket in LDCs cost more than three times that of 2000, not because of the increased volume of food imports, but as the result of rising food prices." These tumultuous developments added 75 million people to the ranks of the hungry and drove an estimated 125 million people in developing countries into extreme poverty.

For some countries, the food crisis was the proverbial straw that broke the camel's back. Some 30 countries experienced violent popular actions against rising prices in 2007 and 2008, among them Bangladesh, Burkina Faso, Cameroon, Côte'd'Ivoire, Egypt, Guinea, India, Indonesia, Mauritania, Mexico, Morocco, Mozambique, Senegal, Somalia, Uzbekistan, and Yemen. Across the continents, people came out in their thousands against the uncontrolled rises in the price of staple goods, which their countries had to import because of insufficient domestic production. Scores of people died in these demonstrations of popular anger.

The most dramatic events transpired in Haiti. With 80% of the population subsisting on less than two dollars a day, the doubling of the price of rice in the first four months of 2008 led to "hunger so tortuous that it felt like [people's] stomachs were being eaten away by bleach or battery acid," according to one account. Widespread rioting broke out that only ended when the Senate fired the prime minister. In their intensity, the Haiti riots reminded observers of the anti-International Monetary Fund (IMF) riots in Venezuela—the so-called Caracazo—almost two decades ago, which reshaped the contours of that country's politics.

In this very timely book, two of the world's most prominent critics of the global food system, Eric Holt-Giménez and Raj Patel, dissect the causes of hunger and the food price crisis, locating them in a political economy of capitalist industrial production dominated by corporations and driven by the search for profits for the few instead of the welfare of the many. Here, greed has played just as destructive a role as in the financial sector.

Holt-Giménez and Patel discuss the contributions of, among other factors, the Green Revolution, export-oriented agriculture, structural adjustment, genetically modified seeds, speculation, and biofuel production. The picture that emerges is a political economy of global production that is failing badly in terms of feeding the world and is itself contributing to the spread of inequalities that promote hunger.

This is not, however, simply a critique of capitalist industrial agriculture. Drawing on the rich experiences of small farmers, peasant communities, indigenous nations, and cooperatives, Holt-Giménez and Patel show that even as the old system unravels, alternative modes of agricultural production are alive and offer the prospect of sufficient food for people along with equity and ecological sustainability. The many people's organizations at the forefront of the struggle for more effective ways of organizing the production and distribution of food, such as Via Campesina, the Landless Movement (MST) in Brazil, and small-scale urban agriculture in the North, are showcased. And an important lesson they are learning—and which this book stresses—is the inseparability of economic organization, technology, equity, sustainability, and democracy.

The aim of the organization of food production, Holt-Giménez and Patel remind us, is to enable people not simply to exist but to live and enjoy the flourishing of the spirit—to eat so they may live in the fullest sense. This is where the capitalist organization of food production has failed so miserably; it has condemned hundreds of millions of people to purely subsisting and millions of others to below subsistence. This is why people throughout the world are, in a multitude of ways, actively organizing to supplant it.

Walden Bello is the recipient of the Right Livelihood Award in 2003, president of the Freedom from Debt Coalition, senior analyst at the Bangkok-based research and advocacy institute Focus on the Global South, and professor of sociology at the University of the Philippines.

1

Introduction to the Global Food Crisis

A "Silent Tsunami"?

The World Food Program's description of the global food crisis raises the specter of a natural disaster surging over an unaware populace that is helpless in the face of massive destruction. With half of the world's population at risk of hunger, the current food crisis is certainly massive and destructive. But the reasons so many people have limited access to food are anything but natural. On the contrary, decades of skewed agricultural policies, inequitable trade, and unsustainable development have thrown the world's food systems into a state of chronic malaise, in which crises are all the more severe. Though hunger comes in waves, not everyone will "drown" in famine. In fact, the planet's food crises are making a handful of investors and multinational corporations very rich—even as they devastate the livelihoods of the poor and put the rest of the world at severe environmental and economic risk. The surge of food "riots" not only in poor countries like Haiti, but in resource-rich countries like Brazil—and even in the industrialized nations of Europe and in the United States—reflects the fact that people are not just hungry, they are rebelling against an unjust global food system.

The food crisis is anything but silent—and as long as we are aware of its true causes, we are not helpless.

The World Bank, the World Trade Organization, and the US Department of Agriculture all carefully avoid addressing the root causes of the food crisis. Accepting the paradigm of the dominant industrial food system, the "solutions" they prescribe are simply more of the same approaches that brought about the crisis in the first place: increased food aid, de-regulated global trade in agricultural commodities, and more technological and genetic fixes. These measures do nothing to challenge the *status quo* of corporate control over the world's food, and there has been little effective leadership in the face of the crisis. Nor has there been any informed public debate about the real reasons the numbers of hungry people are growing, or what we can do about it. The future of our food systems is being decided *de facto* by unregulated global markets, speculators, and global monopolies.

For decades, family farmers, rural women, and communities around the world have resisted the destruction of their native seeds and worked hard to diversify their crops, protect their soil, conserve their water and forests, and establish local gardens, markets, businesses and community-based food systems. There are many highly productive, equitable and sustainable alternatives to the present industrial practices and corporate monopolies holding the world's food hostage, and literally millions of people working to advance these productive methods now. What is missing is the political will on the part of governments, industry and finance to support these solutions.

In 1996 Via Campesina, a world-wide peasant, pastoralist, and fishers federation, launched a global call for *food sovereignty*—the human right of all people to healthy, culturally appropriate, sustainably grown food, and the right of communities to determine their own food systems. The call both echoed and amplified the voices of social movements everywhere that are struggling for land reform, control over local resources, fair markets, neighborhood food systems and sustainable agriculture.

In Europe, smallholder movements, organic farmers, and campaigners from GMO-free (free of genetically modified organisms), anti-hypermarket, and fair trade movements have been fighting to counter the dominance of monocultures and monopolies with local, agroecologically produced and fairly traded food. In the United States, family farmers, students, and neighborhood activists, along with many professionals and socially conscious entrepreneurs have been advocating for fresh and healthy food, and higher incomes to afford it. From the growing food justice movement in underserved communities in the industrial North, to the long-standing agroecological alternatives in Latin America, Asia and sub-Saharan Africa, people are organizing to establish productive, equitable food systems. These movements combine livelihood struggles with activism, and agroecological practice with food advocacy.

The spectrum of activities of these movements runs from the

informed engagement of local citizens in food policy councils and the direct advocacy of civil society in international institutions, to the constructive resistance of community supported agriculture, GMO-free territories, and peasant land invasions. A convergence of wide-ranging and often surprising alliances between farmers, businesses, community organizations, local health departments, food workers, farm laborers, agroecologists, environmentalists, human rights advocates, and indigenous movements are steadily building these sustainable and equitable practices and political will for the democratization of our food systems.

They are racing against time. Agriculture—primarily industrial, petroleum-guzzling, chemical-heavy agriculture—contributes 13%–18% of the world's greenhouse gases (Steinfeld et al. 2006; FAO 2008a) and uses 60%–70% of the planet's diminishing fresh water supplies (FAO 2008b; Pacific Institute 2008). As a sector, agriculture both induces and suffers the most from climate-related hazards. One-sixth of the world's population is desperately hungry—just as many people suffer from obesity (Patel 2007). Cheap, bad food (highly processed and brimming with salt, sugar, fat and high-fructose corn syrup) has become a public health blight on poor and middle-income people alike. Increases in obesity, hypertension, type-2 diabetes and other diet-related diseases—primarily in lower-income sectors—account for 12% of the increase in health spending in the United States alone (Thorpe et al. 2004). This pattern is taking hold in Europe and is increasingly appearing in the emerging economies of the global South.

After decades of policies designed to replace family farms with agribusiness, the flight of farmers from the countryside is massive. In the United States, there are more people in prison than on the land. In addition, huge, for-profit detention centers hold thousands of undocumented immigrants—many of whom left economically devastated farming communities in Mexico and Central America in desperate search of work. As a result of recent food price inflation, many producing countries placed export bans on basic grains—an unsurprising reaction to an unreliable global market, but a disaster for importing countries that have lost the capacity to produce their own food. The industrial agrifoods system has become the bane of the poor and the pork barrel of multinational corporations. A financial cornucopia producing over $6 trillion a year in wealth, industrial agrifood is tragically one of the planet's major drivers of global poverty and environmental destruction.

The global financial crisis, following on the heels of the food crisis, is its decidedly less-silent "tsunami twin," a child of the same deregulated expansion of global capital. The financial crisis deepens the food crisis by restricting production credit and consolidating even more power in the hands of those few corporations influential enough to obtain taxpayer-funded bailouts for their reckless investments. The tsunami twins are reshaping our food and financial systems, and provoking a flurry of high-level agreements between governments and financial houses, even as both farmers and consumers suffer under the squeeze of market volatility and disappearing credit.

This book is an analytical resource for anyone interested in understanding the food crisis. It is also an informational manual for those who wish to do something about it. In Part One, we give a succinct and straightforward analysis of both the proximate and root causes of the food crisis. We provide specific examples of how the people of the global South and underserved communities of the industrial North lost control over their food systems and how this led to the systemic vulnerability that underlies today's crisis. In Part Two, the solutions advanced by the world's main financial, aid, and development institutions are analyzed and critiqued, and the unexamined assumptions and unstated agendas behind these initiatives are exposed. We follow with examples of the "struggle for spaces and places" between these projects and the grassroots efforts advancing equitable, agroecological and locally controlled food production and distribution from around the world. The conclusion of *Food Rebellions!* sets out concrete steps, policies and actions to solve the food crisis and put the world's food systems on the road to food sovereignty.

PART ONE

THE REAL STORY
BEHIND THE WORLD
FOOD CRISIS

2

Hunger, Harvests and Profits: The Tragic Records of the Global Food Crisis

The year 2008 saw record levels of hunger for the world's poor at a time of record global harvests and record profits for the world's major agrifoods corporations. The contradiction of increasing hunger in the midst of wealth and abundance unleashed a flurry of worldwide "food riots" not seen for many decades. Protests were sparked by skyrocketing food prices. In June of 2008, the World Bank reported that global food prices had risen 83% over the previous three years and the UN's Food and Agriculture Organization (FAO) cited a 45% increase in their world food price index in just nine months (Wiggins and Levy 2008). *The Economist's* comparable index stood at its highest point since it was originally formulated (USDA 2008a). In March 2008, average world wheat prices were 130% above their level a year earlier, soy prices were 87% higher, rice had climbed 74%, and maize was up 31% (BBC 2008). The United States Department of Agriculture (USDA) predicted that at least 90% of the increase in grain prices would persist during the next decade (USDA 2008a).

Because they spend as much as 70%–80% of their income on food, the world's poor—particularly women—were hit the hardest. Not surprisingly, people took to the streets in Mexico, Morocco, Mauritania, Senegal, Indonesia, Burkina Faso, Cameroon, Yemen, Egypt, Haiti and over 20 other countries. Scores of people were killed and hundreds injured and jailed. In Haiti, the poorest country in the western hemisphere, food prices increased by 50%–100%, driving the poor to eat biscuits made of mud and vegetable oil. Angry protestors forced the Haitian prime minister out of office. Street rebellions continued to flare in Haiti as successive hurricanes pummeled the island, destroying livelihoods and putting food farther and farther out of people's reach.

The World Bank warned that without massive, immediate injec-

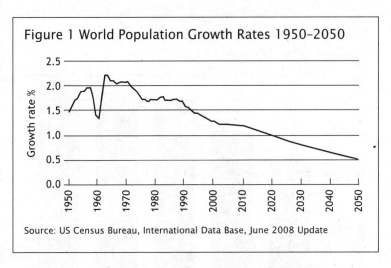

Figure 1 World Population Growth Rates 1950–2050

Source: US Census Bureau, International Data Base, June 2008 Update

tions of food aid, 100 million people in the global South would join the swelling ranks of the word's hungry (World Bank 2008a). But the protests were not simply crazed "riots" by hungry masses. Rather, they were angry demonstrations against high food prices in countries that formerly had food surpluses, and where government and industry were unresponsive to people's plight. Painfully prophetic, they signaled the onset of the global financial crisis and economic recession now gripping the world economy.

The food crisis appeared to explode overnight, reinforcing fears that there are just too many people in the world. But according to the FAO, with record grain harvests in 2007, there was more than enough food in the world to feed everyone—at least 1.5 times current demand. In fact, over the last 20 years, food production has risen steadily at over 2% a year, while the rate of population growth has dropped to 1.14% a year (Hansen-Kuhn 2007; Rossi and Lambrou 2008). Globally, population is not outstripping food supply. According to the World Food Program, over 90% of the world's hungry are too poor to buy enough food. "We're seeing more people hungry and at greater numbers than before," says executive director Josette Sheeran, "There is food on the shelves but people are priced out of the market" (Lean 2008a).

Sheeran's comments were significant, not only because they confirmed that hunger is due to poverty and not a lack of food, but also because they remind us that widespread world hunger is nothing

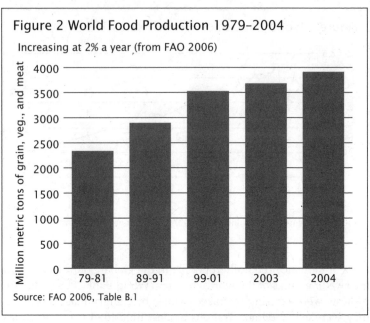

Figure 2 World Food Production 1979–2004

Increasing at 2% a year (from FAO 2006)

Source: FAO 2006, Table B.1

new. Despite the oft-cited production gains of the Green Revolution, and despite repeated development campaigns over the last half-century—most recently, the Millennium Development Goals—the number of desperately hungry people on the planet has grown steadily from 700 million in 1986, to 800 million in 1998, to over 982 million today (Lappé et al. 1986; Lappé et al. 1998; Matthews 2008).

Before the media picked up on the present food crisis there were already 852 million hungry people in the world (De Schutter 2008). Of these, nearly 600 million were women and girls (UNIFEM 2005). Even in the United States—the richest country in the world—35 million people were "food insecure" in 2006: unsure of their next meal or unable to procure sufficient daily calories. Ironically, most of the US's hungry people live in its rural "breadbaskets" working low-wage jobs in the "food industry." Others live in the "food deserts" of its inner cities where low-income residents must travel for miles to find fresh food.

While seen as a serious problem, this situation was not generally referred to as a "global food crisis" by governments, the international aid institutions or the mainstream media. For over 30 years, thanks to market oversupply from Northern grain-producing countries, food

BOX 1

Hunger's Timeline

- 1974—500 million hungry people in the developing world. The World Food Conference pledges to eradicate child hunger in 10 years.
- 1996—830 million hungry people. The World Food Summit pledges to reduce the number of hungry people by half by 2015.
  - 12% of the US population is hungry. US Farm Bill increases food nutrition programs (Food Stamps, Women, Infants and Children in Need) and food banks augment donations of government surplus with locally and industry-donated food.
- 2000 Millennium Summit—World leaders pledge to reduce extreme poverty and hunger by half by 2015.
- 2002—850 million hungry people. The World Food Summit+5 admits to poor progress on the Millennium Development Goals.
- 2009—1 billion hungry people. The FAO High-Level Conference on World Food Security announces that instead of reducing the ranks of the hungry to 400 million, hunger has increased. The World Bank recalculates its projections for extreme poverty upwards from 1 billion to 1.4 billion. Over 3 billion people live on about $2-$5 a day. (These projections were made before the financial crisis engulfed the world, driving down income and ushering in the global recession.)
  - 12% of the US population is still hungry. Despite $60 billion yearly in government food nutrition programs and the explosion of over 50,000 food banks and food pantries across the nation, one in six children in the US go hungry each month and 35 million people cannot ensure minimum daily caloric requirements.

---

prices had been on a steady downward trend. It was widely assumed that eventually—as the promised benefits from liberalized global trade began to kick in—the poor would be able to buy the food they needed.

Not until the dramatic displacement of *food* crops by *fuel* crops began in 2006 did the FAO begin to warn of impending food shortages. But in the winter of 2007, instead of shortages, food price inflation exploded on world markets—in spite of that year's record harvests. As a result, the number of hungry people jumped dramatically to 982 million in just one year (USDA 2008a). The riots that quickly spread across the globe took place not in areas where war or displacement made food unavailable (e.g., Darfur), but where available food was too expensive for the poor to buy.

The overnight reversal of a 30-year global trend in cheap food quickly became known as the "global food crisis."

The immediate reasons for food price inflation were easily identified: droughts in major wheat-producing countries in 2005–06; less than 54 days in global grain reserves; high oil prices; the diversion of 5% of the world's cereals to agrofuels and 70% to grain-fed beef; and, as prices began to rise, financial speculation. Though grain futures and oil prices have recently dropped and an increase in agricultural growth is projected for 2009, retail food prices remain high in much of the global South, and most experts agree they will not drop back to pre-2007 levels. And what if they did? Even at those prices nearly a billion people on the planet were food insecure. The global economic recession will lower real incomes for millions, if not billions, of people, likely offsetting any gains from cheaper oil and grain. Unmanaged supply, unregulated markets and tight credit will continue to provoke chronic price volatility—boom and bust markets that do nothing to stabilize food production or ensure food security. If we focus only on food and oil prices, we are a long way from solving the food crisis.

Why? Because, drought, low reserves, agrofuels, oil prices and speculation are only the *proximate* causes of the food crisis. By themselves, these factors do not explain why—in a dazzlingly affluent global food system—in 2010 up to three billion people will be food insecure. The food crisis has a distinctly feminine face: seven in ten of the world's hungry are women and girls and fully two-thirds of the planet's female population may be at risk. These proximate factors tipped us over the precipice, but to understand how and why we got there in the first place, we need to address the *root* causes of the global food crisis as well. In this book, we'll do both.

Proximate Causes: The Multiple Triggers of Food Price Inflation

The current food price spike is a combination of five distinct factors: the high price of oil, the spread of agrofuels, the consumption of grain-fed meat, weather-related crop failures, and then—after the initial prices increases—market speculation.

The volatile price of oil

Fluctuating wildly between $40 and $140 a barrel, the price of oil exercises a ratchet effect of intermittent, but upward, pressure on food prices. High oil prices increase food production and distribution costs that then drive up food prices. Low oil prices take some of this pressure off, but rather than bring the shelf price of food down, these savings show up as windfall profits on the balance sheets of grain traders and retailers. The net effect is that though consumer food prices may have periods of leveling, they tend to "stick," not fall. Modern industrial food requires many more calories of fossil fuel to produce than the calories people consume. This energy is required not only to transport food considerable distances (an average of 1,200–1,800 miles worldwide), but also for the manufacture of inorganic fertilizers and pesticides, and to operate machinery. The United States Department of Agriculture's price index for nitrogen fertilizers was 118 in 2000, but reached 204 by 2006 (Wiggins and Levy 2008). The USDA projects that over the next decade cereals will cost 15% more per ton to produce (USDA 2008b). The upward production cost trend will continue.

Rising meat consumption

The Northern media has been quick to blame China and India for driving up cereal prices because of increasing consumption of grain-fed meat among growing middle classes. In this view, economic progress in developing economies puts a strain on the world's food supply. But the fact is that both China and India are practically self-sufficient in grain and meat. Some analysts insist that neither country will become a major meat or grain importer (Thompson 2007). (Actually, while less significant in absolute amounts, per capita grain consumption rates in the US are increasing over twice as fast as India's.)[1]

The impact of meat diets on the world's food systems has as much to do with *how* meat is produced and *who* is making a profit as it does with increasing incomes. True, meat and dairy consumption rose an average of 5% a year in China and other Asian countries over the last two decades—five times faster than in the developed world. The so-called 'nutrition transition' has meant that increasing numbers of people in developing countries aspire to the unsustainable diets found in the United States and Western Europe, where consumers currently eat three times more meat than people in the developing world.[2]

BOX 2

Policy Versus Practice: The World Bank's CAFOs

Various World Bank publications address confined animal feedlot operations (CAFOs), pointing to their harmful effects on animals, humans, and the environment. Even the International Finance Corporation (IFC), the private sector lending arm at the World Bank Group published a *Good Practice Note* stating that "Animal welfare is just as important to humans (as to animals) for reasons of food security and nutrition. Better management of and care for livestock can... address nutritional deficiencies and food shortages as well as ensuring food safety" (IFC 2006). Moreover, a book written for the World Bank titled *Livestock Development: Implications for Rural Poverty, the Environment, and Global Food Security* offered a critical view of the current feedlot production of cattle, pigs, and poultry. The document declared that "A sea change will be required from the international livestock community to make people, rather than animals, the focus of livestock development. Focusing on the multiple functions of livestock and including poor non-livestock keepers as potential beneficiaries of livestock development deserve a higher priority than the former exclusive focus on increasing milk and meat output for urban consumers" (de Haan 1999).

However, the livestock projects financed by the World Bank and other development banks (e.g., ADB—Asian Development Bank; IADB—Inter-American Development Bank) conflict directly with these policy recommendations. Numerous instances, past and present, demonstrate flagrant violations of their own stated best practices. Cameroon, People's Republic of China, Croatia, Mexico, Russia, Turkey, and Uruguay all have World Bank projects that work to develop CAFOs. One of the most egregious cases involved a $93.45 million loan to China in 1999 to finance its six-year "Smallholder Cattle Development Project." According to the World Bank, "the project has... accelerated the industrialization process of cattle production, [and has] effectively integrated the dispersed breeding units (feedlots and breeding/fattening households) with the large market, and the big-scale-sequential industrial chain... has come into being" (World Bank 2006). Indeed, the project topped its stated goal of constructing 130 feedlots by actually creating 144 such facilities. Other similar examples involving beef, pork, and poultry include:

However, meat *production* in the global South has grown just as rapidly, and developing countries now supply over half of the world's meat. The increase in global meat production is primarily due to the expansion of industrial feedlots that now produce 40% of all meat—at great social and environmental cost (Delgado et al.

Name of Project*	Lender	Country	Year	$ millions	Product
Animal Feed Project	WB	China	1996	150	feed, pork, poultry
Mironovsky Khleboprodukt CJSC I and II	IFC	Ukraine	2003	110	poultry
Procesadora Nacional de Alimentos C.A. - PRONACA I and II	IFC	Ecuador	2004, 2008	50	poultry
Support New Livestock Products in Uruguay	IADB	Uruguay	2005	15.8	beef
Wadi Holdings I and II	IFC	Egypt	2005, 2007	40	poultry
Agrokor Project I and II	IFC	Croatia	2006, 2008	112	beef, pork
Bertin Ltd.	IFC	Brazil	2006	90	beef
Weishi Integrated Feedlot and Beef Processing	ADB	China	2006	64.3	beef

*All projects can be found at the World Bank, IFC, IADB, and ADB websites. These cases represent only a portion of projects that contrast sharply with the policy recommendations made to the World Bank that explicitly warn of the negative effects of industrial livestock production. The gap between what the World Bank says and the projects it actually finances appears meaty, indeed.

de Haan, Cornelius. 1999. *Livestock Development: Implications for Rural Poverty, the Environment, and Global Food Security*. Washington DC: The World Bank.

IFC. 2006. Animal Welfare in Livestock Operations. In *Good Practice Note* 6. World Bank Group.

World Bank. 2006. Implementation completion report on a loan in the amount of US$93.5 million to the People's Republic of China for a smallholder cattle development project. In *Report* 35962. World Bank.

1999; Nierenberg 2004). According to Henning Steinfeld, senior officer of Animal Production and Health of the FAO, the tremendous growth in industrial feedlots is due to the fact that policies, subsidies and economies of scale all favor large-scale livestock production (Steinfeld et al. 2006).

Industrial meat production is growing in China, thanks to US-based Tyson and Smithfield corporations' rapidly expanding Asian operations. Already China represents 9% of Tyson's international sales (Tyson Foods Inc. 2008). Larry Pope, president and chief executive officer of Smithfield stated, "China is experiencing rapid growth in pork consumption and consumes more pork than the rest of the world combined. COFCO (Smithfield's Chinese affiliate) has introduced Smithfield to many opportunities in China and we look forward to continue working together" (Smithfield Foods 2008). The World Bank is eagerly financing the expansion of feedlots in China through its private-sector arm, the International Finance Corporation (IFC). Not only do feedlots contaminate air and groundwater, they have displaced hundreds of thousands of integrated, mixed farming systems and concentrated control of the world's meat supply in fewer and fewer corporate hands.

Feedlots are steadily depleting the world's grain supply. It takes seven to eight kilos of grain to produce one kilo of beef. As more and more resources are dedicated to producing *feed* for large-scale feedlot production, less land, water and resources are available for *food*: the grains, tubers, and pulses that keep over half the world's population alive. Therefore, it is not China and India's increased meat consumption *per se* that is putting a strain on the food system, it is the Northern model of industrial meat production that has pushed into the global South over the last two decades. Ironically, the growth of feedlots is encouraged by the very countries and development institutions—like the US and the World Bank—that now chastise China and India for eating too much meat!

Unfavorable climate

Poor harvests have been caused by climatic events, like the multiple, devastating hurricanes in 2008 in Burma, Cuba and Haiti. Extreme weather has been responsible for poor harvests, particularly in South East Asia and in Australia. An average of 500 weather-related disasters are now taking place each year, compared with 120 in the 1980s; the number of floods has increased six-fold over the same period (Oxfam 2007). This has at least as much to do with the increasing vulnerability of the environment and human populations as to weather-related hazards. Disasters are as much a function of poverty as climate (Blaikie et al. 1994; O'Keefe 1976).

Current climate models predict that the worst agricultural losses from climate change will be at lower latitudes and tropical climes (IPCC 2007). Small farmers in the developing world will likely suffer much more than their wealthier counterparts in the global North (Cline 2007). In fact, some scientists even predict a windfall for Northern farmers under certain climate change scenarios. This disproportionate effect stands to exacerbate the food crisis enormously. A 2°C–5°C rise in global temperatures stands to make water resources much more scarce and expand the reach of deserts in mid-latitudes (IPCC 2007). Combined with more extreme weather events, climate change is predicted to have "potentially severe" impacts on agriculture in the global South (Cline 2007).

Ironically, it is the small-scale farmers, also largely in the global South, who are doing the most to cool the planet. Agriculture is responsible for at least 13.5% of global greenhouse gas emissions (IPCC 2007)—largely from synthetic fertilizers and large animal feedlots. Greenhouse gas emissions—soil carbon loss, methane, and nitrous oxide—are all largely results of industrial-scale agricultural operations. In small-scale organic systems, carbon is actually stored in the soil at a rate of about four tons per hectare (La Salle and Hepperley 2008). Organic, sustainable agriculture that localizes food systems has the potential to mitigate nearly a third of global greenhouse gas emissions and save one-sixth of global energy use (Ho et al. 2007).

Agrofuels

The agrofuels "boom" touched off a frenzy of venture capital investment in fuel crops, initially driving up the price of grains and food. This attracted further speculation with food. The use of arable land to grow industrial fuel crops is increasingly recognized as a net negative in terms of climate change, water and energy use (Fargione et al. 2008). The World Bank deemed the shift towards agrofuel crop production to be a significant contributor to food price rises (World Bank 2008a). Agrofuels have been criticized for their discriminatory effects against women, who disproportionately shoulder the consequences of the current food crisis (Rossi and Lambrou 2008). While the European Union appears to be retreating somewhat from its bullish agrofuels policy, the US continues to strongly support expansion. By establishing mandatory targets, protective tariffs, and blender's credits, the US provides the agrofuels industry with a guaranteed market for global expansion. However, as we will see, the long-term impact of agrofuels on the food system goes beyond food price

BOX 3

Speculation 101: Gambling with the World's Food

Commodities *futures* markets have existed in the United States since 1865. Futures are standardized legal agreements to transact in a physical commodity at some designated future time. Commodities futures contracts have provided producers and consumers with a mechanism to offset the risk of an asset's changing price, known as *hedging*. A farmer able to sell futures contracts for the expected harvest can lock in a price for his or her crop. Hedging allows those actually trading material goods some protection from price fluctuations and allows them to plan their businesses effectively (Masters and White 2008).

In contrast to hedgers, *speculators* bet on the probability that the price of a commodity will rise or fall in order to profit from changes in prices. Normally, they invest in the debt, equity and real estate markets. However, after the technology and housing bubbles burst, investors sunk their money into commodity futures. While a traditional speculator looks for short-term price shifts from which they can profit, another type of speculator called an *index investor* seeks long-term investments by hoarding commodities futures contracts for extended periods and betting on the continued rise of commodity prices.

There comes a time when index investors must "roll" their commodities futures position in order to avoid delivery of physical commodities (they don't actually want the product—just the change in value). "Rolling"

---

inflation and the "food versus fuel" debate, and concerns the transformation and corporate centralization of key aspects of the world's food and fuel systems under one giant industrial roof. While the agrofuels "boom" may be a proximate cause of the food crisis, the industry itself is structurally one of the root causes of hunger. We'll address agrofuels again later in the book.

Speculation

As the combination of drought, agrofuels and oil prices drove food prices upwards, speculators flocked to the commodities market, eager to take advantage of rising prices. Perceived as safe bets (after the US's sub-prime mortgage meltdown), international investors sunk money into commodity futures in rice, wheat, corn and soy. This drove prices up even further, which in turn attracted more futures investment—

means a trader simultaneously buys a more distant future and sells their closer-to-expiration future. "By periodically rolling over commodity futures contracts, the funds allow investors to gain investment returns equivalent to the change in price of a single commodity, or an 'index' of several commodities" (Collins 2008). The flooding of the commodities futures market by index investors has thrown off the balance between hedgers and speculators, leading to higher prices and creating greater price volatility.

"When hedgers dominate the commodities futures marketplace, prices accurately reflect the supply and demand realities that physical consumers and producers are experiencing in their businesses" (Masters and White 2008, 12). But in a market that is dominated by speculators, trading is not necessarily disciplined by traditional supply and demand considerations. Remember, speculators don't have any interest in physical trading, but in making a profit. When all index speculators roll their positions in unison, it impacts the markets significantly by creating "artificial demand." As money flows into commodities futures markets, the market price goes up. Who initiates a buy order and why it is initiated are irrelevant when it comes to an order's impact on market prices. Since almost all trading is anonymous, an order from a hedger will have the exact same price impact as an index investor. "Today, commodity prices have risen dramatically but *there are few shortages...*" It is *prices*, not *supply*, that has led to food riots around the globe (Masters and White 2008).

Collins, B. 2008. Hot commodities, stuffed markets, and empty bellies. *Dollars & Sense* 9:70.
Masters, M.W., and A.K. White. 2008. The Accidental Hunt Brothers. *Special Report.* www.loe.org/images/080919/Act1.pdf (accessed May 4, 2009).

with little or no oversight or controls coming from governments. After banking deregulation in the 1980s and the Commodities and Futures Modernization Act 2000, banks began to "cross over" into other financial instruments, such as commodities. Commodities traders also began crossing over into financial markets, traditional agribusinesses like Cargill and ADM grew investment arms, and traditional venture capital firms like Goldman Sachs even became importers of physical goods. All these crossovers make it difficult to control food speculation, or to prevent a crisis in one sector of the economy (such as the sub-prime mortgage disaster) from spreading through all sectors. Though rising commodity prices and financial speculation with food have happened before, the "quantity... of money flowing through today's markets is unprecedented in human history" (Collins 2008).

The total holdings of commodity index investors on regulated US exchanges increased nearly 25 fold in five years, from $13 billion in

2003 to $317 billion. In the same time frame, commodity prices tripled (Masters and White 2008). As of April 2008, index investors owned approximately 35% of all regulated corn futures contracts in the US, 42% of all soybean contracts, and 64% of all wheat contracts, compared to minimal holdings in 2001. These holdings are immense: the wheat holdings alone could account for the delivery of two times US annual wheat consumption (Collins 2008). Index speculators are now the single most dominant force in the commodities futures markets, even though their buying and trading has nothing to do with the supply and demand fundamentals of any single commodity.

BOX 4

The Monopolies Controlling our Food Systems

Food industry concentration, through waves of mergers and buyouts, has increased dramatically in the past two decades. Up and down the value chain and across sectors, no area has been immune to this trend. Economists measure the concentration ratio of an industry as the total size of the given market divided by the market share of the top four firms in that market—a measure commonly known as the CR4. In the global food system, each link in the industrial food chain, from production factors to retail, is now in the hands of just a few players:

- 83.5% of all of the beef packing in the United States is in the hands of four firms (Tyson, Cargill, Swift & Co., and National Beef Packing Co.) (Hendrickson 2007).
- Five firms (WalMart, Kroger, Albertson's, Safeway, and Ahold) control 48% of US food retailing (Hendrickson 2007).
- Smithfield, Tyson, Swift & Co., and Cargill pack 66% of all pork in the US (Hendrickson 2007).
- 71% of all soybean crushing is done by three firms—ADM, Bunge, and Cargill (Hendrickson 2007).
- Three firms control nearly 90% of global trade in grains (ADM, Bunge, and Cargill).[i]
- Just two firms, DuPont and Monsanto, control nearly 60% of the United States corn seed market (Hendrickson 2007).
- Monsanto and Dupont together control 65% of the maize seed market and 44% of the soy market (Action Aid International 2005).

Behind the Proximate Causes: Food Systems in Crisis

The proximate causes leading to the food crisis are only the immediate reasons why protests around food are so prevalent. High food prices are only a problem because nearly 3 billion people—half of the world's population—are poor and near-poor. Half of these people—1.4 billion—earn less than $2 a day (of these, the "extremely poor" earn less than $1 a day). Many of those officially classified as poor are subsistence farmers who have limited access to land and water and cannot compete in rigged global markets. Something is

---

Just a quick glance at the list is a who's who of the titans of the industrial agrifoods complex—Bunge, ADM, Monsanto, DuPont, Cargill, WalMart, and others. Not by coincidence, firms in the food industry have seen sky-high profits (De La Torre Ugarte 2008). Control of the global food system by a few powerful corporations is extremely dangerous. Free market dogma states that market competition will lead to overall efficiency and therefore lower prices for consumers. In fact, what the numbers indicate is that the increase in market concentration has led to extreme volatility. Unless we want the world food system to end up like the world financial system, these monopolies must be dismantled.

i. In a speech by Dr. Bill Heffernan at the AAI meeting of agrifood industry researchers, Paris. January 15, 2005. Quoted in O'Driscoll 2005.

Action Aid International. 2005. *Power Hungry: Six Reasons to Regulate Global Food Corporations*. Johannesburg: Action Aid International. www.actionaid.org.uk/_content/documents/power_hungry.pdf (accessed April 9, 2009).

De La Torre Ugarte, Daniel G. and Sophia Murphy. 2008. The global food crisis: Creating an opportunity for fairer and more sustainable food and agriculture systems worldwide. In *Eco-Fair Trade Dialogue* 11. Heinrich Boell Foundation and MISEREOR. http://www.ecofair-trade.org/pics/de/EcoFair_Trade_Paper_No11_Ugarte__Murphy_1.pdf (accessed April 9, 2009).

Hendrickson, Mary and William Heffernan. 2007. *Concentration of Agricultural Markets*. National Farmers' Union. www.nfu.org/wp-content/2007-heffernanreport.pdf (accessed April 9, 2009).

O'Driscoll, Peter. 2005. Part of the Problem: Trade, Transnational Corporations and Hunger. In *Center Focus*. Washington DC: Center of Concern.

deeply dysfunctional when the majority of the world's farmers go hungry. In this sense, high food prices do not constitute a crisis in and of themselves—high food prices combined with widespread poverty are symptoms of a global food system in crisis.

The root causes of the food crisis lie in a skewed global food system that has made Southern countries and poor people everywhere highly vulnerable to economic and environmental shock. This vulnerability springs from the risks, inequities and externalities inherent in food systems that are dominated by a globalized, highly centralized, industrial agrifoods complex. Built over the past half-century—largely with public funds for grain subsidies, foreign aid, and international agricultural research—the industrial agrifoods complex is made up of multinational grain traders, giant seed, chemical and fertilizer corporations, global processors and supermarket chains. These global companies dominate local markets and increasingly control the world's food-producing resources: land, labor, water, inputs, genes, and investments.

While many activists assert that the global food system is "broken," for these companies, it works extraordinarily well. Today two companies, Archer Daniels Midland and Cargill capture three-quarters of the world grain trade (Vorley 2003). Chemical giant Monsanto controls 41% of maize seed and 25% of soy production (GRAIN 2007). Monopolization of the world's food provides these companies with unprecedented market power. This translates into profits in the midst of crisis. In the last quarter of 2007 as the world food crisis was breaking, Archer Daniels Midland's earnings jumped 42%, Monsanto's by 45%, and Cargill's by 86%. Mosaic Fertilizer, a subsidiary of Cargill, saw profits rise by 1,200% (Lean 2008b). Even the livestock sector in the US—supposedly hard hit by soaring grain prices—saw profit increases in the first and second quarters of 2008 up 429% compared to a year earlier.

The trend towards monopoly control over our food systems is particularly visible from within the US, where a handful of transnational corporations in the industrial agrifoods complex mediate the relationship between three million farm operators and 300 million consumers and gobble up the lion's share of the food dollar. Over the last 60 years, the companies that buy, sell, and process farm products, and the chains that distribute and sell food, have steadily eroded farmers' profits. While in the 1950s US farmers received 40%–50% of the food dollar, today they receive around 20% (National Farmers Union 2008; University of Georgia College of Agriculture

Figure 3 The Hourglass: The Concentration of Power and Players in the Food System

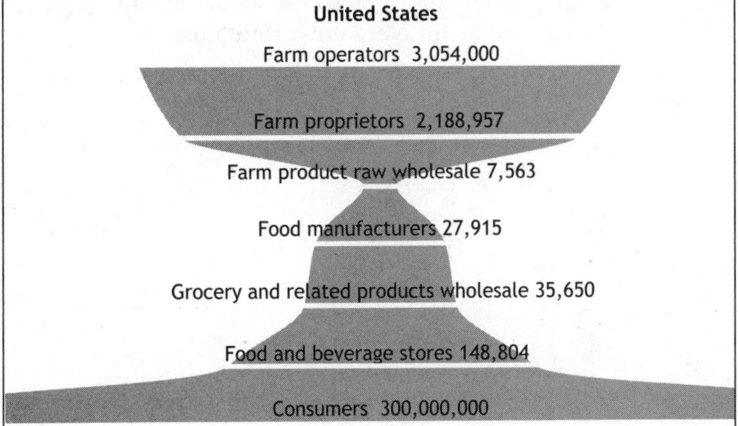

United States

Farm operators 3,054,000

Farm proprietors 2,188,957

Farm product raw wholesale 7,563

Food manufacturers 27,915

Grocery and related products wholesale 35,650

Food and beverage stores 148,804

Consumers 300,000,000

Not to scale

and Environmental Sciences 2008). With this, farmers must still pay for inputs and labor. The erosion of the farmer's share of the food dollar has been accompanied by the steady disappearance of farmers. From a high of seven million farms in 1935, the US now has less than two million. Agricultural land area—around a billion acres—has changed little. This means that tremendous concentration has taken place. Over the last 70 years, the average farm size doubled. US direct payment subsidies amount to billions of dollars a year. Even the US Department of Agriculture concedes that these direct subsidies have the effect of further concentrating land ownership in agriculture (Roberts and Key 2008).

The profits and concentration of market power in the industrial North mirror the import dependence, food deficits and the loss of control over food systems in the global South.[3] Fifty years ago, developing countries had yearly agricultural trade surpluses of US$1 billion. Today, after decades of development and the global expansion of the industrial agrifoods complex, the Southern food *deficit* has ballooned to US$11 billion/year (FAO 2004). The cereal import bill for low income food deficit countries reaching over US$ 38 billion in 2007/2008 (De Schutter 2008). The FAO predicts it will grow to US$50 billion by 2030.

The rise of food dependency and hunger in the global South is not the result of overpopulation, a conspiracy, or the "invisible hand" of the market. As we shall see, it is the result of the systematic destruction of Southern food systems through a series of economic development projects imposed by the Northern institutions.

3

Root Causes: How the Industrial Agrifoods Complex Ate the Global South

The destruction of Southern food systems occurred over time, with starts and stops, and was very uneven, geographically and across social sectors. Moments of breathtaking yield increases in parts of Asia and the Americas were paralleled by flat productivity gains elsewhere on the same continents (even within the same regions), and followed by long periods of grinding stagnation. The flowering of agribusiness was accompanied by the impoverishment of many farming communities; the decline in the dominance of the "dessert" commodities (bananas, sugar, cacao, coffee) was accompanied by the growth in non-traditional exports (cut flowers, winter vegetables). The expansion of agricultural land came at the expense of forests, prairies and wetlands. Cheap, abundant food was dogged by persistent hunger, diet-related diseases and an obesity epidemic. In the process, global forms of industrial production, processing and distribution steadily undermined local, national and regional food systems.

The emergence of the global food system parallels the rise of the industrial agrifoods complex that controls and profits from it. Its history is complicated and often violent, one that stitches the livelihoods, diets, environments and economies of producers and consumers in the industrial North to those in the global South—often to the detriment of both. It was not the result of chance or a "natural" progression of events. There are four key threads to the story that will help us understand how the global system emerged, how the industrial agrifoods complex became dominant, and why both are failing people and the planet:

Development and the Green Revolution (1960–90)

Agriculture was a key component of "development"—the extension of the industrial North's economic model to the "lesser developed countries" of the global South. The modernization of agriculture, based on the industrialization of farm inputs, was deemed the "Green Revolution."[4] Though credited for saving the world from hunger, the Green Revolution led to the monopolization of seed and chemical inputs by Northern companies, the loss of 90% of the South's agricultural biodiversity, the global shift to an oil-based agricultural economy, and the displacement of millions of peasants to fragile hillsides, shrinking forests and urban slums. Contrary to popular belief, the Green Revolution also *produced* as many hungry people as it saved (Lappé et al., 1998).

Overproduction and food aid

Following the Great Depression, the US created a farm price support system to manage supply and make sure farmers' production costs were more or less commensurate with the prices they received for their grain. Surplus production was held in reserves that were used in lean years and sent abroad to allies during World War II. Following the war, the US stepped up agricultural production, filling up the reserves and sending surplus to Europe during reconstruction. European agriculture recovered because governments bought all of farmers' grains at a good price, stimulating supply. With the spread of new technologies like fertilizer, pesticides, and mechanization, Europe and the US began chronically producing more than they could consume. Instead of cutting back on production, Northern governments used combinations of subsidies, tariffs, price supports, and quotas to ensure a continuous oversupply. Why? On the one hand this lowered the price of grains to Northern agro-industries and traders. On the other, these cheap surpluses could be channeled into food aid and "dumped" into overseas markets. Overproduction in the North was used as a battering ram to open up markets in the global South for the benefit of those same agro-industries—to the detriment of farmers in the South who could not compete. In the US price supports were lowered yearly, overproduction increased year after year, and farmers were steadily forced to leave the land.

Because it is designed to ensure overproduction, most of the benefits of government support to agriculture are captured by large corporations who revel in the cheap grain. While the concept of public support for the food system is vital, the way that subsidies and market-price supports have been used in the US and Europe simply exacerbate oversupply, drive farmers from the land, and lead to international dumping and corporate concentration in the food system.

Structural adjustment programs

The structural adjustment programs (SAPs) imposed by the World Bank and the International Monetary Fund (IMF) in the 1980s and 1990s broke down tariffs, dismantled national marketing boards, eliminated price guarantees and destroyed research and extension systems in the global South. By deregulating agricultural markets, the SAPs cleared the way for the "dumping" of agricultural commodities by multinational grain companies into local markets with subsidized grain from the US and Europe. These grains were sold at prices below the costs of production. This tied Southern food security to global markets dominated by multinational agribusinesses from the industrial North instead of encouraging developing countries to increase self-sufficiency through local farm production.

Regional free trade agreements and the World Trade Organization

The rules of the free trade agreements (FTAs) and the World Trade Organization (WTO) then cemented the SAPs into international treaties that overrode national labor and environmental laws and legally prevented countries from protecting their food systems from foreign dominance. While these policies were sold under the banner of "free trade," under WTO rules the US and EU can heavily subsidize their agribusinesses, but other countries are prohibited from doing the same.

The overlapping histories of development, the Green Revolution, Northern subsidies, structural adjustment and free trade agreements constitute an agrarian saga of global proportions and helps to explain why poverty and overproduction—not scarcity and overpopulation—are the main cause of hunger in the world. The tragic story of the world food crisis begins with the introduction of "development," the North's modernization project for the global South.

Development and the Green Revolution

During the Cold War (1950–90) Western countries claimed they could pull underdeveloped nations out of poverty if they followed the industrialized world's path of economic growth. Policymakers in the US and Western Europe were anxious to bring the "third world" into the Western bloc and away from China and the Soviet Union. The problem of underdevelopment was framed as a lack of technology, investment, and entrepreneurial culture. *The Stages of Economic Growth: A Non-Communist Manifesto* was the technocratic cookbook used by development planners (Rostow 1960). The IMF and the International Bank for Reconstruction and Development (World Bank), originally designed to create a fluid and stable trading environment, and provide for the reconstruction of Western Europe, were recruited to develop Western capitalism in the third world (Preston 1996; Rapley 1996). Agriculture was to mobilize a significant social and economic surplus—in the form of low-wage labor and cheap food—from the countryside to the cities for urban industrial growth.

At that time state-led development policies created a favorable financial and institutional climate for the Green Revolution, the blueprint for agricultural modernization (Jennings 1988). But there were also macroeconomic reasons for its success. Through the 1960s, food aid for developing countries was becoming increasingly expensive. In the 1970s OPEC (Organization of Petroleum Exporting Countries) raised the price of oil, creating a shortage. The US responded by trading wheat for oil with the Soviet Union. To do this, US food aid that had previously been shipped to governments to prevent them from developing economic relationships with the Soviet Union was shipped to… the Soviet Union! The US–Soviet food-for-oil program meant that there was less food available for food aid. A new food program was required for the global South so as to keep communism at bay. The Green Revolution fit the bill perfectly.

Led from the 1960s on by scientist Norman Borlaug (who won the Nobel Peace Prize for his work), and initially financed by the Rockefeller and Ford Foundations, the Green Revolution was supported by Western governments through a well-financed campaign that established a massive global research and extension system. Scientists working at the International Center for the Improvement of Maize and Wheat (CIMMYT) in Mexico, and the International Rice Research Institute (IRRI) in the Philippines, developed high-yielding hybrid varieties of grain (HYVs). These hybrids were then adapted to local conditions at national agricultural research stations and disseminated through national agricultural extension programs. Rural banks provided credit with government financing. The HYVs' yields were dependent on "packages" of credit, fertilizers, and timely irrigation. They favored the use of modern agricultural machinery. In Mexico, Asia and India, the Green Revolution raised agricultural productivity on the medium-to-large mechanized farms that had access to agricultural extension, irrigation, and the production credit needed to buy the technological packages.

Production increases were dramatic. From 1970 to 1990, the two decades of major Green Revolution expansion, the total food available per person in the world rose by 11%, while the estimated number of hungry people fell from 942 million to 786 million, a 16% drop. But, in South America, where per capita food supplies rose almost 8%, the number of hungry people went up by 19%. In South Asia there was a 9% increase in food per capita by 1990, but there were also 9% more hungry people. Eliminate China from the global equation—where the number of hungry dropped from 406 million to 189 million—and the number of hungry people in the rest of the world actually *increased* by more than 11%—from 536 to 597 million (Lappé et al. 1986). When the Green Revolution stagnated in the 1990s, cereal yield increases dropped by half and the number of hungry people ballooned to 800 million (World Bank 2003).

The main problem was that poor people couldn't afford all the food being produced and went hungry, despite grain surpluses. The millions of peasant farmers forced off the land to make way for larger, more capital-efficient farms joined the ranks of the hungry.

The social and environmental drawbacks of the Green Revolution were widely documented, including: increased inequality in rural incomes; concentration of land and resources (Frankel 1973; Hewitt de Alcántara 1976; Rosegrant and Pingali 1994); increasing pest problems; loss of agrobiodiversity; massive farm worker poisonings; salinization; depleted and contaminated aquifers; and the erosion of fragile tropical soils (Altieri 2000; Gliessman 1998; Pearse 1980; Pimentel and Pimentel 1990; Shiva 1991; Singh 2000; *The Ecologist* 1996).

Initially, the Green Revolution failed to incorporate poor and middle peasants and rural women. This accentuated existing gender and socioeconomic disparities in the countryside. The high cost of its purchased inputs deepened the divide between large farmers

BOX 5

The Green Revolution in Mexico

The roots of the Green Revolution are found in Mexico during the 1940s, with the policies of President Ávila Camacho and sponsorship from the Rockefeller Foundation, a US philanthropic organization based on the profits from John D. Rockefeller's Standard Oil Company. Rockefeller had already run a public health project in Mexico for decades when in 1941 they sent a survey team of three US scientists to investigate the potential for an agriculture project as well. These scientists recommended a program to train Mexican agronomists, improve weed and pest control, and breed higher-yielding varieties of maize, wheat, and beans. They suggested an initial focus on large commercial growers, with later expansion to reach small-scale peasant agriculture (Merrill and Miró 1996).

Such recommendations contradicted those of Carl Sauer, a respected geography professor at the University of California, Berkeley, who had a great deal of knowledge of the Mexican countryside, and whom the foundation had also sent to evaluate Mexican agriculture (Hewitt de Alcántara 1976). Sauer recommended a primary focus on peasants' actual needs, noting that their agricultural and nutritional practices were "excellent" and that the main problems were economic (e.g. isolation from markets and lack of access to credit) rather than technical. Sauer's suggestions generated little discussion or enthusiasm within the foundation (Merrill and Miró 1996; Jennings 1988).

In 1941, two foundation officials met with US Vice President Henry A. Wallace and stated that one of Mexico's most important problems was the need for greater agricultural production. Wallace too expressed concern about low productivity in the face of a high birth rate, and encouraged the creation of the Mexican Agriculture Program (MAP) as a joint effort between the Rockefeller Foundation and Mexican government (Merrill and Miró 1996). The MAP established crop research stations throughout Mexico, where scientists began collecting the highest-yielding strains of corn and wheat (from within Mexico and abroad) and cross-breeding them to create new varieties with greater disease resistance and higher yield. Over time, the scientists bred new varieties capable of responding to high doses of fertilizer that when grown on irrigated land under favorable conditions yielded far more than traditional varieties (Merrill and Miró 1996; Hewitt de Alcántara 1976).

Over the following two decades, Mexican agricultural production grew tremendously and the country became self-sufficient in its grain supply (Hewitt de Alcántara 1976; Wright 2005). However, this success was not solely due to chemicals and higher-yielding crop varieties, but to government policies supporting domestic agriculture and ensuring affordable food for the entire population (Barry 1995). Self-sufficiency was not simply the result of greater quantities of food being produced, but of government intervention and programs making sure everyone had access to food (Barry 1995).

This changed during the 1970s. In response to a growing demand for meat by the urban middle and upper class, the government prioritized the production of feed grains (for livestock) over that of food grains (for human consumption), and the availability of basic grains as a food source began to decline. Even though agricultural growth had made it possible to provide 2,623 calories and 80 grams of protein per day to the entire population, an estimated one-third of Mexicans in 1970 (mainly in the countryside or in migrant settlements just outside cities) still could not obtain an adequate diet and suffered from malnutrition. This illustrated the project's failure, in spite of increased productivity, to actually reach the poorest segments of society (Barry 1995; Jennings 1988).

Today, critics of the Green Revolution argue that the "food shortage" of the early 1940s was also the result of inadequate policies and distribution rather than low productivity. It's clear that urban demand for food in the early 1940s was growing faster than total output, prices were rising, and a short crop of corn in 1943 led to public protests and riots throughout the country (Barry 1995; Merrill and Miró 1996). But according to Cynthia Hewitt de Alcántara of the UN Research Institute for Social Development, this was not the result of a lack of agricultural capacity so much as a "sudden shift in consumption priorities at the turn of the decade." Hewitt de Alcántara asserts that production in the countryside had actually been increasing and that food was plentiful, but that it would have taken time and investment to build the infrastructure for channeling that production to urban consumers. The proponents of industrialization, however, were unwilling to provide such investment to smallholder agriculture. As a result, the majority of food entering the national market during the 1940s came from large commercial farms, while vast numbers of smaller growers remained isolated from markets they might have supplied (Barry 1995).

Adapted from Dori Stone, *Beyond the Fence: A Journey to the Roots of the Migration Crisis*, Food First Books, 2009

Barry, Tom. 1995. *Zapata's Revenge: Free Trade and the Farm Crisis in Mexico*. Boston: Interhemispheric Resource Center.

Hewitt de Alcántara, Cynthia. 1976. *Modernizing Mexican Agriculture: Socioeconomic Implications of Technological Change 1940-1970*. Geneva: United Nations Research Institute for Social Development.

Jennings, Bruce H. 1988. Foundations of International Agricultural Research: Sciences and Politics in Mexican Agriculture. Boulder: Westview Press, Inc.

Merrill, Tim and Ramón Miró. 1996. Government Agricultural Policy. In *Mexico: A Country Study*. Washington DC: Federal Research Division, Library of Congress.

Wright, Angus. 2005. *The Death of Ramón González: The Modern Agricultural Dilemma*. 2nd ed. Austin: University of Texas Press.

BOX 6

Sub-Saharan Africa's Population Factor

The population of sub-Saharan African has grown from 230 million in 1961 to 673 million in 2000—a 292% increase over 39 years (WRI 2007). Domestic food production has not kept pace. Agricultural exports have fallen and imports are up tenfold. Why? Poor soils, poor seeds, and poor people are the stock answers. These explanations do not look at why African family farmers have to farm poor soils, why their access to seeds is limited, or why so many people on such a resource-rich continent are poor.

Through its structural adjustment policies, the World Bank and the IMF pressured African countries to abandon small-farm agriculture, which was seen by these institutions as unproductive. Development policies pushed people to the cities, where they were to provide labor to manufacturing and industry. African industrial agriculture would produce export crops (e.g., coffee, cacao, cotton) to pay off their foreign debt and Africans would use revenues from industry to import their food. The bank insisted that this development strategy would result in increased family incomes and economic security, thus leading to lower population growth rates. This strategy failed miserably. The urban population increased seven-fold, swelling from 18% to 33% of the population. Millions of poor and unemployed workers crowded into the cities—with two-thirds of them living in slums (WRI 2007). The manufacturing and industrial sector did not "take off" in African countries; the percentage of the GDP coming from industry was 30% in 1961 and 32% in 2000 (WRI 2007).

In the countryside, as plantations for agro-exports expanded, food production for local consumption plummeted and poverty grew. Within the rural population, density increased by 180% as more farmers were crowded onto smaller plots. While the rest of the developing world lowered the amount of export earnings they spent on food imports from 42% to 24%, African countries increased the share they spent on food imports from 42% to 54% (Azarnert 2004). The industrial transition did not slow population growth because it actually increased poverty and insecurity in both rural and urban areas. This rise in population was not the cause of hunger, per se, but the result of poverty—brought on by the programmed destruction of African food systems.

Azarnert, L. 2004. *Foreign Aid and Population Growth: Evidence from Africa.* http://www.commerce.uct.ac.za/Research_Units/DPRU/DPRU-Conference2004/Papers/Foreign_Aid_and_Population_Growth_Leonid_Azarnert.pdf (accessed January 3, 2009).

WRI. 2007. *World Resource Institute. Earthtrends 2007.* http://earthtrends.wri.org/searchable_db/index.php?theme=8 (accessed October 1, 2008).

and smallholders because the latter could not afford the technology. Women also had less access to credit, inputs and extension services than their male counterparts, placing the Green Revolution's economies of scale largely out of reach for rural women (IFPRI 2000).

In both Mexico and India, seminal studies revealed that the Green Revolution's expensive "packages" favored a minority of economically privileged farmers, put the majority smallholders at a disadvantage, and led to the concentration of land and resources (Hewitt de Alcántara 1976; Frankel 1973; Jennings 1988; Pearse 1980). In fact, a study reviewing every research report published on the Green Revolution over a 30-year period all over the world—more than 300 in all—showed that 80% of those with conclusions on equity found that inequality increased (Freebairn 1995).

With the help of development institutions, governments implemented integrated rural development projects (IRDPs) in an attempt to address these social problems. Strikingly similar to Jeffrey Sachs' high-profile "Millennium Villages" in Africa today, IRDPs attempted to improve agriculture by addressing all aspects of rural development on a village scale. The IRDPs failed as a development strategy because they were too expensive, logistically complicated and institutionally cumbersome. Because of this, in the few instances where IRDPs had partial successes, the actual factors of success were difficult to identify and the results were impossible to reproduce on a large scale. Nevertheless, they were good vehicles for introducing what became known as the "second" Green Revolution, in which smallholders were offered credit and agricultural extension in order to facilitate widespread adoption of commercial hybrids. It was assumed that early adopters would "make it" in modern agriculture. Non-adopters and late adopters would be forced out of production and into the labor market. Higher efficiencies would make basic grains cheap and bring down urban food prices for industrial expansion.

An unspoken objective of the Green Revolution was to avoid implementing agrarian reform. In this sense, the Green Revolution was less a campaign to feed the urban poor than a strategy to prevent the rural poor from seizing land to feed themselves. Rather than raise production through redistribution of land to smallholders, the Green Revolution favored raising production through technological intensification.

This strategy, a thinly veiled attempt to eliminate the "surplus" peasantry, forced millions of smallholders to migrate to the misery

BOX 7

As You Sow: Farmer Suicides and Structural Violence in the Green Revolution's Breadbasket

No greater misfortune could perhaps befall the people of India than that their land should be poisoned with artificial fertilizers.

M.K. Gandhi, 1947

Never before in the history of agriculture has a transplantation of high-yielding varieties coupled with an entirely new technology and strategy been achieved on such a massive scale, in so short a period of time, and with such great success.

N. Borlaug, Nobel Prize acceptance speech, 1970

A farmer allegedly committed suicide after failing to sell off his paddy crop in the Nadala Mandi premises in Kapurthala district on Sunday night. Heavily indebted, Kuljit Singh killed his wife and teenage son with a machete and then committed suicide by consuming a poisonous fumigant. Kuljit Singh… could not take the humiliation, tension and the pressure of the money lender and found escape only in suicide.

(Newman 2007)

Alongside India's tremendous middle class growth and the much-celebrated boom of its IT sector, a quiet emergency of debt-driven suicide has taken hold in the countryside. Since 1993, as many as 150,000 indebted Indian farmers have taken their own lives (Mishra 2006). Many of these farmers died consuming the very same pesticides they had bought to use on their fields. The government of Punjab concedes that 2,116 indebted Punjabi farmers committed suicide between 1988 and 2004 (Aditi 2006). Many farmers' rights activists claim this figure may be a severe underestimation.

Suicides are ripping the countryside apart, but so is hunger and poverty. In 2001, with granaries so full of surplus that Indian authorities proposed dumping them into the sea, hunger deaths were reported in 12 Indian states—deaths unheard of since the 1960s. In 2008 India ranked 66th out of 88 countries on the International Food Policy Research Institute's Hunger Index (IFPRI 2008). Unemployment, especially among youth, is rampant (Singh et al. 2003). Once credited with transforming India from the world's "begging bowl to a bread basket," (Agarwal 1979) the seemingly endless abundance of Punjab was the poster child for the Green Revolution. So what failed India's miracle state?

The introduction of Green Revolution technologies into Punjab—India's historical bread basket—while succeeding in growing significantly more food for the rest of India, has brought about economic, environmental and social disasters to Punjabi farmers. Punjab's agrarian crisis consists of three interconnected factors:

- Rampant and widespread debt among farmers due to shrinking markets, flat support prices, stagnating crop yields, and increasing production costs
- Social inequalities exacerbated by the exclusionary policies of the Green Revolution and its aftermath
- Ecological breakdown in both soil and water systems.

Small and marginal Punjabi farmers, the rural majority, are the most indebted, unable to stay afloat amid liberalizing economic reforms geared toward their larger counterparts and transnational agribusiness. Yet even the largest farmers in Punjab have not been completely immune to the environmental and economic damage caused by 40 years of industrial agriculture. Punjabi agriculture as a whole appears to be crashing.

In 1961 the Ford and Rockefeller Foundations launched an Intensive Agricultural Development Program in India, bringing the Green Revolution that had been rolled out in Mexico and the Philippines to the north Indian state of Punjab. The program set out to feed India's angry masses through chemical intensive farming—and in the process to avert the possibility of a "Red India."

As early as 1969, nearly 70% of Punjab's wheat and 20% of its rice were from Green Revolution seeds. Only three years later, over 75% of rice, and almost 80% of wheat grown in Punjab were of the new varieties. Between 1960 and 1979, total statewide yields in wheat increased by 124%, while rice yields shot up by 175% (McGuirk and Mundlak 1991).

However, total statewide yield does little to indicate the yields of the majority of Punjab's farmers. For those with marginal, small and medium-sized land holdings, the costly new inputs—fertilizers, pesticides, tubewell irrigation, etc.—priced the Green Revolution far beyond their means. While the majority of Punjab's farmers worked only ten acres or less, the economics of the Green Revolution were such that only those farmers owning at least 20 acres were in a position to purchase the new inputs (Frankel 1973).

As the Green Revolution progressed (1970-90), land holdings of small farmers decreased by almost 40%, while those of large and "extra-large" farmers increased by over 50% (UNDP 2004). Today, a significant number of cultivators still work small and marginal pieces of land in the Punjab; nearly 400,000 holdings of two hectares or less were recorded in a 1996 state agricultural census (UNDP 2004). These small farmers have almost no ability to secure credit through conventional banks and must turn to money lenders. The high interest rates that these agents charge, combined with the low annual income of the small farmer, has created a "debt trap." Once caught in the debt trap, there is almost no alternative for the small farmer but to sell or mortgage their land—a step taken by about 14% of small farmers as well as a few entire villages.

The new seeds introduced into Punjab since the 1960s have been completely dependent on intensive irrigation. The combined force of one million tubewells, while propelling forward the crops of the Green Revolution, has devastated Punjab's fragile ecosystem. Sixty-one percent of Punjab is now an official "black zone," an area where irrigation use—which has increased 200 times over the last three decades—is greater than its rate of recharge (Agnihotri 2004). Punjab's water table has been estimated by R.S. Narang and M.S. Gill of the normally conservative Punjab Agricultural University to be retreating by two meters annually over two-thirds of the state, leading them to conclude that, "this [situation] has now reached such alarming proportions that questions are now being asked as to what extent rice cultivation should be permitted in the irrigated Indo-Gangetic Plains" (Agnihotri 2004).

If the Green Revolution was a success, what are we to make of the dying soils, shrinking water tables, increased inequality and skyrocketing debt that have become part and parcel of its legacy in rural Punjab? Can a program be described as economically "successful" if it destroys the wealth and livelihoods upon which it rests?

In 1986 a resolution was passed at the all-Sikh convention condemning the inequalities of the Green Revolution. It read:

> If the hard-earned income of the people or the natural resources of any nation or the region are forcibly plundered; if the goods produced by them are paid for at arbitrarily determined prices while the goods bought are sold at higher prices and if, in order to carry this process of economic exploitation to its logical conclusion, the human rights of a nation, region or people are lost then the people will be like the Sikhs today—shackled by the chains of slavery.
>
> (Shiva 1992)

The Indian scholar Vandana Shiva sees increased inequality in the Punjab not only as injustice, but a type of violence. In her 1992 book she says the Green Revolution in the Punjab:

> changed the structure of social and political relationships, from those based on mutual (though asymmetric) obligations—within the village to relations of each cultivator directly with banks, seed and fertilizer agencies, food procurement agencies, and electricity and irrigation organizations. Further, since all the externally supplied inputs were scarce, it set up conflict and competition over scarce resources, between classes, and between regions... this generated on the one hand, an erosion of cultural norms and practices and on the other hand, it sowed the seeds of violence and conflict.
>
> (Shiva 1992)

Shiva blames the Green Revolution for the outbreak of Sikh-on-Sikh violence in the late 1980s that left 550 people dead in four months (Weismann 1987), for the disaster at the Union Carbide pesticide plant in 1984 that killed over 30,000 people in Bhopal and most recently for the rash of farmer suicides (Shiva n.d.). But aside from manifestations of physical violence, the legacy of the Green Revolution in Punjab is a quieter kind of destruction—a structural violence that enforces hunger in times of plenty, extracts water and soil from an ever-shrinking resource base, dispossesses small-farm families, and forges an expensive dependency on multinationals that has cost many farmers their lives.

Partially adapted from Bryan Newman, A Bitter Harvest: Farmer Suicide in India, *Food First Development Report*, no. 15, January 2007.

Aditi, Tandon. 2006. The Kin of Indebted Farmers Finally Get to Speak. *The Tribune*. April 2.

Agarwal, Anil. 1979. From Begging Bowl to Bread Basket. *Nature* 281:250-51.

Agnihotri, Peeyush. 2004. Tubewells, Drilling for Deep Trouble. *The Tribune*, February 16.

Frankel, Francine R. 1973. Politics of the Green Revolution: Shifting Peasant Participation in India and Pakistan. In *Food, Population, Employment: The Impact of the Green Revolution*. Edited by Thomas T. Poleman and Donald K. Freebairn. New York: Praeger Publishers.

IFPRI. 2008. *India Faces Urgent Hunger Situation*. Press release. Delhi: International Food Policy Research Institute.

McGuirk, Anya and Yair Mundlak. 1991. Incentives and Constraints in the Transformation of Punjab Agriculture. *Research Report* 87. International Food Policy Research Institute.

Mishra, Pankaj. 2006. The Myth of the New India. *The New York Times*. July 6.

Newman, Bryan. 2007. A Bitter Harvest: Farmer Suicide in India. *Food First Development Report* 15. Quoting from Gruesome Tale of Sikh Farmer Who Could Not Pay the Interest on His Loan to the *Bania* (Moneylender). Washington DC: Khalistan Affairs Center. August 26, 1998. www.khalistan-affairs.org.

Shiva, Vandana. n.d. In *The Practice of Earth Democracy*. Research Center for Science, Technology, and Ecology. http://www.navdanya.org/about/practice_earth_dem.htm (accessed January 30, 2009).

Shiva, Vandana. 1992. *The Violence of the Green Revolution: Third World Agriculture, Ecology, and Politics*. London: Zed Books.

Singh, Baldev, Sukhwinder Singh and Jaswinder Singh Brar. 2003. *Extent of Unemployment in the Border Districts of Punjab: A Case Study of Rural Ferozepur District*. Patiala: Center for Research of Economic Change, Punjabi University.

UNDP. 2004. *Human Development Report*. Punjab: United Nations Development Program with the Government of Punjab.

Weismann, Steven. 1987. Sikh Violence in Punjab a Threat to Indian Unity. *The New York Times*. October 5.

belts around the larger cities where they provided an endless supply of cheap and part-time labor to the industrial, construction, and
manufacturing sectors. When labor supply outstripped demand, the
former peasants did not go back to farming but joined the growing
"informal sector" of the underemployed. Another part of the peasantry moved to the fragile hillsides and forest perimeters of the global South, opening up new but highly vulnerable areas to subsistence
agriculture. Here, the seeds and fertilizers of the Green Revolution
provided only a few years worth of good harvest, which steadily
declined as soil degraded, then eroded and disappeared altogether.
Pesticides killed off beneficial insects, leading to pest outbreaks that
became too severe and expensive to control. This initial increase in
overall food production (due in part to the increase in land area)
was claimed by Green Revolution advocates as proof of its success.
However, they had little to say and even less to offer when yields
crashed and production stagnated.

As the Green Revolution was being implemented, several key geopolitical events were taking place. In the wake of the oil crisis, Middle
Eastern countries found themselves flush with cash. Unable to spend
it all, they invested in Northern banks. With these so-called 'petro-
dollars,' Northern banks were happy to lend to all comers, including Northern farmers and Southern governments. In the US, farmers were showered with cheap credit and directed to save the world
from hunger by planting "fencerow to fencerow." The World Bank
helped prepare the investment terrain in the global South, disbursing
billions in public funds for massive infrastructure projects and bold
colonization schemes.

The oil price shocks in the late 1970s and the global North's economic recession sent the global South into a severe economic crisis in
the 1980s. Northern banks raised their interest rates and began to call
in their loans. Unfortunately, debtor countries were asked to pay up
precisely at the time their products had lost their value and their market share, sending the global South into a profound economic crisis
that resulted in negative economic growth and an unprecedented—
and unpayable—foreign debt (Sonntag et al. 2000). In this context,
with commercial banks unwilling and unable to extend further credit,
institutions like the World Bank moved to fill the gap. But the bank
used this opportunity to foist structural adjustment policies (SAPs)
on the global South and, with no other alternative, the governments
of the global South were forced to comply.

Neoliberal economics came to the fore in this period, signifying a dramatic reversal in strategy away from planned, state-led development to "spontaneous" market order. This ideology embraced the neoclassical economic model of a pure market system at the center of human development, with minimal interference from the state (Balassa 1971; Bauer 1981; Friedman 1968). Neoliberals focused on trade as the engine for growth and prescribed trade liberalization, privatization, currency devaluation, deregulation, and fiscal austerity. The new neoliberal development paradigm was soon enshrined in what became known as the "Washington Consensus," implemented through the structural adjustment policies applied in the 1980s to the global South by the World Bank and the IMF. Under the guise of macroeconomic stability, the IMF and the World Bank forced countries of the South to open up their economies to foreign investment and their markets to foreign products by making debt relief and foreign aid contingent upon the liberalization of markets, the deregulation of controls on international finance capital, the privatization of state-held industries and services, and the deregulation of labor (Gore 2000; Pieterse 1998).

Structural Adjustment and the Sins of the World Bank

The World Bank began its institutional life by more or less ignoring agriculture. It needed to prove its creditworthiness to a skeptical bond market, and did so by investing in projects with guaranteed high rates of return. As a result, early on it heavily favored industrial projects over agricultural ones. In 1961 there were only 12 staff charged with agricultural programming at the bank. Funding for agriculture received a boost under bank President Robert McNamara, who pledged himself to support agriculture, "the stepchild of development" (Kapur et al. 2007). Under his tenure, the bank invested in and supported the creation of grain marketing boards, agricultural extension services and food storage and distribution services, particularly in Africa.

The debt crisis in the early 1980s ushered in a political transformation of the World Bank's economic policies. Previously, the bank had relied on the state to advance development. Suddenly, the state was considered an obstacle to development. Development would come about by unleashing the market and "getting the prices right." This

BOX 8

Haiti: Showcase for Free Trade

"Basketcase" rather than "showcase" is the word most consistently used to describe the Caribbean half-island nation of Haiti. Seventy-six percent of the Haitian population subsists on less than US$2 per day, the majority of which lives below the extreme poverty level of US$1 per person, per day (IMF 2008). The country's high level of dependence on imports of major grains such as rice, wheat and corn earned Haiti a place on the FAO's list of the 22 countries most vulnerable to increases in food and fuel prices.

Haiti has not always been so highly dependent on imports. Haiti's integration into the global economy began in earnest in 1986, after the fall of dictator Jean-Claude "Baby Doc" Duvalier (who inherited power from his father, the ruthless Francois "Papa Doc" Duvalier). Under US tutelage, the military junta that replaced Baby Doc—the National Governing Council (CNG)—implemented a radical neoliberal program which included slashing tariffs, closing state-owned industries, opening the agricultural market to US producers and cutting spending on agriculture by 30% in the fertile, rice-producing Artibonite Valley. The policies were designed to meet conditions required by the International Monetary Fund (IMF) for acquiring a $24.6 million loan, desperately needed after the Duvalier dynasty had plunged the country into debt.

Rice and other imports, particularly highly subsidized US agricultural products, immediately flooded the Haitian market. In 1987, Haiti met three-quarters of its rice needs through domestic production (Haiti Info 1995). Today, of the 400,000 tons of rice consumed in Haiti each year, three-quarters consists of "Miami Rice"—the Haitian nickname for the cheap US rice sold at half the price of local grain (Williams 2008). This is the root of the current crisis, acknowledged current president René Préval: "In 1987 when we allowed cheap rice to enter the country a lot of people applauded 'Bravo'... But cheap imported rice destroyed the Artibonite rice. Today, imported rice has become expensive, and our national production is in ruins" (Lindsay 2008).

The second wave of Haitian economic liberalization occurred in the mid-1990s. Haiti's first democratically elected president, Jean-Bertrand Aristide, had been removed in a military coup in 1991. As a condition for his return, the US, IMF and World Bank required that he further open up the Haitian economy. If the radical priest wanted help, he had to play by neoliberal rules.

In 1995, under Aristide, tariffs on rice were reduced from 35% to 3%, the lowest in the Caribbean region, and government funding was diverted from agricultural development to servicing the nation's foreign debt. Without government support or protection, Haitian farmers were in no position to compete with their highly subsidized US counterparts. According to a 2004 Oxfam report, subsidies for rice producers in the US totaled approximately $1.3 billion in 2003 alone, amounting to more than double Haiti's entire budget for that year (Oxfam International 2004).

In fact, Haitian farmers were never meant to compete with US farmers. Rather, Haiti's economic growth was to be predicated on a shift from agriculture to manufacturing. Since the 1980s, the economic strategy pursued by USAID and the international financial institutions has been to capitalize on Haiti's primary competitive advantage—cheap labor—to increase exports in manufactured goods and in agricultural products such as mangoes and coffee to Northern markets. Instead, Haiti experienced massive rural to urban migration, compounding poverty, unemployment and crime in urban slums.

Haiti's food "riots" are food rebellions, challenging the very logic of free trade. Frantz Thelusma, a community organizer, articulates the protesters' demands: "First, we demand the government get rid of its neoliberal plan. We will not accept this death plan. Second, the government needs to regulate the market and lower the price of basic goods" (Carlsen 2008). Although President Préval, an agronomist by training, announced subsidies to cut the cost of rice by 15% in an attempt to appease protesters, the government has shown no signs of reversing the tide of liberalization that has left Haitians so vulnerable to the global food crisis.

Haiti, the most impoverished nation in the Western hemisphere is one of the most open economies in the world.

Carlsen, Laura. 2008. Behind Latin America's Food Crisis. *Hungry for Justice: How the World Food System Failed the Poor* 11. Americas Policy Program, Center for International Policy.

Haiti Info. 1995. Neoliberalism in Haiti: the Case of Rice. *Haiti Info* 3 (24).

IMF. 2008. Haiti: Joint Staff Advisory Note of the Poverty Reduction Strategy Paper. *IMF Country Report* 08/114. Washington DC: International Monetary Fund.

Lindsay, Reed. 2008. Haiti on the Death Plan. *The Nation.* http://www.thenation.com/doc/20080602/lindsay (accessed October 14, 2008).

Oxfam International. 2004. Kicking Down the Door: How Upcoming WTO Talks Threaten Farmers in Poor Countries. *Oxfam Briefing Paper* 72. Oxfam International.

Williams, Carol J. 2008. Haiti's Food Crisis Rooted in Rice. *Seattle Times.* May 15.

new free market doctrine demanded a complete reversal of policy. Instead of building domestic industries, developing countries were forced to open their markets to the world. The bank's approach ignored the real economic trajectory of the first world (which developed both agriculture and industry behind protective tariffs), and plunged developing countries straight into the cauldron of international competition (Chang 2007).

This approach had some very specific consequences for agriculture. For this food regime to work, existing marketing boards and support structures in the global South needed to be dismantled. The World Bank set off around the world, destroying the very state bodies it formerly supported (McMichael 2004). These new policies were based on the unproven assumption that the private sector would be more efficient and less wasteful than the public sector. Not only did this assumption turn out to be wrong, but mass privatization in agriculture had serious drawbacks. As one report observed: "Farmers suffered negative consequences because key products and marketing costs rose rapidly, fertilizer prices and transport costs soared and labor costs declined. [For example] producer prices showed greater volatility in Cameroon, Côte d'Ivoire and Nigeria—countries that dismantled their marketing boards—than in Ghana (which kept its marketing boards)" (Alexander 2005).

Even the World Bank's own Independent Evaluation Group notes two key failures in the bank's operations in agriculture. First, the bank has neglected agriculture to the detriment of many developing countries: "Underperformance of agriculture has been a major limitation of Africa's development. For most of the past two decades, both governments and donors, including the World Bank, have neglected the sector. The Bank's limited and—until recently—declining support to agriculture has not been strategically used to meet the diverse needs of a sector that requires coordinated interventions across a range of activities" (World Bank 2007). Second, the dismantling of agriculture was intended to create opportunities for the private sector, but invariably, "the invisible hand of the market" was nowhere to be seen. The Blair Commission for Africa concurs with the Independent Evaluation Group's evaluation. In its report, the commission states, "Domestic stabilization schemes and associated institutions have been dismantled under the banner of market efficiency, and this has created an institutional void with adverse consequences for the livelihood of millions of African farmers" (Alexander 2005).

BOX 9

Ghana's Import Surge

In 1998, Ghana's local rice production accounted for over 80% of domestic consumption. By 2003, that figure was less than 20% (ActionAid International Ghana 2006). Nor is this the only commodity in which Ghana has suffered an erosion in domestic production. As one report notes: "Until the early 1990s, local industry supplied all the chicken and eggs consumed in Ghana, and in 1992, 95% of the domestic poultry requirement was met through local production... this trend did not continue through the 1990s, as imports of poultry products such as legs, wings and thighs from Europe attracted consumers. The consumption pattern of Ghanaians gradually changed from whole chicken to chicken parts, particularly the thighs. Thus, from 2000 onwards the share of local poultry had dropped to 11 percent" (Monsalve et al. 2007). This outcome was predicted in advance by Ghanaian civil society and members of the Ghanaian Department of Agriculture, but it was taken to be an acceptable consequence of liberalization policies that farmers in tomatoes, rice and poultry should compete unprotected against billions of dollars of annual subsidy in the European Union and North America. The consequence is that public monopolies have been transformed into private ones, without any of the benefits of competition and, now, without even the benefit of recourse to elected officials.

ActionAid International Ghana. 2006. *Agro-Import Surge Study: The Case of Rice in Ghana*. Johannesburg: ActionAid International.
Monsalve, Sofia, M. Issah, B. Ilge, A. Paasch, K. Lanje and Patrick Mulvany. 2007. *Right to Food of Tomato and Poultry Farmers: Report of an Investigative Mission to Ghana*. Heidelberg: FoodFirst Information Action Network (FIAN).

Over the years, the banks' combination of strategic neglect of agriculture and the active dismantling of agricultural supports went hand in hand with further efforts to liberalize economies, a prerequisite to receive loans from the bank. For example, the World Bank forced the Nicaraguan legislature to approve the controversial Central American Free Trade Agreement as part of its Poverty Reduction Support Credit (IDA 2006a). In accepting these conditions, however, countries were effectively forced to abandon domestic policies and institutions that might have been bargaining tools in multilateral trade negotiations. Broadly, the adoption of these structural adjustment policies kept Southern countries from negotiating trade outcomes favorable to agriculture and the rural poor (Paasch et al. 2007).

The result of these interventions and conditions was to accelerate the decline of agriculture in the global South. One of the most striking consequences of liberalization has been the phenomenon of "import surges" (FAO 2003). These happen when tariffs on cheaper (and often subsidized) agricultural products are lowered, and a host country is then flooded with those goods. There is often a correspond-

BOX 10

Philippines: The Death of Rice

As the world's largest rice importer, the Philippines has been hit hard by the skyrocketing price of rice on the global market—a 76% increase between December 2007 and April 2008 (FAO 2008). Two of the most commonly cited culprits are the rising price of oil and farm inputs, and climatic events such as Myanmar's Cyclone Nargis and Australia's drought, which devastated rice production. As a result, rice-exporting countries, including India and Vietnam, imposed export restrictions to ensure their domestic consumption, while rice-importing countries (including the Philippines) scrambled to meet their import requirements at inflated costs. The Philippines' rush on the market to fill a 500,000-ton rice tender in May was blamed for sparking even higher prices.

Filipinos took to the streets to protest the upsurge in the cost of rice, the country's primary food staple. The government of Gloria Macapagal-Arroyo responded with measures ranging from appeals to fast food chains to reduce their rice portions to pledges of support for biotechnology.

But how did the Philippines, at the heart of the world's rice bowl, lose the ability to produce enough to feed itself?

The Green Revolution, launched in Asia in the 1960s, succeeded in increasing rice yields in the Philippines. However, this increase came at the cost of significant use of chemical inputs and hybrid seeds. Between 1976 and 1988, total fertilizer consumption rose from 668 tons to 1,222 tons—an increase of over 80% (Dolan 1991). These resource-intensive farming practices generated long-term soil degradation and contamination, threatening future productivity (Rosegrant and Pingali 1994). Worse, starting with 1,400 rice varieties, Filipino agrobiodiversity was reduced to just four varieties of rice because farm credit was conditioned on planting only Green Revolution hybrids.

By the 1980s, the rate of increase in input use was greater than the rate of increase in yields. In Central Luzon, for example, a 13% yield increase between 1980 and 1989 was achieved with a 21% increase in fertilizers and a 34% increase in seeds (Rosegrant and Pingali 1994). As the cost of these inputs rose and the price to rice farmers decreased, smallholders found themselves mired in debt. Many abandoned farming. Consequently, the Philippines

ing decline in domestic production. In Senegal, for example, tariff reduction led to an import surge in tomato paste, with a fifteen-fold increase in imports, and a halving of domestic production. Similarly, Chile experienced a three-fold surge in imports of vegetable oil, and a halving of domestic production.

The World Bank has never been held accountable for these policy

---

reached one of the highest rates of urban population growth in the developing world, at an annual rate of 5.1% between 1960 and 1995 (World Bank 2009). Meanwhile, the amount of land devoted to rice production fell an average of 2.4% per year during the first half of the 1980s (Dolan 1991).

Farmers were not the only ones facing an economic squeeze. By the 1980s, the Philippine government faced mounting debt, rising inflation and deteriorating terms of trade. In 1982 the Ferdinand Marcos regime borrowed $200 million conditioned upon an IMF structural adjustment program that lifted import restrictions, cut government funding for agriculture and abolished price stabilization mechanisms. In following years, debt repayment remained a national priority and spending on agriculture plummeted.

The country's entrance into the WTO in 1995 delivered yet another blow to agriculture. Under the Agreement on Agriculture, the Philippines was required to eliminate quotas on all agricultural imports except rice. In fact, rice production was already so weakened that the grain was massively imported to meet demand, thus further discouraging domestic production. From 1996 to 1998 rice production dropped by 24% (Bernardino-Yabut 2000). Similarly, a flood of cheap corn imports—costing one-third the price of the locally produced grain—devastated corn production, which dropped by 20% from 1993 to 1998 (Bernardino-Yabut 2000). Meanwhile, from 1993 to 2003, the national food import bill increased from $714 million to $2.38 billion (Chavez et al. 2004).

Bernardino-Yabut, Natividad. 2000. *An Impact Study of Agricultural Trade Liberalization in the Philippines*. Quezon City: ISGN.

Chavez, Jenina Joy, Mary Ann Manahan and Joseph Purugganan. 2004. *Hunger on the Rise in the Philippines*. Bangkok: Focus on the Global South.

Dolan, Ronald E. 1991. *Philippines: A Country Study*. Washington DC: GPO for the Library of Congress.

FAO. 2008. *FAO Rice Market Monitor* 11 (1).

Rosegrant, M. W., and Prabhu L. Pingali. 1994. *Confronting the Environmental Consequences of the Green Revolution in Asia "Urban Development in the Philippines"*. Washington DC and Philippines: World Bank and International Food Policy Research Institute.

World Bank. 2009. *Urban Development and the Philippines*. http://go.worldbank.org/GLZOIMN160 (accessed January 30, 2009).

decisions. By conditioning their loans on the economic restructuring, it exercises enormous control over food systems in developing countries. The bank's conditions continue to be enforced. In the World Bank's Poverty Reduction Support Credits (PRSCs), for instance, loans are contingent on specific policy demands. To take four agricultural examples among dozens of economic transformations in areas as diverse as water, housing, government procurement and labor law: four crop boards were prepared for sale in Tanzania; Benin's cotton sector is being privatized; all agricultural support programs are being liberalized in Moldova; and Yemen is being forced into a land reform policy that has failed everywhere else it has been attempted (IDA 2006b, 2007a, 2007b). If these conditions resulted in alleviating poverty and hunger, the bank would have a case for its infamous "conditionality." But these loans are failing. In an assessment by the OECD none of these loans received an A grade and the majority received C or D grades (OECD 2007).

A main consequence of the combination of market liberalization, government subsidy programs in developed countries, and the capital advantage of multinational agribusiness was a dramatic increase in the "dumping" of commodities: the sale of goods at prices below the cost of their production. Import surges, in which local producers are swamped by cheaper imports, have destroyed local production capacity in countries like Haiti and Mexico. As a result, by 2005, 72% of countries in the global South had become net food importers (Ng 2008).

The steady increase in developing countries' hunger reflects the loss of national food producing capacity as international finance institutions continue to pressure developing countries to purchase on the global market rather than grow their own food (World Bank 2008a).

In its *2008 World Development Report on Agriculture* (the first of the bank's World Reports to deal with agriculture in decades) the bank admits to the need for broader policies. But instead of following a well-proven and successful path of state-led land reform—a path that the bank acknowledges as key to the ongoing economic success of South Korea, Taiwan and Japan—the bank is keen to turn its back on the lessons of history, let markets loose, distort the reporting on the success of these experiments, and offer instead to remedy this by siphoning "excess" rural people out of agriculture completely.

This is perhaps the most controversial recommendation in its 2008 report, in which the bank takes the view that smallholder agriculture is not an economically viable activity. This is evinced by the market's tendency to move land from the hands of poor farmers to richer ones, leading to the current situation where the majority of export agriculture is carried out on a few large farms while the majority of poor farmers live on relatively small plots. The bank suggests in the report that this land concentration is a sign that land is being transferred to 'more efficient' farmers—with the concomitant recommendation that the rural poor should be helped to leave agriculture and switch to non-agricultural labor. That smallholder agriculture has, for the first time in human history, ceased to be a viable economic activity has much to do with the policies instituted by the bank itself.

Yet the emptying of the countryside is now the only option that the bank can see to solve the problem of agriculture and development. In reality, this policy offers economic cover for the political expropriation of the rural poor. Nowhere is this clearer than Colombia—where the countryside has been emptied through political violence, smallholders expropriated, and where large landowners are able to take over land through a process which commentator Hector Mondragón calls "fake agrarian reform." To suggest that the processes at work here are those of efficiency is, at best, disingenuous. And while Colombia presents an extreme example, the bank's policy is explicitly aimed at removing the poorest people from agriculture, a policy that has been called "de-peasantization." These rural workers, already disenfranchised from property, are cast off under this policy, to face uncertain futures either in the rural non-agricultural employment market, or in the swelling shantytowns of the cities. It is a strong-arm policy that shrugs off evidence suggesting that comprehensive agrarian reform, as demanded by the world's poorest farmers, can offer alternatives within agriculture.

The Dismantling of African Agriculture[5]

De-peasantization is at an advanced state in Latin America and Asia. And if the World Bank has its way, Africa will travel in the same direction. *The World Bank Development Report for 2008*, which touches extensively on agriculture in Africa, is practically a blueprint for the transformation of the peasant-based agriculture of the continent into large-scale commercial farming (Havnevik et al. 2007).

At the time of decolonization in the 1960s, Africa was not just self-sufficient in food; it was actually a net food exporter with exports averaging 1.3 million tons a year between 1966 and 1970 (BBC 2006).

Today, the continent imports 25% of its food, with almost every country being a net food importer (Green Revolution 2008). Hunger and famine have become recurrent phenomena, with the last three years alone seeing food emergencies break out in the Horn of Africa, the Sahel, Southern Africa, and Central Africa.

While much agricultural work was traditionally women's domain, poverty, conflict, and migration have left women with an ever greater share of agricultural labor as male heads of households migrate to cities or follow seasonal wage jobs. Globally, women are responsible for 50% of food production. In sub-Saharan Africa, women make up 60%–80% of the farm labor force yet are still disproportionately affected by hunger and malnutrition (FAO 2008c). Our broken food system leaves rural women and their children doubly vulnerable: once as consumers with disproportionately fewer resources with which to buy food, and again as producers vulnerable to volatile price swings.

Agriculture is in deep crisis, and the causes range from wars to bad governance, lack of productivity-enhancing agricultural technology, and the spread of HIV-AIDS. However, a very important contribution to the crisis is the bank's structural adjustment policies. Instead of triggering a virtuous spiral of growth and prosperity, structural adjustment has imprisoned Africa in a low-level trap in which low investment, increased unemployment, reduced social spending, reduced consumption, and low output interact to create a vicious cycle of stagnation and decline.

Lifting price controls on fertilizers while simultaneously cutting back on agricultural credit systems is reducing fertilizer applications, lowering yields, and reducing investment. Moreover, reality refuses to conform to the doctrinal expectation that the withdrawal of the state will pave the way for the market and private sector to dynamize agriculture. Instead, the private sector has seen reduced state expenditures as creating more risk and failed to step into the breach. In country after country, the opposite of that predicted by neoliberal doctrine occurred: the departure of the state "crowded out" rather than "crowded in" private investment. In those instances where private traders did come in to replace the state, an Oxfam report noted, "they have sometimes done so on highly unfavorable terms for poor farmers," leaving "farmers more food insecure, and governments reliant on unpredictable aid flows" (Oxfam 2006). The usually pro-private sector *Economist* agreed, admitting that "many of the private firms brought in to replace state researchers turned out to be rent-seeking monopolists" (*The Economist* 2008).

What support the government has been allowed to muster was channeled by the World Bank to export agriculture in order to generate the foreign exchange earnings that the state needed to service its debt to the bank and the IMF. But, as in Ethiopia during the famine of the early 1980s, this has led to the dedication of good land to export crops, with food crops forced into more and more unsuitable soil, thus exacerbating food insecurity. Moreover, the bank's encouragement of several economies undergoing adjustment to focus on export production of the same crops simultaneously often led to overproduction that then triggered a price collapse in international markets. For instance, the very success of Ghana's program to expand cocoa production triggered a 48% drop in the international price of cocoa between 1986 and 1989, threatening, as one account put it, "to increase the vulnerability of the entire economy to the vagaries of the cocoa market" (Abugre 1993). In 2002–03, a collapse in coffee prices contributed to another food emergency in Ethiopia (Oxfam 2006).

As in Mexico and the Philippines, structural adjustment in Africa was not simply underinvestment but state divestment. But there was one major difference. In the Philippines and Mexico, the World Bank and IMF confined themselves to macromanagement, or supervising the dismantling of the state's economic role from above, leaving the dirty details of implementation to the bureaucracy. In Africa, where they dealt with much weaker governments, the bank and fund *micromanaged*, reaching down to make decisions on how fast subsidies should be phased out, how many civil servants had to be fired, or even, as in the case of Malawi, how much of the country's grain reserve should be sold and to whom. In other words, bank and IMF resident proconsuls reached to the very innards of the state's involvement in the agricultural economy to rip it up.

Compounding the negative impact of adjustment were unfair trade practices on the part of the EU and the United States. Trade liberalization simply allowed low-priced, subsidized EU beef to enter and drive many West African and South African cattle raisers to ruin. With their subsidies legitimized by the WTO's Agreement on Agriculture, US cotton growers offloaded their cotton on world markets at 20%–55% of the cost of production, bankrupting West African and Central African cotton farmers in the process (Business World 2003).

According to Oxfam, the number of people living on less than a dollar a day more than doubled to 313 million between 1981 and 2001—or 46% of the whole continent (Oxfam 2006). The role of structural adjustment in creating poverty, as well as severely weakening the continent's agricultural base and consolidating import dependency, was hard to deny. As the World Bank's chief economist for Africa admitted, "We did not think that the human costs of these programs could be so great, and the economic gains would be so slow in coming" (Miller 1991).

That was, however, a rare moment of candor. What was especially disturbing was that, as Oxford University political economist Ngaire Woods pointed out, the "seeming blindness of the Fund and Bank to the failure of their approach to sub-Saharan Africa persisted even as internal studies by the IMF and the World Bank failed to elicit positive investment effects" (Woods 2006).

Owing to the absence of any clear case of success, structural adjustment has been widely discredited throughout Africa. Even some donor governments that used to subscribe to it have distanced themselves from the bank, the most prominent case being the official British aid agency DFID, which cofunded the latest subsidized fertilizer program in Malawi (DFID 2007).

Unable to deny the obvious, the bank has finally acknowledged that the whole structural adjustment enterprise was a mistake, though it buried this admission in the middle of the *2008 World Development Report*, perhaps in the hope that it would not attract too much attention. Nevertheless, it was a damning admission:

> Structural adjustment in the 1980's dismantled the elaborate system of public agencies that provided farmers with access to land, credit, insurance, inputs, and cooperative organization. The expectation was that removing the state would free the market for private actors to take over these functions—reducing their costs, improving their quality, and eliminating their regressive bias. Too often, that didn't happen. In some places, the state's withdrawal was tentative at best, limiting private entry. Elsewhere, the private sector emerged only slowly and partially—mainly serving commercial farmers but leaving smallholders exposed to extensive market failures, high transaction costs and risks, and service gaps. Incomplete markets and institutional gaps impose huge costs in forgone growth and welfare losses for smallholders, threatening their competitiveness and, in many cases, their survival.
>
> (World Bank 2008b)

Had the World Bank listened to the growing chorus of civil society organizations, progressive think tanks, hundreds of peasant and farm organizations (and even its own reports) that began criticizing the bank's policies as early as two decades ago, this admission—still far from an apology—would not ring so hollow.

Global Trade: A Free Straitjacket for the Poor

Free trade is credited with providing everything from abundance to democracy. In fact, what is called "free" trade today is not free but rather forced, and has yet to demonstrate any positive correlation with either reducing hunger or ensuring democratic practice. On the contrary, the ideology and discourse of free trade has been used to establish global institutions, regional agreements and sets of rules that favor strong over weak trading partners. While certain sectors and business interests within a particular country may benefit, and while GDP may rise as the result of increased trade, even in the "emerging markets" of countries like India, Mexico, and Brazil, this increase in wealth has been accompanied by an even larger increase in poverty and hunger. Researcher-activist Vandana Shiva (2008) notes that even while India's economy is growing at the astonishing rate of 9%, over the last 17 years the per capita availability of food has declined by 14%. Today's global trade regime rests on the institutional pillars of the World Trade Organization (WTO), and North–South free trade agreements (FTAs).

The World Trade Organization

[The] idea that developing countries should feed themselves is an anachronism from a bygone era. They could better ensure their food security by relying on U.S. agricultural products, which are available, in most cases, at much lower cost.

John Block, US Secretary for Agriculture, Uruguay Round, General Agreement on Tariffs and Trade, 1986

While the World Bank and the IMF act as the North's financial henchmen, the WTO, formed in 1995, has tried to play the role of chief trade enforcer. Built on the principles of free market fundamentalism and dominated by rich countries, the WTO is a permanent negotiating forum for global trade policy. While the WTO is the prized creation of the Northern countries, Southern countries participate because they feel they cannot afford to be left out of negotiations.

Following World War II, in 1948 Western powers formed the General Agreement on Tariffs and Trade (GATT) to facilitate international trade among non-socialist countries. At the time, because of food security concerns, agriculture was not included in the agreement. In 1995, following the Uruguay Round of GATT negotiations (1986–94), the WTO was formed and agriculture, services, and intellectual property rights were officially added to the trade agenda. The stated purpose of the WTO was to reduce trade barriers and establish non-discriminatory mechanisms to enforce global trade rules. This market-led approach to development would "lift all boats." In its 13 years of existence the WTO has not established the "level playing field" that would ensure benefits for all its members, and has favored the profits of Northern corporations much more than the economies of the global South. Proponents claim the WTO exists to iron out these problems. Critics claim favoring Northern corporations was the unstated purpose of the WTO all along.

In WTO ministerial meetings, held biannually, trade and finance ministers from around the world negotiate world trade policies. These meetings have produced only a few new agreements. The repeated failures of the ministerial meetings are usually due to a combination of disagreements between developed and developing countries, combined with massive public protests from labor, farmer, environmentalist, food justice and fair trade activists opposed to corporate globalization. Market access, domestic subsidies, dumping, and special safeguards are among the major issues that have broken down negotiations in the past.

The WTO has a comprehensive Agreement on Agriculture (AoA)—an agreement that was largely written between the US and Europe. (The WTO's founding talks, the Uruguay Round, looked like they were going to fail until Europe and the US worked out a way to keep their agricultural interests protected. Under a separate negotiation called the Blair House agreement, the EU and US agreed to continue to subsidize their respective agricultural sectors, while also agreeing that such protection be denied developing countries.) Though developing countries were successfully strong-armed into signing the AoA in 1995, it quickly became clear they were receiving a raw deal. The WTO talks collapsed in Seattle in 1999 in part because of a rebellion from these countries and in part from massive civil protests (the "Battle of Seattle") by farmers, unions, environmentalists and food activists.

Doha: the death round

To avoid any civil protest, the next round of talks in 2001 was held in bunker-like conditions in Doha, Qatar, an expensive destination that put the WTO safely beyond the reach of most international public protest. Christened the "Development Round" the ministerial meeting's title reflected the concern on the part of the industrialized world that unless they were able to convince the global South of the economic merits of free trade, the WTO might never move forward. In Qatar, the Northern countries agreed to address the possibility of special treatment for Southern countries, if they agreed to consider new, less trade-related issues as part of the WTO (Rosset 2007).

However, the next ministerial meeting in Cancún, Mexico in 2003 was the site of massive public protests, profound disillusionment on the part of Southern countries, and a weak agreement to "continue negotiating." The sixth ministerial meeting in Hong Kong in 2005 also left the WTO in limbo. In July of 2008, an emergency mini-ministerial meeting was held in Geneva as a "stepping stone" to conclude Doha in 2008. After a week of intensive negotiations, WTO Director General Pascal Lamy reported that the meeting had failed to reach agreement on the "modalities" to be used to cut Southern tariffs and Northern agricultural subsidies. Despite the deadlock, the director general insisted that "no one is throwing in the towel" (Lamy 2008). True to his word, Lamy attempted to revive Doha at the G8 summit in Hokkaido, Japan in August 2008. Leaders at the summit linked the Doha agenda to the world food crisis. In their Statement on Food Security they insisted,

> Food security also requires a robust world market and trade system for food and agriculture. Rising food prices are adding inflationary pressures and generating macroeconomic imbalances, especially for some low-income countries. In this regard, we will work toward the urgent and successful conclusion of an ambitious, comprehensive and balanced Doha Round.
>
> (G8 2008)

The ministers did not say aloud what everyone at Hokkaido knew: that the WTO's "free" market was actually undermining food security by making poor countries dependent on a volatile world market for their food.

Agreements were not forthcoming. Developing countries attempted to get the US and the EU to curb their tariffs and subsidies, and to allow Southern countries to protect themselves against import surges from the North. The lead countries on either side of the negotiations, the US and India, were both facing elections and neither was willing to risk losing the political support of their agricultural sector by making concessions. (Granted, the South had little left to concede.) Yet again, WTO negotiations ground to a halt.

Southern countries are not the only ones fed up with the WTO. Smallholders in the global North have not benefited from corporate globalization either. Montana farmer Dena Hoff (US), North American co-chair of Via Campesina states flatly:

> We have a food crisis, water crisis, climate crisis, but the WTO continues to promote export-oriented agriculture that only leads to increased deforestation, land concentration, soil erosion, biodiversity destruction and water contamination. Farmers producing food for local domestic markets have now been replaced by agro-export industries such as cut-rate flowers in Kenya and Colombia and devastating agrofuel plantations in Brazil and Indonesia producing sugar, soya and palm oil instead of actual food to feed their citizens. Here in the U.S., this has led to monoculture production of corn and soybeans and factory farms instead of diversified farms producing healthy food for local markets.
>
> (NFFC 2008)

Some observers think the failure of the Doha rounds spells the end of the WTO. Its successful conclusion, however, could be the last straw for smallholder farmers around the world. At the explosive Cancun ministerial meeting in Mexico, on September 16, 2003, Lee Kyung Hae, a Korean farm leader, committed suicide on the fence separating thousands of farmers and protestors from government negotiators. His last, desperate words were both chilling and prophetic:

> My warning goes out to all citizens that human beings are in an endangered situation. That uncontrolled multinational corporations and a small number of big WTO members are leading an undesirable globalization that is inhumane, environmentally degrading, farmer-killing, and undemocratic. It should be stopped immediately. Otherwise, the false logic of neoliberalism will wipe out the diversity of global agriculture and be disastrous to all human beings. WTO kills farmers!

What's next?

Protecting family farmers from the goliath of global trade is literally a matter of life and death for over a billion smallholders trying to compete with subsidized industrial agriculture. In an ideal world, the function of the WTO would be to prevent unfair trading practices like dumping and monopoly control over markets. Instead the WTO agreements have cemented corporate control over the world's food systems.

George Naylor, a corn and soybean farmer from Churdan, Iowa, US, asserts:

> The deregulation of agriculture as advocated by the WTO has decimated family farms both here and abroad. The U.S. commodity farm groups, backed by agribusiness, have propagandized for years that export markets would help family farmers when in reality it just fattens agribusiness's profits. Farmers don't export. Archer Daniels Midland and Cargill do… The WTO promotes a globalized market where all farmers in different countries are pitted in a 'race-to-the-bottom' that only benefits agribusinesses that get access to the cheapest commodities possible. We need domestic farm and food policies that respond to the needs of local communities.
>
> (NFFC 2008)

The evidence from 30 years of these policies is in: farmers, peasants, fishers, migrant workers, urban poor, women, and indigenous people around the world are worse off than they were 40 years ago, and the countries of the global South as a whole are less food secure. Though the food crisis seems to G8 leaders as an opportunity to push the WTO agenda, the world peasant federation, Via Campesina, sees it as a chance to take agriculture out of the WTO altogether:

> In Geneva the talks collapsed on a very big and fundamental issue: the protection of the livelihoods of billions of peasants worldwide against the aggressive pressure by the U.S.A. and the EU to open markets for more food dumping by their multinationals. The… WTO should get out of agriculture! [We] urge the governments not to waste time and resources to find compromises to finalize the Doha round anymore.
>
> (La Via Campesina 2008)

The intractability of the Northern countries in the Doha round succeeded in unifying developing countries against the WTO, with the broad support of smallholders around the world. In this sense, the food crisis and the failing WTO talks may have a positive effect by spurring resolve for real change in the way agriculture is treated in global markets, and by demonstrating that the global South can speak with one voice.

But the WTO is not the only way Northern governments control trade in favor of agribusiness. In fact, whenever the WTO has actually come close to leveling the trading field between Northern and Southern countries, Northern countries have fallen back on bilateral and regional free trade agreements to ensure their market dominance.

BOX 11

The Geneva Doha Package: Third World Pushback

The first wave of stories about the collapse of the talks had to do with China's and India's unreasonable demands. The US daily *The Washington Post* painted a picture of these intransigent upstarts:

> High-level delegations from the United States and the European Union showed fresh willingness at the World Trade Organization talks to make concessions that would have gradually curbed the subsidies and tariffs they have long employed to protect First-World farmers. But India and China dug in their heels, insisting on the right to keep protecting their farmers while accusing the United States and other rich countries of exaggerating the generosity of their concessions.
>
> (Faiola 2008)

India and China maintained that fragile economies should be allowed to protect their agriculture with a special safeguard mechanism (SSM). Broadly speaking, the SSM allows countries to impose duties higher than the agreed ceiling level on farm imports if import volumes rise above their three-year average by an agreed percentage. The goal is to protect poor farmers against import surges.

US Trade Representative Susan Schwab proposed an astronomical 150% volume surge trigger before duties could be imposed. WTO Director General Pascal Lamy offered a 140% trigger. According to historical models the 140% figure means that the SSM would only be invoked in one half of the cases of import surges (ICTSD 2008a). This would cause tremendous harm to poor farmers in the global South. Both of these figures would allow significant commodities dumping from wealthy industrial countries with no legal

The Tyranny of the FTAs

In 1994, just before the formation of the WTO, the North American Free Trade Agreement (NAFTA), an agreement between Mexico, Canada, and the US, entered into effect. This was the first FTA that would be enforced by the WTO, and it became the model for more FTAs to come.

NAFTA evolved from the Commission for the Study of International Migration and Cooperative Economic Development, which was designed by the Immigration Reform and Control Act of 1986 to investigate the causes of immigration into the US. In 1990, a report was issued to President George Bush, Sr. and Congress saying that

---

remedy (which may be the point). Speaking on behalf of the G33 and other developing countries, India proposed a 110% volume trigger, leaving the sides far apart. The US representative later "compromised" by endorsing Lamy's position (ICTSD 2008b). When India proposed compromise positions, the US refused to budge from the 140% figure. The US used China and India as the scapegoats, but in reality the two represented a coalition of nearly 100 countries.

Ben Burkett, president of the National Family Farm Coalition in the US had little sympathy for the US position: "The WTO bears much responsibility for dismantling domestic and tariff protections and leaving countries at the mercy of volatile, speculative markets for their food security. As a U.S. farmer, I fully support the right of India and the G33 countries to implement a special safeguard mechanism (SSM) to protect their farmers and consumers from below-cost imports flooding their markets" (NFFC 2008).

Adapted from Rick Jonasse, The Doha Collapse: Time to Get Agriculture out of the WTO, *Food First Policy Brief*, no. 15, August 2008, http://www.foodfirst.org/en/node/2224.

Faiola, Anthony and Rama Lakshmi. 2008. Bitter Rift Halts Free-Trade Talks: Emerging Nations India, China Insist on Right to Tariffs. *The Washington Post*. July 30.

ICTSD. 2008a. *Agricultural Safeguard Controversy Triggers Breakdown in Doha Round Talks*. International Centre for Trade and Sustainable Development. http://ictsd.net/i/news/bridgesweekly/18034/ (accessed August 7, 2008).

ICTSD. 2008b. *G7 Talks on Special Safeguard Mechanism Inconclusive as Blame Game Heats Up*. International Centre for Trade and Sustainable Development. http://ictsd.net/i/wto/englishupdates/15018/ (accessed August 15, 2008).

NFFC. 2008. *Press Release: U.S. Family Farmers Applaud Demise of Doha Negotiations*. National Family Farm Coalition. http://www.foodfirst.org/en/node/2208 (accessed August 14, 2008).

BOX 12

NAFTA: Effects on Agriculture

The North American Free Trade Agreement (NAFTA) required the immediate removal of all non-tariff barriers for agricultural goods, and a gradual five-year phase-out of tariffs for "sensitive" crops such as corn, beans, and milk. However, the Mexican government eliminated tariffs much sooner than required, and agricultural trade—particularly exports of US grain and Mexican fruits and vegetables—grew very rapidly (Carlsen 2007; de Ita 2008; Henriques 2004). The USDA Foreign Agriculture Service describes this as "one of the most successful trade agreements in history" (Carlsen 2007). Opponents maintain that NAFTA has only benefited a few large-scale growers and food processing corporations, while devastating smaller producers. In Mexico, small farmers (who still comprised 25% of the population prior to NAFTA) had historically grown corn as a staple for home consumption as well as for the domestic market, supplying up to a quarter of total national production in some years. But as imports of cheaper US corn entered the market, these farmers could no longer find buyers for their crops (de Ita 2008; Scott 2006).

The architects of NAFTA predicted that market signals would prompt farmers to switch to other crops such as fruits and vegetables, in which Mexico—due to its cheap labor force and winter growing season—has a comparative advantage over the US (de Ita 2008). But only large land-holders in the north—located on flat, fertile, irrigated land with access to credit, technology, and established marketing channels—were able to make such a shift. These farms are typically contracted out by US produce companies that prefer to deal with large commercial growers rather than peasant farmers. Meanwhile, the vast majority of producers live in central and southern Mexico, on small rain-fed plots that are generally unsuitable for horticulture due to steep slopes, poor soil, and irregular rainfall. These farmers are also unable to afford the high initial start-up costs of shifting to agro-export production, and are therefore excluded from the new export market. In addition, those who assumed that farmers would readily shift away from basic grain failed to consider the dietary and cultural significance of corn in rural Mexico. The success of a few large-scale growers masks the plight of small farmers throughout the country, just as higher overall GDP can mask the declining incomes of the poor (de Ita 2008; Scott 2006).

Throughout the course of NAFTA, rural Mexico has faced ever-increasing poverty, environmental degradation, social unrest, and out-migration (de Ita 2008). Over two million farmers have fled the countryside (Stiglitz and

Charlton 2005), and each year hundreds of thousands more risk their lives to cross the border in search of work (Barry 1995). Rather than profiting from new markets, these displaced farmers have become the labor force for large agro-export farms, picking tomatoes and peppers for US markets under some of the worst living and working conditions in North America (Wright 2005). While their incomes may have increased (contributing to higher overall GDP), these workers also face declining nutrition, separation from their families, job instability, and higher living costs due to the loss of self-provisioning (de Ita 2008).

Advocates of NAFTA point to Mexico's increased GDP as an indicator of success, arguing that poverty and uneven distribution of wealth are the failure of domestic policies rather than free trade. Opponents reply that NAFTA has prevented the governments from enacting better policies, and has increased corporate influence over national politics (Meléndez Salinas 2007). Many also point out that the impacts of NAFTA have been unevenly distributed among nations, as the US imports mainly nonessential products like coffee and fruit, while Mexico imports vast quantities of basic staple foods. Such trade has a greater impact on food security in Mexico, where a large percentage of the population is involved in agriculture and depends upon it for both income and daily sustenance (de Ita 2008).

Adapted from Dori Stone, *Beyond the Fence: A Journey to the Roots of the Migration Crisis*, Food First Books, 2009.

Barry, Tom. 1995. *Zapata's Revenge: Free Trade and the Farm Crisis in Mexico*. Boston: Interhemispheric Resource Center.

Carlsen, Laura. 2007. *NAFTA Inequality and Immigration: Americas Policy Program*. Mexico City: Interhemispheric Resources Center.

de Ita, Ana. 2008. *Fourteen Years of NAFTA and the Tortilla Crisis: Americas Policy Program*. Mexico City: Interhemispheric Resources Center.

Henriques, Gisele and Raj Patel. 2004. *NAFTA, Corn, and Mexico's Agricultural Trade Liberalization: IRC Americas Program Special Report*. Mexico City: Interhemispheric Resources Center.

Meléndez Salinas, Claudia. 2007. Mexican Farmers Struggle to Survive: NAFTA, Farm Bill, Lack of Other Economic Opportunities Force Subsistence Producers to Find Work Elsewhere. *Monterey County Herald*. December 5.

Scott, Robert E. et al. 2006. *Revisiting NAFTA: Still Not Working for North America's Workers*. Economic Policy Institute. http://www.epi.org/content.cfm/bp173 (accessed July 23 2008).

Stiglitz, Joseph E. and Andrew Charlton. 2005. *Fair Trade for All: How Trade Can Promote Development*. New York: Oxford University Press.

Wright, Angus. 2005. *The Death of Ramón González: The Modern Agricultural Dilemma*. 2 ed. Austin: University of Texas Press.

the main incentive for immigration was economic need. The report prescribed more economic integration through free trade to stall this flow, specifically suggesting that the US encourage the development of a free trade area for all of North America (Bacon 2008). What NAFTA actually did was to force Mexican farmers, especially corn farmers, to compete with the cheap prices of subsidized commodities being dumped in Mexico from the US.

Thanks to NAFTA, by the late 1990s Mexico had gone from being self-sufficient in corn to becoming a corn importer. NAFTA outlawed price supports for Mexican farmers, which made it impossible to sell their products at prices covering the costs of production. According to the Mexican government, one million Mexicans became unemployed in NAFTA's first year alone, creating larger—not smaller—waves of immigration to the US (Bacon 2008).

NAFTA addresses both trade-related issues, such as import tariffs and quotas and non-trade-related issues, such as investment and competition between domestic and foreign companies. Reductions in tariffs and quotas, cuts in agricultural subsidies and price supports, privatization of government-sponsored marketing mechanisms, and the evaporation of accessible credit for small farmers under NAFTA have created more poverty and malnutrition, and led to the separation of families through migration (Rosset 2006).

NAFTA has also allowed many US factories and other transnational companies to move to Mexico, where they regularly abuse labor laws and threaten to relocate overseas if laborers demand better treatment (Scott 2003). Furthermore, corporations are allowed to sue a government if its laws or policies limit their profits under NAFTA's 'investor protection' provisions (Brown 2004). This includes situations where a government implements public health, labor, and environmental protections mandated by voters.

In 2004 the Central America–Dominican Republic–United States Free Trade Agreement (CAFTA–DR) was put into effect. This agreement was modeled after NAFTA and includes Costa Rica, Guatemala, El Salvador, Honduras, and Nicaragua, in addition to the Dominican Republic and the US. The signing of CAFTA provoked mass protests throughout Central America. CAFTA hits the poor even harder than NAFTA because Central America is less industrialized, has lower skill levels, and fewer major national firms than does Mexico (Moore 2005).

The US has FTAs with 14 countries and is aggressively negotiating with Colombia, Korea, Oman, Panama, and Peru. Agreements in Latin America are part of a strategy to establish a continent-wide free trade agreement for the Americas. According to the US Department of Commerce's official website for free trade agreements, "Free trade agreements (FTAs) have proved to be one of the best ways to open up foreign markets to U.S. exporters." Free trade agreements now account for over 42% of US exports (International Trade Administration 2008).

4

The Overproduction of Hunger: Uncle Sam's Farm and Food Bill

The US Farm Bill is a mammoth piece of legislation passed by the US Congress every five to seven years. It funds a wide range of government programs including food stamps and nutrition, agricultural research, animal welfare, forestry, rural electricity and water supply, foreign food aid, and—importantly—subsidy payments to commodity crop producers.

Year-to-year fluctuation in crop yields and prices makes farming financially risky. Farmers are also caught in a perennial cost–price squeeze because they use expensive industrial inputs to produce cheap raw materials. Further, farmers must invest heavily up front in inputs and labor and then hope that the weather cooperates. When they take their crops to market months later, they often find crop prices have fallen. Subsidy payments, price guarantees, crop insurance, set-asides, grain reserves and other measures have historically been used to provide more stability to farmers under agriculture's inherently adverse conditions.

Food crises and farm crises are never far apart. In the 1970s, the US government had been managing grain supply and market fluctuations by maintaining national reserves and paying farmers to idle their land. But when oil shortages and inflation pushed up food prices—provoking widespread hunger abroad—the US Secretary of Agriculture Earl Butz told US farmers to save the world from hunger by planting "fence row to fence row" and putting their entire harvest on the market. Prior policies that curbed overproduction and protected farmers from price swings were replaced by ones that encouraged maximum production and low prices.

When it turned out the hungry people of the world were too poor to buy all the food US farmers produced, markets became glutted with grain and prices crashed. Secretary Butz then told farmers to grow their way out of the crisis. The only option was to "get big or

BOX 13

The Perils of the Unregulated Market

by George Naylor, National Family Farm Coalition—USA

Farmers produce commodities (especially grains) because they are not perishable, can be stored, and act virtually as money throughout the year. The boom and bust cycle is inherent in an unregulated agricultural economy. In years of abundance and low prices, individual farmers will increase production in an attempt to maintain their income. This only drives the market price even lower, leading to wasteful consumption—such as feedlots or ethanol plants. In years of scarcity, the increased demand that grew in the abundant years will push prices ever upwards. Both farmers and poor consumers suffer under this unregulated market.

The solution is to first recognize the natural tendency of the market to discount the environmental costs and social costs that are inevitable with unregulated commodity production. A price floor has to be set to internalize these costs and adjust it to inflation (this higher price would discourage their use as livestock feed and as a feedstock for ethanol). Then the government needs to implement conservation and supply management programs to limit wasteful overproduction and encourage biodiversity. Finally, we need to provide for a government-held reserve that keeps surpluses off the market in years of bounty so as to not break the price floor, and to release grain in times of scarcity to ensure food security. This needs to be done internationally among all countries able to produce commodity surpluses. Every country should have the right to eliminate any imports that disrupt the agricultural policy they have chosen which lets them respect their traditions, environment, food security and need for economic opportunity in rural areas.

---

get out." The result was widespread bankruptcy and the wrenching exodus of over half of the US's farming families from the countryside. The average farm size went from 200 to 400 acres, reflecting a steady shift to megafarms. Large-scale corporate and non-family farms now control 75% of agricultural production in the US (Rosegrant 1994; Banker et al. 2007).

Under new agricultural policy, farmers were guaranteed a minimum price for their grain. True to its word, over the next two decades, the government paid out billions of dollars to maintain surpluses of cheap grain. Cheap grain became the bulwark not only of a feedlot explosion, but of US foreign policy as well. This strategy was

BOX 14

The US: The Food Crisis Comes Home

Few people think of the United States when they think of the food crisis. However, hidden from international attention is the fact that even before the global food crisis, over 35 million Americans—12% of the population—were going hungry. With the crisis, they were joined by people living just over the poverty line, making 50 million people food insecure in the richest country in the world. In a moderately populated land of massive wealth, rich soils, abundant water and cutting-edge technology, these numbers fly in the face of assertions that hunger is due to "overpopulation," "under-development," or "scarce resources." The food crisis is hitting the US and with the economic crisis, will soon become a domestic political issue.

US retail prices of food increased 5.5% between 2007 and 2008. The USDA claims prices will increase another three to four percentage points throughout 2009, amounting to the steepest increase in 19 years. Many food insecure people in the US live in the "food deserts" and must travel long distances to buy fresh food. The triple squeeze of a declining economy and food and energy inflation are affecting the poor and the middle class alike. Last year, over 28 million people—a national record—were driven into the national food stamp program (Winne 2008). A dozen eggs in 2008 cost 50 cents more than in 2007, a loaf of bread, 20 cents more. Most small retailers operate on a slim margin of 1%-3%, cannot absorb these cost increases, and so pass them on to consumers. However, because they make their money on high volume and low margins—and because they can source directly from producers—larger chains and big box stores are posting sizable crisis profits. Safeway showed a 15.7% increase in net income between 2006 and 2007. UK-based Tesco's profits rose by a record 11.8% last year. Other major retailers, such as WalMart, also say that food sales are driving their profit increases.

Food Banks: Canaries in the Mineshaft

Recent trends in the nation's food banks are a good indicator of the dimensions of the crisis: there is less food available, it is more expensive, and the lines outside the food banks are growing. A 2008 survey done by Feeding

---

later baked-in to the rules of the World Trade Organization (WTO) that prevented developing countries from raising tariffs to protect their agriculture from cheap US imports.

But membership in the WTO also required the US to drop *its* farm subsidies. The 1996 Farm Bill called for a phase-out by 2001. The so-called, "Freedom to Farm" Act abandoned our national grain reserves

America (the nation's food bank coordinating agency, distributing two billion pounds of food annually) revealed that 99% of food banks had significant increases in the number of people served since last year (America's Second Harvest 2008). Though the demand for food has increased, food stocks are down. USDA surplus has declined by $200 million (Leibtag 2008) and local food donations are down nationally about 9% (Fraser 2008). (The USDA distributes surplus when stocks are high or commodity prices fall below a certain level. Like international food aid, they respond to the needs of the grain market first, tending to decrease distribution when food is most needed and increase it when it is less needed.) Because many food banks across the nation rely heavily on government surplus, the decline in USDA bonus commodities has pressured them to find alternative suppliers and sources of food. Food Banks are also suffering due to decreased monetary donations from middle class Americans who are tightening their belts in response to the national financial crunch, and decreased food donations from food corporations due to the emergence of lucrative "secondary markets" (e.g., Big Lots, Dollar Tree, Grocery Outlet). In California—the richest agricultural state in the US—the California Association of Food Banks in the summer of 2008 asserted that food banks are at the "beginning of a crisis" (California Association of Food Banks 2008).

Adapted from Conner et al., The Food Crisis Comes Home: Empty Food Banks, Rising Costs—Symptoms of a Hungrier Nation, *Food First Backgrounder*, vol.14, no. 3, 2008.

America's Second Harvest. 2008. *New Survey Underscores Urgent Need for Farm Bill as Demands Are Up, Food Down: More Hungry Americans Turn to Nation's Food Banks for Help*. Chicago: America's Second Harvest.

California Association of Food Banks. 2008. *International Food Crisis: Food Bank Clients in Peril*. Oakland: California Association of Food Banks.

Fraser, R. 2008. Media Relations Manger. Telephone interview with H. Conner. in The Food Crisis Comes Home: Empty Food Banks, Rising Costs—Symptoms of a Hungrier Nation. *Food First Backgrounder* 14 (3). June 30. Oakland: Food First.

Winne, Mark. 2008. Leading the Charge, Leading the Change. Keynote address given to the Northwest Harvest Food Bank Annual Meeting, Seattle WA.

and gutted the positive, New Deal aspects of the US Farm Bill (like price floors to rural economies, and conservation and diversified livestock programs). Counting on unimpeded exports, US farmers borrowed heavily to crank up production—too quickly, as it turned out. When global grain prices crashed, government responded with billions of dollars in "emergency payments" that they claimed were "not technically" subsidies. In 2002 corn and wheat exports from the US were priced at 13% and 43% below the cost of production. It is no surprise that these "non-subsidies" became the foundation of the 2002 Farm Bill.

The main beneficiaries of such policies were large farms, multinational grain traders like Cargill and Archer Daniels Midland, and the feedlot industries (e.g., Tyson and Smithfield) that gained access to cheap, abundant grain supplies for their processed foods and animal feed.

The 2008 Food, Conservation and Energy Act

This act, also known as the Farm Bill, weighed in at $307 billion over five years. On the food side, 68% of the bill is for the Supplemental Nutrition Assistance Program (Mitchell 2008). Thanks to years of tireless lobbying on the part of food and farm activists in the US, there is also $100 million a year to be split between programs that rebuild local food systems, increase access to healthy food in underserved communities and support organic, beginning and minority farmers (Banker et al. 2007).

Unfortunately, the Farm Bill also includes $74 billion of the same commodity programs that benefit megafarms and corporate agribusiness, and undermine public health, the environment, and farming communities worldwide including:

- $12.6 billion in commodity programs with $8.7 billion in direct payments regardless of a grower's need (CCC 2008)
- $300 million a year for agrofuel programs that will continue to push up grain prices (Posey 2008).

The boom: are farmers benefiting?

While the food crisis sent grain prices on the global market skyrocketing, the family farmers growing the grain didn't see much of this windfall for long. The spectacular increase in the price of corn (from $2 to $8 a bushel) was quickly followed by a tripling in the price of farm inputs—then a crash in commodity prices when the world financial crisis hit.

Farmers receive less than 20 cents of the food dollar, out of which they must pay for production costs that have increased by 45% over the last six years. The prices of most fertilizers have tripled in a

Demonstration and rally for food justice in San Francisco, 2008

year and a half. The price of urea, the most common nitrogen fertilizer, rose from an average of US$281 per ton in January 2007 to $402 in January 2008, then to $815 in August, an increase of 300% (IFDC 2008). Diesel prices to farmers have increased 40% in two years (Energy Information Administration 2008).

Organic farmers report an increase in their input costs such as organic fertilizer, seeds, and plastics used for irrigation, and general costs such as electricity and water. Many organic milk producers can no longer find organic feed grains. Some small-scale producers selling at farmers' markets have seen an increase in customers and in the short run, community supported agriculture (CSA) farmers appear to be the best off (because their consumers help shoulder production costs), but this can shift due to anxiety over next year's crop or the overall economy. In the Midwest and the South, the crisis has been compounded by flooding and hurricanes, forcing replanting and loss of crops to sell at farmers' markets or to local distributors.

The bust

Due to the global financial crisis, grain is sitting in freighters overseas because buyers can't get the letters of credit they need to purchase it. Farmers are having just as much difficulty finding credit to cover their production costs (Weitzman 2008). Market prices for grain after two years of boom are now crashing by 47% to 62% (CBOT 2008; Cha and

McCrummen 2008). Ten-dollar (a bushel) corn was devastating for poor consumers. Three-dollar corn will now devastate producers.

The volatility of the world grain market is the bane of today's globalized food systems. In the boom and bust of the 1970s, the US lost half of its farming population. What will it lose if agriculture goes bust again?

Europe's Common Agricultural Policy[6]

In Europe, more than a thousand farms disappear every day (Coordinadora Europa de la Via Campesina 2008). The main reason behind this trend is the lack of political will on the part of governments and international institutions to back local, family-scale and smallholder agriculture. Similar to the Farm Bill in the US, in the European Union the Common Agricultural Policy (and the agricultural rules of the WTO) serve the interests of agro-industry, not family farmers. These policies put corporate profit ahead of people's food needs and local, sustainable production.

The current Common Agricultural Policy (CAP) is a combination of poor policies and bad reforms dating back to 1992. The CAP, with its focus on industrial agriculture and subsidies, generated a boom in agricultural production, resulting in falling prices and highly negative ecological and social impacts (Soler 2007). The CAP directs the majority of its assistance to large producers, to the detriment of small family farms. As the report *Goliath Against David: Who Wins and Who Loses with the CAP in Spain and in Poor Counties* (Intermón Oxfam 2005) states, "The CAP sustains a model of intensive production that rewards those who have the most and causes important distortions in international markets, often at the expense of developing countries." The report adds that "behind the legal and technical maze that accompanies the functioning of the system is hidden a simple principle: the more you produce and the more land you own—which is to say, the richer you are—the more public assistance you receive."

According to data from the European Commission, in 2000 some 2.3 million European farmers received only 4% of EU farm subsidies, while 5% of the largest producers took half the subsidies. In Great Britain, families in the wealthiest ranks of society received heavy subsidies from the EU: the Duke of Westminster, €470,000, Sir Adrian Swire, €300,000 for his farm in Oxfordshire, and the Duke of Marlborough, €535,000 for his production of cereals, among others.

The same logic is repeated in France, Germany, and Spain. According to data from the French government, a quarter of its farmers receive no assistance, while 15% of the largest farms take in six of every ten euros in French subsidies (Watkins 2003). In Spain 17% of the proprietors of the largest farms receive much greater than average income, while the 60% of the smallest holdings receive below average income (Intermón Oxfam 2005).

The battle over food in Europe is also being fought over genetically modified organisms. Spain is the only country in Europe that cultivates genetically modified organisms (GMOs) on a large scale, and as a consequence has become the back door for GMOs' entry on the continent. Spain imports some nine million tons of soy and maize annually from countries with massive GMO production including the US, Argentina, and Brazil. Importers Cargill, Bunge, Simsa, and ADM do not separate conventional from genetically modified grain, thus causing massive genetic contamination (Greenpeace España 2004). In Europe there is no systematic protection of conventional and organic seed, and a loose threshold of accidental contamination is legally acceptable. This puts the free choice of farmers and consumers at risk and endangers conventional and organic production.

The European Union's model of industrial agriculture has had profound social and environmental impacts in the region. In Spain between 1999 and 2003, 147,000 family farms disappeared, resulting in the depopulation of rural areas, their impoverishment, and a withdrawal of essential public services (Intermón Oxfam 2005). Environmental degradation has proceeded apace: soil erosion; excessive use of pesticides and fertilizers; soil depletion from the absence of crop rotation and fallow periods; the loss of biodiversity due to the spread of monocultures; desertification, and the depletion and contamination of water resources through excessive irrigation have all been among the disastrous consequences of the CAP.

5

Agrofuels: A Bad Idea at the Worst Possible Time

In 2007 Lester Brown of the Earth Policy Institute shocked the world by stating flatly: "The grain it takes to fill a 25-gallon tank with ethanol just once will feed one person for a whole year" (Brown 2007). The UN special rapporteur on the right to food, Jean Ziegler, was just as critical. He called agrofuels a "crime against humanity" and urged governments to implement a five-year moratorium on production (Ziegler 2007). These statements were the first fractures in the "agrofuels consensus," the widely held belief that fuel crops hailed the next transition to a renewable fuel economy, one that would lower greenhouse gas emissions and usher in a new era of rural prosperity.

Faith in agrofuels helped unleash an investment boom in research, processing plants, and the conversion of millions of acres of land into sugarcane, corn, oil palm and jatropha plantations worldwide. The desire for an alternative fuel to confront "peak oil" forged an unspoken social agreement on the need for agrofuels, even as scientific evidence contradicted the claims of energy savings and environmental benefits enthusiastically promoted by the industry (Crutzen 2007; Searchinger et al. 2008). The protests of poor peasants losing land to palm-oil expansion in Colombia, of pastoralists losing land to jatropha plantations in Africa and India, of sugarcane workers living and dying in slave-like conditions in Brazil, or of Malaysian conservationists struggling to preserve forest habitat for endangered orangutans, were drowned out by the "Green Gold Rush." Politicians of every stripe lined up behind the flush agrofuels lobby, voting for billions of dollars in subsidies, tariffs and tax incentives.

Not until the global food crisis burst upon the scene were the world's governments forced to question the wisdom of using food resources for fuel production.

While food price inflation was not caused solely by agrofuels, the explosive expansion of the ethanol market had a direct effect on grain

Leonor Hurtado

Food or fuel? Agrofuels in our food system

price surges (De La Torre Ugarte and Murphy 2008). Between 2001 and 2006, the amount of corn used in US ethanol distilleries tripled from 18 million tons to an estimated 55 million tons. Between 2006 and 2007, the increase in demand for corn from US ethanol distilleries—from 54 to 81 million tons—was over twice the annual increase in global demand for the world's grain. By 2008 a quarter of the US corn harvest was being diverted to ethanol production (*Financial Times* 2008).

Despite industry claims to the contrary, agrofuels do raise food prices. After all, their original purpose was to add value to cheap, surplus grain. (In this respect, they worked a little too well…) Because US corn accounts for some 40% of global production, increasing the value of US corn as fuel-stock impacts global markets for corn as food. As market demand for fuel corn increases, not only do all corn prices rise, but more corn is planted, crowding out other food grains such as wheat and soybeans. With less land available for cultivation, the price of these products also increases.

The International Food Policy Research Institute (IFPRI) predicts that depending on rates of agrofuels expansion, by 2020, the global price of corn will increase by 26% to 72% and the price of oilseeds between 18% and 44% (von Braun 2007). With every 1% rise in the cost of food, 16 million people are made food insecure (Runge and Senauer 2007).

However, agrofuels don't just drive up food prices, they concentrate corporate monopoly power and pull our food and fuels systems under one giant industrial roof.

How? Overproduction of grains has led to a steady decline in food prices and profit margins over the last 30 years. In the past, corporations offset this falling rate of profit by increasing productivity through technological improvements (e.g., the Green Revolution), or by adding value to raw commodities by transforming them (e.g., corn into beef), and by vertically integrating—expanding their operations to include production, processing and retail, thus capturing more of the food value chain. Grain companies simply traded and transported larger and larger volumes of grain.

Agrofuels accomplish *all* of these things in one operation.

In this way, they are like an industrial "one-stop-shop" to solve agribusiness' problem with the falling rate of profit. The transformation of food into fuel (a) opens up new market space for overproduced commodities like corn and sugarcane, (b) inflates the value of those commodities in both food and fuel markets, (c) creates more processing steps that allow corporate players to both add and capture more value, and (d) increases the total amount of grain being traded. Little wonder that agrofuels steam full speed ahead, despite their serious social and environmental drawbacks.

Proponents of agrofuels argue that fuel crops planted on ecologically degraded lands will improve rather than destroy the environment. Perhaps the government of Brazil had this in mind when it reclassified some 200 million hectares of dry tropical forests, grassland, and marshes as "degraded" and apt for cultivation. In reality, these are the biodiverse ecosystems of the Mata Atlantica, the Cerrado and the Pantanal, occupied by indigenous people, subsistence farmers, and extensive cattle ranches. The introduction of agrofuel

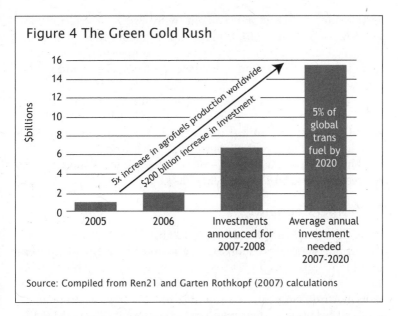

Figure 4 The Green Gold Rush

5x increase in agrofuels production worldwide

$200 billion increase in investment

5% of global trans fuel by 2020

$billions

16
14
12
10
8
6
4
2
0

2005   2006   Investments announced for 2007-2008   Average annual investment needed 2007-2020

Source: Compiled from Ren21 and Garten Rothkopf (2007) calculations

plantations will simply push these communities to the "agricultural frontier" of the Amazon where the devastating patterns of deforestation are all too well known. Soybeans supply 40% of Brazil's biodiesel. NASA has positively correlated their market price with the destruction of the Amazon rainforest—currently at nearly 325,000 hectares a year. Called "The Diesel of Deforestation," palm oil plantations for biodiesel are the primary cause of forest loss in Indonesia, a country with one of the highest deforestation rates in the world. By 2020, Indonesia's oil palm plantations will triple in size to 16.5 million hectares—an area the size of England and Wales combined—resulting in a loss of 98% of forest cover. Neighboring Malaysia, the world's largest producer of palm oil, has already lost 87% of its tropical forests and continues deforesting at a rate of 7% a year.

The big players in the agrofuels boom are no longer environmentalists or family farmers, but multinational corporations and investors, who have increased their investments in the industry seven-fold in just three years (CNBC 2007). This investment is creating new corporate partnerships between agribusinesses, biotechnology, oil and automotive companies: ADM with both Monsanto and Conoco-Phillips; BP with DuPont and Toyota, as well as with Monsanto and Mendel Biotechnology; Royal Dutch Shell with Cargill, Syngenta, and Goldman-Sachs; and DuPont with British Petroleum and Weyerhauser. In June 2007, BP, Associated British Foods, and chemical giant DuPont Co. announced they were investing $400 million to build an agrofuels plant in England (Holt-Giménez and Kenfield 2008).

Despite bumps and busts within the industry, the targets, subsidies, tariffs, and tax benefits hold agrofuels firmly in place. US subsidies for ethanol are as much as $1.38 per gallon. By early 2009 they accounted for over half its wholesale market price. In 2006, the combined state and federal support for the US ethanol industry was between $5.1 and $6.8 billion (IISD 2006).

Do farmers benefit?

In the tropics of the global South, 100 hectares dedicated to family farming generates 35 jobs. Oil palm and sugarcane plantations provide 10 jobs, eucalyptus two, and soybeans a scant half-job per 100 hectares, all poorly paid. The establishment of palm oil plantations in Afro-Colombian communities has driven peasants off thousands of hectares of their own land at gunpoint (Zimbalist 2007). The "Jatropha Explosion" in India and Africa, far from occupying idle, unproductive land, or serving as a hedgerow cash crop for peasant farmers, has become a major plantation monocrop, driving herders out of browsing lands and peasants into low-income contract farming.

Until recently, agrofuels supplied primarily local and sub-regional markets. Even in the US, most ethanol plants were relatively small, and farmer owned. With the agrofuels boom, big industry is quickly moving in, centralizing operations and creating gargantuan economies of scale. Big Oil, Big Grain, and Big Genetic Engineering are rapidly consolidating control over the entire agrofuel value chain. The market power of these corporations is staggering: Cargill and ADM control 65% of the global grain trade, Monsanto and Syngenta a quarter of the $60 billion genetech industry. This market power allows these companies to extract profits from the most lucrative and low-risk segments of the value chain, e.g., inputs, processing and distribution. Farmers producing fuel crops will be increasingly dependent on a tightly organized cabal of companies for their seed, inputs, services, processing, and sale. They are not likely to receive many benefits. More likely, smallholders will be forced out of the market and off the land, just as hundreds of thousands have already been displaced by the corporate soybean plantations in the "Republic of Soy," a 50+ million hectare area covering southern Brazil, northern Argentina, Paraguay, and eastern Bolivia.

There is overwhelming support for agrofuels in the corn-growing regions of North America. The US Corn Growers Association, the American Corn Growers Association, and the Canadian Oilseed Association all promote agrofuels. This is because decades of low prices turned many rural communities in North America into economically depressed ghost towns with few jobs, failed businesses, crumbling infrastructure, and painful deficits in basic human services like hospitals, schools, fire departments, banks, and grocery stores. Hunger in the US is actually worse in rural areas than urban centers, making the rural Midwest the largest "food desert" in the world.

When the agrofuels industry drove up the price of corn to levels not seen in decades, farmers finally received a price for their grain that not only covered the cost of production, but generated profits. The burgeoning ethanol plants brought in jobs and new investments in hotels, restaurants and other services. Unsurprisingly, farmers unable to get a fair price when their grain was sold for food were ecstatic when grain sold as fuel drove up prices paid to them by 300%.

With the global economic recession, oil and grain prices are crashing, agrofuel plants are folding, and the agrofuels industry (now consolidating into the usual corporate hands) is operating on slimmer margins, despite subsidy and tariff supports. Because inflated farm inputs are not coming down in price, Northern farmers can look forward to a cost-price squeeze once again.

Many family farm groups are tired of putting their livelihoods at risk in the volatile, unregulated market and want to move away from subsidies, which they consider benefit industry more than farmers. They are calling for something very simple: a fair price. If farmers received a fair price for their crop, they would not need subsidies. Neither would they have to resort to agrofuels. The government has many ways of ensuring a fair market price for farmers, including a guaranteed price floor and supply-side controls to prevent overproduction and price volatility. Grain companies are staunch opponents of these mechanisms. They prefer to buy on the cheap, even though it costs taxpayers and hurts farmers.

BOX 15

The RFS Targets: The Obligatory Market Driving the Agrofuels Boom

The Renewable Fuel Standards (RFS) targets in the 2007 US Energy and Security Act—36 billion gallons per year by 2022—far exceed the US's current capacity for fuel crop production. Of the mandate, less than half—15 billion gallons—will come from corn ethanol. Achieving this volume will require 45 million acres—nearly 50% of the country's current corn acreage. Even if all of the US's 90 million-acre corn crop were converted to ethanol, just 12%-16% of our gasoline would be replaced—barely enough for current 10% ethanol blends (E-10), much less the 98% blends suggested in the Energy Bill (Hill et al. 2006).

The remaining 21 billion gallons in the RFS are defined as "advanced biofuels." This futuristic sounding term actually includes any fuel crop other than corn, including soybeans, oil palm, sugarcane and jatropha. While politicians have pinned their hopes on cellulosic ethanol made from native grasses or genetically engineered fast-growing trees, by most accounts these fuels will need years and billions of dollars in research and infrastructure development to become commercially viable. The 36-billion-gallon mandate only replaces some 7% of the US's current fuel use—about 1.5 million barrels of oil per day (Goodell 2007). Regardless of the technology, the inconvenient truth lurking in the 2007 US Energy Bill is that the United States is geographically incapable of producing enough agrofuel to meet the RFS mandate.

This is why in 2006 the US imported 13.5% of ethanol used. Countries that export ethanol to the US include Costa Rica, El Salvador, Jamaica, Trinidad-Tobago, and Brazil. In 2005, the US imported 31 million gallons of

The corporate concentration in the agrofuels industry is rapidly pushing out the small farmer-owned ethanol cooperatives. According to the Renewable Fuels Association (RFA), out of a total of 193 operational ethanol processing plants in the US, 39 are local, farmer owned, accounting for 15% of the nation's total capacity. Farmers' share of production dropped 13 points from 28% between 2007 and 2008 (Hasan 2007; RFA 2009). Out of a total of 20 plants now under construction, none are farmer-owned. The top four companies now control 33% of US production capacity (RFA 2009). Because of the economies of scale of its plants, and the fact that it can dominate the grain market in both food and fuel crops, ADM is emerging as the dominant player. As the

ethanol from Brazil. By 2006 Brazilian imports jumped to 434 million gallons (Renewable Fuel Association 2008). Rather than ensuring energy independence, the RFS mandate reflects an agreement between industry and politicians to legislate the US's dependency on imported agrofuels.

The liquid fuel targets in the RFS are the keystone of the agrofuels boom. They frame the economic context by legally forcing US consumers to buy agrofuels. Without the targets, neither agrofuels' substantial subsidies nor their protective tariffs can sustain the industry. Remove the 36-billion-gallon-per-year targets and agrofuels come to a grinding halt. This is why many concerned citizens in the US are calling for a suspension of agrofuel targets. A coalition of progressive environmental and social justice groups in the US launched a global call for a US moratorium in 2008.[i]

The call for an agrofuels moratorium in Europe has forced European Commission officials to acknowledge the dangers of agrofuels expansion, leading to a move to down-size Europe's agrofuels mandates from 10% to 4%.

Adapted from Eric Holt-Giménez and Isabella Kenfield, When Renewable Isn't Sustainable: Agrofuels and the Inconvenient Truths Behind the 2007 US Energy Independence and Security Act, *Food First Policy Brief* 13, 2008.

i. See http://ga3.org/campaign/agrofuelsmoratorium.

Goodell, Jeff. 2007. The Ethanol Scam: One of America's Biggest Political Boondoggles. *Rolling Stone* 1032.
Hill, Jason, Erik Nelson, David Tilman, Stephen Polasky, and Douglas Tiffany. 2006. *Environmental, Economic and Energetic Costs of Biodiesel and Ethanol Biofuels*. Paper read at National Academy of Sciences, July 12.
Renewable Fuel Association. 2008. *Industry Statistics. Renewable Fuel Association*. http://www.ethanolrfa.org/industry/statistics/ (accessed October 14, 2008).

boom–bust cycle of food and fuel unfolds, the industry continues to consolidate. ADM's stock options now dwarf all major competitors by 3:1 (*Financial Times* 2008).

Agrofuels: Renewable… but not Green

Before the advent of electricity and hydropower, much of the Western world lit their lamps with oil rendered from the blubber of whales, a "renewable" resource that the whaling industry nearly drove to extinction. (Even after the commercialization of petroleum, the industry continued to hunt whales, marketing perfumes and baleen corsets in an attempt to save the industry.) Confusing the term

BOX 16

Yes, We Have No Tortillas

While they may well be suffering under the current financial crisis due to speculation, big grain companies were not hit by food price inflation. Corporations like ADM and Cargill both buy and sell grain, so they stand to gain from either low or high grain prices. When grain prices drop, they buy. Because of their market power they can withhold grain from the market—hoarding supplies until the price goes up again. When grain prices rise, they sell. This speculation was at the heart of the Mexican "Tortilla Crisis" in 2007. It makes no difference that white corn is used for tortillas and yellow corn for cattle feed. As agrofuels cut into the acreage planted to yellow corn, white corn was fed to cattle, taking it off the tortilla market and inflating its price. Grain merchants, like ADM and Cargill, and corn processors, like Mexico's binational Maseca, raised their prices. When the Mexican government attempted to intervene with a price cap, these corporations responded by witholding grain from the market (hoarding), which made the problem worse. This incident illustrates how the agrofuels boom increases the market power of these corporations—a power summarily unchecked by governments.

"renewable" with the notion of sustainability hides an inconvenient truth: agrofuels targets in the industrial North are leading to massive environmental destruction in the global South. Millions of hectares of tropical forests, grasslands, and peat lands around the world are rapidly being cleared and burned to plant fuel crops for export.

But when the full "life cycle" of agrofuels is considered—from land clearing to automotive consumption—the moderate emission savings are undone by far greater emissions from deforestation, burning, peat drainage, cultivation, and soil carbon losses (Searchinger et al. 2008). Every ton of palm oil produced results in 33 tons of carbon dioxide emissions—10 times more than petroleum (Monbiot 2007). Tropical forests cleared for sugarcane ethanol emit 50% more greenhouse gasses than the production and use of the same amount of gasoline (Tillman and Hill 2007). Commenting on the global carbon balance, Doug Parr, chief UK scientist at Greenpeace, states flatly, "If even five percent of biofuels are sourced from wiping out existing ancient forests, you've lost all your carbon gain" (Holt-Giménez 2007).

There are other environmental problems as well. To produce a liter of ethanol takes three to five liters of irrigation water and produces up to 13 liters of waste water (Aslow 2007). It takes the energy equivalent of 113 liters of natural gas to treat this waste, increasing the likelihood that it will simply be released into the environment to pollute streams, rivers and groundwater. Intensive cultivation of fuel crops also leads to high rates of erosion, particularly in soy production—from 6.5 tons per hectare in the US to up to 12 tons per hectare in Brazil and Argentina (Altieri and Bravo 2007).

Nonetheless, the agrofuels boom also offers biotech companies, including Monsanto and Syngenta, the opportunity to irreversibly convert agriculture to genetically engineered crops worldwide. In 2008, 80% of corn, 92% of soy and 86% of cotton in the US was genetically modified (GM) (USDA 2008c). In the EU, consumer resistance has, to a large extent, kept GM crops out. But with agrofuels, the biotech industry has a chance to gain access through the back door by presenting GM crops as energy crops, not food crops. Like a Trojan horse, the expansion of GM corn and soy for special ethanol processing plants will remove geographical barriers to the contamination of non-GMO crops.

Second Generation Fuel Crops: Greening the Parachute?

Proponents of agrofuels argue that present-day agrofuels made from food crops will soon be replaced with environmentally friendly crops like fast-growing trees and switchgrass. This myth, wryly referred to as the "bait and switchgrass" game, invites us to accept present inefficient and polluting agrofuels on the chance that a better, greener alternative is in the works. This is a bit like being asked to jump out of a plane on the assurance that parachutes will be invented before you hit the ground...

Second generation agrofuels will do nothing to decrease the monopoly power in the food and fuel industries. They won't avoid the ecological problems of industrial fuel crop monocultures, nor will they resolve the problem of resource competition between food and fuel. This is because the issue of which crops (food or non-food) are converted to fuel is irrelevant. If and when fuel crops like switchgrass and eucalyptus trees become viable agrofuel commodities, they will migrate from hedgerows and woodlots into the field where the main crops are grown. Here they will compete with food crops for land, water, and resources. Additionally, second generation agrofuels will

BOX 17

Biotechnology: "Stacking" Agrofuels' Market Power

Monsanto and agribusiness giant Cargill recently launched a joint venture called Renessen, a whole new agribusiness corporation with an initial invest- ment of nearly half a billion dollars. Renessen is the sole provider of the first commercially available, genetically modified, energy-dedicated crop, "Mavera High-Value Corn." Mavera corn is "stacked" with foreign genetic material for increased oil content, amino acid production, Monsanto's standard Bt pesticide, and its Roundup Ready gene. The genius of this operation, and the danger to farmers, is that farmers must sell their crop of Mavera corn to a Renessen-owned processing plant to recoup the higher value of the crop (for which they paid a premium on the seed). Cargill's agricultural processing division has created a plant that only processes their brand of corn. Further, due to the genetically engineered presence of lysine, an amino acid lacking in the standard cattle feedlot diet, they can sell the waste stream as a high-priced cattle feed. Renessen has achieved for Monsanto and Cargill nearly perfect vertical integration. Renessen sets the price of seed, Monsanto sells the chemical inputs, Renessen sets the price at which to buy back the finished crop, Renessen sells the fuel, and farmers are left to absorb the risk. This system robs small farmers of choices and market power, while ensuring maximum monopoly profits for Renessen, Monsanto and Cargill.

From Annie Shattuck, The Agrofuels Trojan Horse, *Food First Policy Brief*, no. 14, Institute for Food and Development Policy, 2008.

not be commercially available for at least a decade (if ever), because they require major scientific discoveries in plant physiology to break down lignin, cellulose and hemi-cellulose—not simple refinements of existing technology.

A recent study from Iowa State University indicates that under the RFS targets, the expansion of cellulosic feedstock for ethanol produc- tion will worsen, not lessen, the competition for land and resources between food and fuel, sending prices skyrocketing. Further, they determine that, "In order for switchgrass ethanol to be commercially viable, it must receive a differential subsidy over that awarded to corn-based ethanol." In other words, subsidies to second-generation fuels must be even greater than those presently artificially propping up corn ethanol. The same study estimates that a 3%–4% increase in

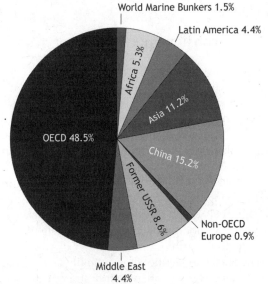

Figure 5 Key World Energy Statistics: World Energy Use

World Marine Bunkers 1.5%

Latin America 4.4%

Africa 5.3%

Asia 11.2%

OECD 48.5%

China 15.2%

Former USSR 8.6%

Non-OECD
Europe 0.9%

Middle East
4.4%

Source: International Energy Agency 2007 © OECD/IEA 2007. Head of
Communication and Information Office, Paris, France.

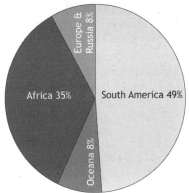

Figure 6 Key World Energy Statistics: Additional Land
Available for Agrofuels

Europe &
Russia 8%

Africa 35%

South America 49%

Oceana 8%

North America 0%

Source: International Energy Agency 2007 © OECD/IEA 2007. Head of
Communication and Information Office, Paris, France.

fuel economy would save the same amount of fuel as that expected to be replaced by agrofuels—without massive taxpayer subsidies (Baker et al. 2008).

Can we really consume our way out of over-consumption?

The need to reduce Northern dependence on foreign oil has led many people to embrace agrofuels as a replacement for fossil fuels and "energy independence." A quick look at where most of the world's energy is consumed and where the available land for agrofuels is found dispels this myth (see Figures 6 and 7). The truth is, nearly half of the planet's energy is consumed in the industrial North, while almost all of the available land for agrofuels (including forests, peat bogs, and browsing land) is found in Africa and Latin America. The tragedy of agrofuels is that the global South will sacrifice its forests, savannas, peat bogs and productive land to satiate the energy appetite of the industrial North.

There is no reason to sacrifice the possibility of sustainable, equitable food and fuel systems to an industrial strategy that compromises both. Many successful, locally focused, energy-efficient and people-centered alternatives are presently producing food and fuel in ways that do not threaten food systems, the environment, or livelihoods. The question is not whether agrofuels *per se* have a place in our future, but whether or not we will allow a handful of global corporations to determine our future by dragging us down an environmentally devastating dead end. To avoid this trap we have to abandon the cornucopian myths left over from the age of abundant oil. We must dare to envision a different, steady-state agrarian transition linked to diverse, resilient local food systems.

6

Summing Up the Crisis

The global monopolies of the industrial agrifoods complex, with the help of the international finance institutions and the complicity of governments, have served up a major planetary crisis. Further, the global institutions ostensibly in charge of monitoring and protecting the world's food and financial systems completely failed to anticipate the food and financial system meltdowns.

The food crisis is rooted in a vulnerable global food system that has become socially, environmentally and financially dysfunctional. Food has become another commodity subject to financial speculation. The trade regime serves predatory markets instead of human needs. Agriculture has become an industrial mode of corporate accumulation rather than the basis for productive livelihoods and a sustainable supply of good, healthy food. Local and national food systems have been mercilessly uprooted to make way for global corporate interests. Land, labor, water, and the planet's genetic patrimony have been privatized and commodified. Even diet has been colonized by agrifoods corporations in their relentless drive for profit. Because the food system and the financial system have coevolved, the twin crises are inextricably linked.

The human dimensions of these crises are often lost in a sea of abstrusely large numbers: one billion starving people, 1600% profit increases, $306 billion in subsidies, multi-trillion dollar bailouts... But as they merge and deepen, the concrete realities of the twin crises become unavoidable. A food system in crisis does not just hurt "the poor" in the abstract, but directly affects our families, our neighborhoods, our diets, our health, the soil, the water, the forests, and the air. It affects our own future as well as that of our children, and it damages our planet earth.

Popular US author-journalist Michael Pollan claims that the US's pressing challenges of climate change, the energy crisis, and the health care crisis are impossible to solve without reforming the food system. We would go further to say that solving the world's financial and food crises is impossible without transforming the global food system.

If crises can be globalized, so can opportunities. Indeed, there may never be a better time than now to positively transform the global food system. We have an opportunity to address the root causes of poverty and hunger, to build fairness, sustainability and local resilience into the way we produce, process, transport and consume food. In doing so, we can reconstruct and build resiliency into our economies and communities by rebuilding our food systems.

If the food crisis also presents us with a wide array of opportunities, the question is: Who benefits? If opportunities are seized by the existing international institutions and multinational corporations to implement the same political, technological, and neoliberal approaches that got us into these messes in the first place, then not only will we not solve the root problems of hunger, we will be unable to advance equitable, lasting and sustainable alternatives. Distinguishing between proximate and root causes of the crisis is the first step in being able to choose genuine solutions.

Part Two of *Food Rebellions!* will analyze different approaches to solving the food crisis by describing the socioeconomic and political terrain of struggle in which different actors actively attempt to capture the opportunities with their own solutions. Some seek to solve the crisis by reaffirming the mandates of existing institutions, by reforming existing programs, or by advancing new technologies. Others are transformative in outlook. All will play a decisive role in the outcomes for our food systems.

PART TWO

WHAT WE CAN DO ABOUT IT

7

Overcoming the Crisis: Transforming the Food System

To overcome the food crisis, we need to transform the food system.

Sound ambitious? Yes, but there has never been a better time to end hunger. In spite of decades of globalization, people around the planet continue to save local seeds, hold on to family farms, build local economies, establish fair markets, and stubbornly keep their civic organizations alive.

At the same time, hundreds of thousands of activists worldwide are working tirelessly to ensure the transparency and accountability of our public and international institutions, struggling to roll back the monopoly power of the agrifoods corporations, and are fighting for the "triple bottom line" of social, economic, and environmental sustainability. Though systemic changes are difficult to see, these efforts have not only put constant pressure on governments, international finance institutions and multinational corporations, they have created important social and political infrastructures for the growing practice of *food sovereignty*: the democratic control over our food systems.

Taken together, these movements and organizations number in the tens of thousands. Made up of advocates and practitioners, over the years they have developed a wealth of political, technical and entrepreneurial skills that work in concert to put food first—before monopoly megaprofits. Islands of sanity in a dysfunctional global sea, these experiences are steadily building bridges between organizations and communities, linking sustainable production practices, equitable trade relationships and new, locally centered businesses around the globe.

Despite their steady growth, sustainable agriculture and community food systems approaches find it hard to "scale up," to become the rule rather than the exception. Big agribusiness, international processors and multinational retail chains insist that only they have the efficiencies of scale needed to feed the world. According to them, a world without Yara, Cargill, ADM, Monsanto, Tyson, Tesco and

WalMart is a world doomed to starvation. However, these arguments conveniently fail to mention that the agrifood industry's dominance comes not from their superior productivity, but from their access to vast expanses of land, immense market power, cheap oil, taxpayer subsidies, protective tariffs, tax breaks, and an underpaid and exploited labor force. Furthermore, industrial agrifoods corporations almost never pay the costs of the extensive social and environmental damage resulting from the overuse of chemicals, labor abuses, product dumping and unhealthy foods. Given the skewed playing field, it is remarkable that alternatives to the industrial agrifoods complex even exist, much less scale up. But they do exist, they are growing, and we need to help them make the systemic leap from being the hopeful "alternatives" to becoming the norm. The task is not about making small projects bigger or simply creating more and more small projects—though both of these things should and will happen. The challenge is to remove the structural barriers that are holding back all these promising alternatives. Most of the technology, business models, and organizational experience already exist. The next step is to change the outdated rules of our food systems so that rather than favoring monopoly control over our food, they ensure the diversity, resilience, sustainability and democratic control of our food systems.

If there is a silver lining to the recent food and financial crises it is that together they can be leveraged to change how we produce and consume our food. The institutional pillars of our global food systems are buckling under the weight of decades of unsustainable production and consumption, and changes are inevitable. But, as we shall see, rather than changing the architecture, our governments and international institutions are busy propping up the fraying system with bailouts, subsidies, and shaky promises of "just-in-time" technical fixes. This puts everyone at risk. We can, and must, do better.

Though the titans of the industrial agrifoods complex are stronger now than they have ever been, the public institutions that do their bidding are not, and the current crisis is a crushing indictment against the industrial agrifoods model. It has shaken public faith in the international institutions that govern our global food and financial systems. Not only were the World Bank, the International Monetary Fund (IMF), the World Trade Organization (WTO) and Northern governments unable to prevent the food and financial meltdowns, they were caught completely off guard. After years of vigorously promoting trade liberalization, the WTO is unable to muster agreement or enthusiasm for the Doha round. The World Bank and the IMF—widely detested even before the crises—are struggling to re-invent themselves. These institutions have not only failed the developing world, they have failed the very system they were designed to serve.

This crisis of confidence has plunged these institutions into a political crisis of their own. Internationally weakened and internally fractured, the solutions they advance to solve the food and financial crises are compromised by political maneuvering to ensure each institution's own survival. (Unsurprisingly, one of the few results of the disappointing G20 Summit in London in 2009 was a tripling of the IMF's budget to $750 billion. This major injection of cash is part of a desperate attempt to re-establish the fund's financial dominance over developing economies.)

Encouragingly, broad-based movements for food sovereignty—literally, people's self-government of the food system—are widespread and growing rapidly. First defined by the international peasant federation Via Campesina as "people's right to healthy and culturally appropriate food produced through ecologically sound and sustainable methods, and their right to define their own food and agriculture systems," food sovereignty proposes that people, rather than corporate monopolies, make the decisions regarding our food. Food sovereignty is a much deeper concept than food security—the term usually employed by governments, the UN's Food and Agricultural Organization (FAO) and the World Food Program—because it proposes not just guaranteed access to food, but democratic *control* over food: from production and processing, to distribution, marketing and consumption. Whether applied to countries in the global South working to re-establish national food production, to farmers protecting their seed systems from genetically modified organisms (GMOs), or rural–urban communities setting up their own marketing systems, food sovereignty aims to democratize our food systems.

Food Rebellions! will address both official and grassroots solutions to the food crisis. By understanding the interests behind the solutions being proposed, we are better able to visualize and act upon the opportunities before us. While the range of solutions proposed for solving the food crisis is diverse and sometimes confusing, our informed, democratic engagement is the key to identifying and advancing sustainable solutions that restore resiliency and equity to our ailing food systems.

Reviving Aid to Agriculture: The Arsonist's Try to Put Out the Fire

The weak, more-of-the-same response syndrome

Official responses to the global food crisis have resulted in a policy patchwork with shortsighted mitigation efforts from the North, and desperate emergency actions from the global South.

When food price inflation first hit, countries that could afford it offered cash subsidies, vouchers, food-for-work, health and nutrition, and school feeding programs to those sectors hardest hit by high prices. Some governments tried to bring down prices by lowering tariffs on food imports. Others imposed export restrictions to keep their grain at home. The former measure hurt local farmers and reduced essential state revenues. The latter took food off the global market and was a disincentive to countries whose farmers depend on exporting their products. A few countries re-established national grain reserves.

Global institutions were quick to provide some food aid, but slow to look at the causes of the crisis. Unfortunately, their mitigation efforts fell woefully short of addressing the enormity of the problem.

In December 2007, the FAO introduced the Initiative on Soaring Food Prices. This initiative has spent $24 million in 54 countries to improve smallholder access to chemical and organic farm inputs and irrigation. The International Fund for Agricultural Development contributed $100 million in 2008 and made $200 million more available by redirecting existing funds to improve poor farmers access to seeds and fertilizer in 37 countries (IFAD 2008). This is all still just a drop in the bucket. The FAO estimates that rebuilding agriculture in these countries will take over $30 billion a year.

In April 2008—over a year into the global food crisis—World Bank President Robert Zoellick called for a "New Deal for a Global Food Policy." The bank promised to double its low-interest loans for agriculture to $800 million in Africa, offered $200 million in grants, urged for a conclusion to the Doha round, and called on the $3 trillion industry in sovereign wealth funds to create a "One Percent Solution" for equity investment in Africa (Zoellick 2008). In late May, the bank announced the billion-dollar Global Food Response Facility. This is a rapid financing mechanism (loans) for governments to

BOX 18

The Politics of Food Aid

In 2007, despite growing hunger, food aid fell globally by 15% to 5.9 million tons for the year—the lowest level since 1961. This reflects the tendency of food aid to respond to international grain prices—and not to the food needs of the poor. When the price of cereals is low, Northern countries and transnational grain companies sell their commodities through food aid programs. When grain prices are high, they sell their grains on the global market. So when people are less able to buy food, less food aid arrives (WFP 2007).

The World Food Program expected to feed 70 million people in 2008 (WFP 2008). By mid-year, with the explosion of food price inflation, it had revised this estimate up to 80 million. Towards the end of the year they said they would feed 90 million people—one in ten of the world's hungry—at a cost of $6 billion, twice as much as they had budgeted (De La Torre Ugarte and Murphy 2008).

Most of the WFP's budget and most of their food comes from governments. Official food aid is dominated by the US model, initiated in 1954 with the passing of Public Law 480. The US's objective with PL 480 was "to lay the basis for a permanent expansion of our exports of agricultural products with lasting benefits to ourselves and peoples of other lands" (USAID 2008). The modalities of food aid from the US reflect its commercial interests in providing food:

- By law, 75% of food aid from the US must be purchased, processed, transported, and distributed by US companies (Melito 2007).
- In 2002, just two US companies—ADM and Cargill—controlled 75% of the global grain trade, with US government contracts to manage and distribute 30% of food aid grains. Only four companies control 84% of the transport and delivery of food aid worldwide (Barret 2006).
- Bilateral trade agreements control 50%-90% of global food aid. For example, US aid requires recipient countries to accept genetically modified grains (FAO 2006).
- In 2007, 99.3% of US food aid was "in-kind," that is, food procured in the US and shipped to recipient countries on corporate ships, rather than purchased with cash or coupons closer to recipients (WFP 2007).

Apologists for this kind of food aid insist that the private sector is the most efficient way to distribute food. This assertion ignores not only the huge state subsidies, but also the enormous inefficiencies and inherent manipulations in food aid dominated by corporate monopolies:

- In general, the delivery of food aid from vendor to village takes four to six months (Melito 2007).
- Transaction costs take over 60% of the total emergency food aid budget (Melito 2007).
- This food aid frequently adds 30% efficiency losses due to "tying" purchases to US companies (Melito 2007).
- Food aid reaches less than one-quarter (a mere 200 million people per year) of the 850 million people who are hungry. If evenly distributed, recipients would receive only 50 kilograms each. If all food aid were divided amongst the 850 million hungry of the world, it would amount to less than 12 kilograms per person annually—falling far short of urgent needs (FAO 2006).

There are three types of food aid: program aid, project aid, and emergency aid. Program aid is not really food aid, but cheap food sales to help the donors dispose of surplus commodities. Project aid is used for projects including food for work and food for school programs, most often distributed by the World Food Program and nonprofits. The third is emergency aid, originally used to mitigate hunger accompanying natural disasters and wars. This emergency aid is primarily distributed by the World Food Program and three North American NGOs: CARE, World Vision, and Catholic Relief Services.

Since 1996, emergency aid has been replacing program and project aid, becoming a permanent factor in the economy of many countries (in Africa, for example). Ten years ago, program aid accounted for 70%, and emergency only 10% of total food aid. Now the relationship is completely inverted—donors distribute 10% of food aid as program aid and 70% as emergency aid.

Barret, Christopher B. 2006. *Food Aid's Intended and Unitended Consequences*. Rome: Agriculture and Development Economics Division (ESA) of the Food and Agriculture Organization of the United Nations.

De La Torre Ugarte, Daniel G. and Sophia Murphy. 2008. The Global Food Crisis: Creating an Opportunity for Fairer and More Sustainable Food and Agriculture Systems Worldwide. *Eco-Fair Trade Dialogue* 11. Heinrich Boell Foundation and MISEREOR. http://www.ecofair-trade.org/pics/de/EcoFair_Trade_Paper_No11_Ugarte__Murphy_1.pdf (accessed April 9, 2009).

FAO. 2006. *The State of Food and Agriculture: Food Aid for Food Security?* Rome: Food and Agriculture Organization of the United Nations.

Melito, Thomas. 2007. *Various Challenges Impede the Efficiency and Effectiveness of U.S. Food Aid*. Washington DC: United States Government Accountability Office.

USAID. 2008. *The History of America's Food Aid*. USAID. http://www.usaid.gov/

our_work/humanitarian_assistance/ffp/50th/history.html (accessed October 14, 2008).

WFP. 2007. Food Aid Flows, 2007, Food Aid Monitor. In *International Food Aid Information System*. Rome: Office of the Executive Director, World Food Program.

WFP. 2008. *Overview of Operations 2008*. World Food Program. http://www.wfp.org/appeals/projected_needs/documents/2008/Overview.pdf (accessed October 29, 2008).

establish food for work, conditional cash transfers, and school feeding safety net programs. The bank would also loan money for seeds, fertilizer, irrigation improvement, and provide budget support to offset tariff reductions for food and other unexpected revenue shortfalls. The bank promised to increase its overall support for global agriculture and food to $6 billion in 2009, up from $4 billion (World Bank 2008c). For its part, the IMF provided additional balance of payments support to 12 countries under the Poverty Reduction Growth Facility in early 2008. However, as the global financial crisis and recession hit, the food crisis fell off the agenda. The IMF is offering up to $250 billion in conditional lending for balance of payments shortfalls in developing economies—about a third of the amount the US Congress gave its financial houses in the 2008 financial bailout package.

In June of 2008, the FAO organized a High-Level Conference on Food Security in Rome. Instead of the promised "roadmap" to food security, the conference produced disagreement and paltry funds. This was followed by another "food summit" in Madrid in January of 2009, that basically reiterated the agreements (or lack thereof) from the Rome meeting. The weak response from international institutions prompted the International Planning Committee (a coalition of farmer's unions, NGOs, and civil society groups working for food sovereignty) to declare a "People's State of Emergency" and called on the UN to create a commission on food made up of smallholder farmers and marginalized producers. (See the IPC Declaration in Appendix 6.)

On the basis of emergency appeals, in late 2008 the World Food Program (WFP) raised $1.2 billion—nearly half its yearly budget—and distributed food aid to a record 80 million beneficiaries. However, the WFP estimates the cost of feeding a projected 93.3 million hungry people will be $6.2 billion in 2009. This will require an 80% increase in new donor resources (WFP 2008). This massive increase in food aid will still reach less than one-tenth of the people going hungry on the planet.

Considering that food prices began to rise in 2005 and spiked in early 2008, the response from international institutions was decidedly slow. It was not fast enough to avert the export bans from food-deficit countries (that in many ways made the global situation worse), and just slow enough to allow commodity speculators and grain hoarders (like ADM and Maseca) the perverse opportunity to make money on the price rises, aggravating the situation, driving the system even faster towards a full-blown food crisis.

Though the WFP quickly received the funding it needed to make up its $700 million shortfall in buying power (largely thanks to a $500 million donation from Saudi Arabia), international plans to bring the crisis under control did not get under way until the leaders of the UN, World Bank, IMF and WTO met in Bern, Switzerland, in late April 2008. The World Bank's freshly formulated "New Deal for a Global Food Policy" set the tone for the high-level agreements to beef up the World Food Program and establish immediate safety nets and long-term production-enhancing measures, particularly in Africa.

Throughout July and August of 2008, as the architecture for the global food system was being propped up, hopeful public statements referring to the "Global Partnership for Food," and the "New Deal for a Global Food Policy" emanated from the halls of power in Rome, New York and Washington DC.

In late September of 2008, the global financial crisis hit Wall Street—and then exploded on the rest of the world.

Suddenly, the food crisis was forgotten. Financial giants Lehman Brothers, Merrill Lynch, the American International Group (AIG) and Bear Stearns, their reserves overwhelmed by toxic securities, tumbled towards bankruptcy. Between $1–$3 trillion worth of financial assets evaporated. Credit was tied up as banks refused to lend to each other. Trading and markets ground to a halt, and oil and commodity markets crashed. After letting Lehman Brothers fail, the US Treasury called for an immediate $700 billion bailout of the nation's favored banks and insurance companies. The US Congress gave then Treasury Secretary Henry Paulson—a former CEO of Goldman Sachs, one of the last two major investment banks left on Wall Street—unprecedented discretionary power over these funds. Soon thereafter, US banks received another $2 trillion in emergency loans from the US Federal Reserve. There were no conditions placed on the Treasury's bailout and what (if any) collateral US banks put up in order to qualify for these loans has yet to be disclosed. In 2008 alone the US government committed $243.7 billion of taxpayer money to bail out international financial institutions (*Economist* 2009). As the financial crisis reverberated around the world, Great Britain, France and Germany followed suit with similar, if more modest, conditional bailouts of their own.

The trillion-dollar difference in the response to the food crisis and the financial crises is revealing. Six months after the June 2008 Food Summit in Rome only $2 billion of the $20 billion that was eventually promised for food and agricultural aid had actually arrived. Meanwhile, US banks and insurance companies received half of their $700 billion bailout in a matter of weeks. Insurance giant AIG got $85 billion right off the bat. When they later admitted they could not account for $24 billion of their bailout money, they were nonetheless rewarded with another tranche of $37.8 billion (Williams-Walsh 2008). Wells Fargo and JP Morgan received $25 billion in bailouts. Citigroup got $40 billion (*Economist* 2009).

When Kenyan farmer Stephen Muchiri, head of the Eastern Africa Farmers Federation, heard of the US and European financial bailouts he lamented, "People here are saying that [the bailout] money is enough to feed the poor in Africa for the next three years!" (Eunjung Cha and McCrummen 2008). Actually, the bailouts are over 30 times the amount needed to rebuild smallholder food systems worldwide.

Concerned that even the limited promises made at the food summits will now not be met at all, FAO Director Jacques Diouf fairly pleaded with world leaders, "The global financial crisis should not make us forget the food crisis."

The financial crisis has already plunged 119 million people into severe poverty, signaling that its impact on the world's food systems will be extensive and severe. As the crisis reverberates in the "real economy," the centrality of agriculture will become increasingly evident. How the majority of the world's population weathers the economic crisis will depend in large part on the strength of small-holder agriculture and the resiliency of local—rather than global—food systems. In the long run, how well our economies recover will also depend on the nature of the transformations taking place in agriculture. If these transformations are based on the equitable and sustainable recovery of the world's local food systems, they will go a long way to ensuring economic recovery, the end of hunger, and the well-being of the world's majorities—without which any real global economic recovery is highly doubtful.

The Comprehensive Framework for Action: Not All Opportunities are Solutions

> The current situation creates opportunities. But opportunities should not be mistaken for solutions… If a new global partnership for agriculture and food is to emerge from the current crisis, it is crucial to ensure that this partnership does not simply seek to boost supply by promoting technology-driven recipes, but also empowers those who are hungry and malnourished and whose livelihoods may be threatened by precisely this renewed interest in encouraging agricultural production.
>
> **Olivier De Schutter (2008, p. 25), United Nations Special Rapporteur on the Right to Food**

In his report to the United Nations Human Rights Council, Dr. De Schutter, a human rights expert and professor at the Center for the Philosophy of Law at the Catholic University in Louvaine, Belgium, was responding to the official proposals that see in the food crisis investment opportunities for "public–private partnerships." Referring to the controversial agricultural development projects being advanced in Africa, De Schutter warns, "The difficulty in identifying the best options in this regard is best illustrated by the ongoing discussion on the impacts to be expected from the work of the Alliance for a Green Revolution in Africa (AGRA)." The special rapporteur is concerned with "[How these] investments will be channeled, towards whom, and for which purpose" (De Schutter 2008).

While the food system is changing in response to the crisis, whether state, big philanthropy or private sector investments will benefit the poor and underserved, or reverse industrial agriculture's destructive impact, is still up for discussion. Unfortunately, these discussions have been anything but public, taking place in high-level sessions and behind closed doors. The *Comprehensive Framework for Action*, the main international document outlining the official response to the food crisis, is an example of this.

In April 2008, the United Nations established a High-Level Task

Force (HLTF), headed up by the World Bank, the IMF and the FAO, to address the global food crisis.[7] At the FAO's High-Level Conference on World Food Security held in Rome in June 2008, the HLTF released the draft of the *Comprehensive Framework for Action* (CFA), proposing joint actions to overcome the food crisis. The final document, released in July, is a consensus of the global institutions in the High-Level Task Force. It proposes outcomes and actions to meet the immediate needs of vulnerable populations as well as to build long-term resiliency into the global food system for food security.

The CFA was a turning point in the international response. On the one hand, it brought the mitigation efforts of concerned nations under one roof. On the other, it re-asserted the dominant roles of the World Bank, the IMF and the WTO in defining the rules of the global food system. This arrangement was endorsed by world leaders at the G8 Summit in Hokkaido Toyako in July 2008.

In the short term the CFA encourages governments, philanthropies, the private sector and the international institutions to enhance emergency food assistance, nutrition interventions and safety nets and boost smallholder food production. Governments are expected to adjust trade and tax policies to protect food security. The CFA envisions continuing these policies in the future to ensure local food availability and improve international food markets. While the CFA takes no position on the issue, it urges governments to come to an "international agrofuels consensus."

The HLTF calls for US$25–$40 billion a year to reactivate the slow progress towards the Millennium Development Goals (one-third for immediate needs and two-thirds for long-term actions). This would require developed countries to actually keep their promises of increasing overseas development assistance (ODA) to 0.7% of their gross national income. They also call on developed countries to double food aid and increase agricultural development assistance from 3% to 10% of all ODA within five years. The document asserts that "the key to achievement of the outcomes set in the CFA will be close partnerships between national governments, HLTF members, civil society and private sector organizations, donors as well as other vital actors."

The CFA generally reflects the World Bank's shift in thinking about agricultural development, as laid out in the *World Development Report 2008: Agriculture for Development* (World Bank 2008b). On the one hand, after decades of neglect, the bank finally recognizes that neither poverty nor hunger can be addressed without supporting smallholders. The bank now claims that agricultural policies should be pro-poor and environmentally sound, and that they should ensure women's rights to own and access productive resources. The CFA goes somewhat beyond this position by calling for an equitable international trading system and by recognizing the human right to food. In doing so, they imply—but do not specify—that governments have a legal obligation to ensure the food security of their citizens.

However, the bank's 2008 report and the CFA both studiously avoid addressing the root causes of the crises and fall back on assumptions that have proven false in light of the food crisis. Both renew the call for the liberalization of trade, a swift conclusion to the WTO's Doha round, and assume that integrating farmers into global commodity market chains will benefit smallholders (when the last 20 years of privatization and global commodity markets demonstrate exactly the opposite). The loss of agrobiodiversity and farmers' dangerous dependence on a few commercial (and increasingly expensive) seed varieties is patently ignored. In a masterful stroke of reductionism, both documents assume that "leveling the playing field" between large and small producers simply means improving rural infrastructure and providing smallholders with access to fertilizer and improved seed. There are no concrete strategies to ensure access in light of the skyrocketing increase in input prices and the restriction of agricultural credit presently squeezing world agriculture. Nowhere do these documents seriously consider the ways that the global trade and finance regimes discriminate against smallholders nor do they address the deleterious market distortions caused by corporate oligopolies. They refrain from suggesting any regulation of agribusiness' monopoly power as a way of decreasing volatility and building in resilience to the food system. There is no suggestion that the way to ensure fair prices to farmers and affordable prices to consumers might be to reduce the 80% share of the food dollar going to the middlemen of the industrial agrifoods complex. Neither the *World Development Report* nor the CFA see a role for redistributive agrarian reform, and there is no mention of the growing trend in "land grabbing" by large-scale investors taking place throughout the world (for example, for agrofuels plantations). Regrettably, neither the *World Development Report* nor the CFA recognizes the inherent potential in the rapid and highly productive spread of low-input, agroecological and organic agriculture worldwide.

BOX 19

Land Grabs!

The food and financial crises have sparked a flurry of land grabs. Corporations and governments are buying up tracts of farmland on foreign soil. These land grabs are both a food security strategy for nations rich in capital and poor in agricultural land, like Saudi Arabia, and a low-risk investment hedge in troubled financial times.

Where in the midst of a food crisis can free agricultural land be found? It can be found in nations like Sudan, a country now synonymous with suffering, violence and hunger where the World Food Program fed 5.6 million people this year (World Food Program 2008); Cambodia, where 19% of the population lives on less than a dollar a day (World Bank 2009); and Pakistan, where rampant poverty is a direct cause of political violence and instability. Under the "all-investment is good investment" logic of the World Bank and the International Finance Corporation, capital-starved nations without adequate supports for their own agriculture are opening their lands to foreign ownership.

For Gulf States including Oman, Qatar, Saudi Arabia, and the United Arab Emirates that are largely dependent on food imports, the need to insulate their populations from price shock has become painfully clear. When food prices skyrocketed in 2007 and 2008, the food import bill of the Gulf states more than doubled (GRAIN 2008). Governments acted almost immediately. Between March and August 2008 Gulf Coast Consortium governments began leasing millions of hectares of agricultural land abroad to secure food for their populations (GRAIN 2008).

The government of Kuwait for example, leased land in Cambodia, Thailand, Burma, and Sudan, mostly to insulate the nations' low-paid Filipino laborers from the skyrocketing price of rice on the global market. The out-sourcing of food production is not limited to desert states, either. Japanese, Korean, and Egyptian firms are securing land for food production overseas as well (GRAIN 2008).

All of these omissions spring from the development ideology espoused by the World Bank. For the bank, economic development remains a process that eventually eliminates most of the world's smallholders. At best, the bank envisions smallholder strategies as contributing to "poverty alleviation," while strategies for "serious" economic development are reserved for plantation agriculture, agrofuels, manufacturing, and extractive industries (Havnevik et al. 2007). The World Bank paradigm and the CFA framework run the risk of condemning smallholders to the role of cheap providers of

Not to be left out of the boom, private capital is racing in. Deutuch Bank and Goldman Sachs are buying up livestock operations in China. BlackRock of New York City recently created a $200 million agricultural hedge fund (GRAIN 2008). In a particularly egregious example, Jarch Capital, a US-based private investment firm, recently leased 400,000 hectares in southern Sudan—not through any official channels, but from a Sudanese warlord whose son had laid claim to the territory (Blas and Walls 2009). With over three million people dependent on international food aid, misery-ridden Sudan seems an unlikely ground zero for the land grab craze.

Governments and private firms in Bahrain, Egypt, Kuwait, Qatar, Jordan, Saudi Arabia, South Korea, and the United Arab Emirates are all grabbing up land in relatively water-rich regions of Sudan with the blessing of the Khartoum government (Blas and Walls 2009). Saudi Arabia's Hadco leased 25,000 hectares of cropland, Abu Dhabi launched a project to develop 28,000 hectares in the north, and Qatar's Zad Holding Company is looking into an agricultural venture there as well (Blas and Walls 2009).

All of this amounts to a new round of colonialism in Africa. Sparked by high food prices and risky financial markets, this new round of enclosures—effectively a land reform in favor of corporate agribusiness—is leaving small farmers landless and eroding the foundation on which to build sovereign food systems.

Blas, Javier and William Walls. 2009. U.S. Investor Buys Sudanese Warlord's Land. *Financial Times*. January 9.

GRAIN. 2008.*Siezed! The 2008 Land Grab for Food and Financial Security*. http://www.grain.org/go/landgrab (accessed November 1, 2008).

World Bank. 2009. *Frequently Asked Questions about Poverty in Cambodia*. http://go.worldbank.org/T2890U8730 (accessed January 31, 2009).

World Food Program. 2008. *Where We Work: Sudan*. http://www.wfp.org/country_brief/indexcountry.asp?country=736 (accessed December 30, 2008).

emergency food in the short run, and a rural reserve for poverty and underpaid labor in the long term. The CFA does not see the food crisis as an opportunity to reform the food system, but as an occasion to mitigate the negative impacts of the existing system.

An assessment carried out by the FoodFirst Information and Action Network (FIAN 2008) claims the CFA's approach will, "[Contribute] to cementing existing power structures which are the source of violations of the human right to food worldwide…" Pointing out the undemocratic way in which the CFA's platform was formulated, FIAN observes that, "[The] decision on the CFA has not been taken by governments, let alone parliaments, and relevant [Community Service Organizations] have never been consulted in a meaningful way."

The disappointing response of governments and international institutions to the crises is itself a reflection of the dysfunctional global food and finance systems. As rights activist Shalmali Guttal from Focus on the Global South points out:

> The four fold crisis of food, finance, energy and climate [are] interrelated dimensions of a meta crisis... a larger systemic crisis. They are recurrent crises, they have happened before and they will happen again. The impact of the crisis now is bad. But the response of governments, industry and the international agencies... are equally bad and are going to make the current situation much, much worse.
>
> (Guttal 2009)

What can be done if the institutions that are supposed to guide our economies and food systems are part of the problem, rather than the solution? Luckily, while bad, these responses have also opened up governments and institutions to increasing social scrutiny. People are beginning to question the leadership, the policies, and the structures of the global food system. The multiple crises are hitting people hard across the North–South divide—a boundary that, with globalization, has become increasingly permeable. Important social and political spaces for informed engagement and public debate on the issues are being steadily pried open by people acting locally and transnationally.

Transforming our Food Systems: Advocacy and Practice

To solve the food crisis, we need to transform the food system. Rather than simply increasing aid, imposing more "free trade," applying technical fixes, or otherwise propping up a dysfunctional food system, ending hunger will require restructuring the ways we produce, process, distribute and consume our food.

These transformations are already underway. Like green grass breaking through the asphalt, local, equitable and sustainable alternatives are thriving in the cracks of the global food system. Helping food system alternatives grow and give fruit requires creating favorable structural conditions to unleash their transformative potential. The following section focuses on the principles and practices that form the basis for these emerging transformations.

The Science and Practice of Agroecology

Agronomy, genetics, and molecular biology are the sciences of choice for agribusiness because they are able to generate a steady stream of marketable products for industry. In the developing world, these products—such as genetically engineered crops—have yet to demonstrate higher yields, superior drought-resistance, or more effective pest control than what ecological farmers have already developed. Promises of future productivity from transgenic "super-seeds" are based on heroic assumptions and hopeful projections—not actual past performance. Ironically, it is industry's faith in science, rather than science *per se,* that provides the basis for their projections.

While sustainable agriculture has frequently been dismissed by the international agricultural research centers as "lacking science,"

Emiliano Juarez of Mexico explains the importance of organic matter

Leonor Hurtado

BOX 20

The Right to Food

The right to be free from hunger is a fundamental human right. Though the right to food has been enshrined in international law for over 60 years, it is systematically violated for nearly a billion people.

The 1948 Universal Declaration of Human Rights, the International Covenant on Economic, Social and Cultural Rights (ICESCR), and the Convention on the Rights of the Child, among others, all uphold the right to food. The right was legally defined by the UN Committee on Economic, Social and Cultural Rights (1999) as: 'the right of every man, woman and child alone and in community with others to have physical and economic access at all times to adequate food or means for its procurement in ways consistent with human dignity.'

With the large majority of the world's hungry being small farmers or landless workers, the right to food must be understood as the right to feed oneself and one's family (Claeys 2009). The ICESCR outlines three specific responsibilities of the state: to respect, protect and fulfill the right to food. The first two imply that governments must ensure that neither the state nor individuals take any action that deprives people of the means to feed themselves. The responsibilities to respect and protect are fundamental to understanding the legal right to food—which is often falsely interpreted as the right to receive food or food aid. The obligation to fulfill the right to food means that governments must facilitate access to food and food producing resources, and where access is not possible by one's own means, governments have a responsibility to provide it directly. In 2004 the General Council of the FAO laid out a road map for implementing the right to food. The guidelines specifically mention land reform, access to and sustainable management of resources, and sustainable agricultural development (FAO 2004).

The human right to food is universally accepted (it has been accepted by 155 countries) and legally binding, but it is routinely violated by national

---

the fact is that the practices of many ecological farmers have been racing ahead of industrial science's understanding of sustainability for some time. The science of agroecology, developed through close ecological observation of traditional farming systems, has become the science for sustainable agriculture. Agroecologists have documented remarkable management practices around the world in which farmers restore and improve farm ecosystem functions. These practices have resulted in stable, high-yielding food production, soil and water conservation, and the enrichment of agricultural biodiversity.

and international policy. In what former UN Rapporteur Jean Ziegler called 'schizophrenia in the United Nations system' (Zeigler 2008), international financial institutions promote economic policies that systematically violate the right to food, while institutions like the World Food Program and UNICEF work to alleviate hunger. The same is true of states. National trade and investment policies routinely destroy people's ability to feed themselves in contradiction to international human rights commitments and development goals.

Despite tooth-and-nail resistance from the World Bank and others, the right to food is making legal headway. Activist groups and NGOs are working towards the justiciability of the right to food. Justiciability—when violations can be brought to court, and victims can be compensated for damages and are guaranteed that the right will not be violated again—is essential to implementing the right to food. In addition to international efforts, 22 countries have now included an explicit mention of the right to food in their constitutions.

Claeys, Priscilla. 2009. Personal communication. Special Advisor to the UN Special Rapporteur on the Right to Food. February 3.

FAO. 2004. *Voluntary Guidelines to Support the Progressive Realization of the Right to Adequate Food in the Context of National Food Security*. Rome: Food and Agriculture Organization of the United Nations.

FIAN. 2009. *Justiciability of the Right to Food*. Heidelberg: Food First Information and Action Network. http://www.fian.org/programs-and-campaigns/justiciability-of-the-right-to-food (accessed May 4, 2009).

UN Committee on Economic Social and Cultural Rights. 1999. *General Comment 12: The Right to Adequate Food*. Geneva: Economic and Social Council of the United Nations.

Zeigler, Jean. 2008. Promotion and Protection of all Human Rights, Civil, Political, Economic, Social, and Cultural Rights, Including the Right to Development. In *Report of the Special Rapporteur on the Right to Food*. Geneva: United Nations General Assembly.

By studying the ecological principles at work behind these practices, agroecologists have been able to learn and contribute to the practices of sustainable agriculture worldwide.

The social, economic and environmental superiority of farmers' agroecological alternatives as compared to conventional or "semi-technical" farming (part traditional, part chemical) are dramatic. The superior resilience of sustainable farms when subjected to extreme weather hazards (such as drought and hurricanes); their enhanced ability to capture carbon (and cool the planet); their provisioning of

BOX 21

Agroecology—Some Definitions

In the most basic sense, agroecology is "the application of ecological concepts and principles to the design and management of sustainable agroecosystems" (Altieri 1995).

Agroecological agriculture can cover a broad range of approaches, including sustainable agriculture, ecological agriculture, ecofarming, eco-agriculture, low-external-input agriculture, organic agriculture, permaculture, and biodynamic agriculture.

In general, these terms all refer to roughly the same thing. They all try to use natural processes and eliminate or significantly reduce the use of external inputs, especially the more toxic and widely contaminating ones (e.g., poisons and transgenic seeds). Organic agriculture can thus be seen as a specific instance of ecological agriculture, in which chemicals are rejected entirely. Permaculture and biodynamic agriculture are, in turn, specific types of organic agriculture. Sustainable agriculture is often used as if synonymous with ecological agriculture, but also gets used by conventional, chemical agriculture people for systems that use chemicals, but which they claim will endure for a long time without damaging the environment.

In this book we will interchange the terms ecological agriculture and agroecological agriculture to refer to farming systems that:

- Make the best use of nature's goods and services as functional inputs
- Integrate natural and regenerative processes, such as nutrient cycling, nitrogen fixation, soil regeneration and natural enemies of pests into food production processes
- Minimize the use of non-renewable inputs (pesticides and fertilizers) that damage the environment or harm the health of farmers and consumers
- Make better use of the knowledge and skills of farmers, improving their self-reliance
- Make productive use of people's capacities to work together to solve common management problems, such as pest, watershed, irrigation, forest and credit management.

This definition is from Jules Pretty and Richard Hine, *Reducing Food Poverty with Sustainable Agriculture: A Summary of New Evidence*, Centre for Environment and Society, Essex University, UK, 2001.

Altieri, Miguel. 1995. *Agroecology: the Science of Sustainable Agriculture*. Boulder: Westview Press.

well-balanced diets; and, yes, their ability to consistently produce more food per hectare than conventional farming methods, have all been measured in a wide diversity of ecosystems around the world — particularly in the global South, where the need is greatest. As we will see in the following sections, unlike agribusiness's expensive promises to develop "climate-ready" seeds some time in the future, these farmer-led alternatives exist now, are comparatively inexpensive, highly effective, and easily transferable farmer-to-farmer.

Can Ecological Agriculture Feed the World? Smashing the Myth of Low Productivity[8]

For years, critics claimed that ecological agriculture might be able to address environmental concerns, but couldn't produce sufficient food to sustain an exploding human population. Such skepticism was understandable—the Green Revolution had been widely credited with "saving a billion people" from starving. The social upheaval and environmental damage it provoked were generally ignored or underemphasized. Questioning the Green Revolution seemed almost heretical... How could we criticize technologies that produced more food?

Now, years later, with the insights available to us in seminal works like Rachel Carson's *Silent Spring* and Frances Moore-Lappé's *World Hunger: Twelve Myths*, as well as more recent critiques like Michael Pollan's *The Omnivore's Dilemma*, Paul Roberts' *The End of Food*, and Raj Patel's *Stuffed and Starved*, the inescapable social and environmental costs of the industrial food system have led many to question Green Revolution strategies for ending hunger. Sustainable alternatives are receiving greater attention. Organic agriculture is fast on the rise, and the call to buy local, buy seasonal, and buy fair is growing louder. But critics, such as geographer Vaclav Smil and the conservative Hudson Institute's Dennis and Alex Avery, see sustainable agriculture as a "liberal fetish" that would bring hunger and ruin to millions.

Such concerns would be valid if agroecological methods were as unproven or unproductive as often portrayed. However, besides the thousands of years of small-scale and family agriculture that developed and field-tested the antecedents of many modern sustainable practices, over the past 40 years a significant amount of scientific literature has compared "conventional" and "sustainable" agriculture. What were valid and important doubts among some scientists about sustainable agriculture four decades ago have since turned

BOX 22

The MST and Agroecology

by José Maria Tardin and Isabella Kenfield

Brazil has emerged as an agro-industrial superpower. It is also a global epi-center for well-organized rural social movements. Indeed, the two phenomena are intricately related. As more land has been devoted to monocultures and production for agro-export, expulsion of family farmers from their lands has increased, along with poverty and hunger in rural areas, leading peasants and workers to organize and resist. The most important rural social movement to have emerged in Brazil is the Movement of Landless Rural Workers (MST).

The MST was founded in the southern state of Paraná in 1984 where it organized landless families and rural workers. The MST's primary tactic is the non-violent occupation of unproductive lands belonging to large landowners. These occupations are based on a constitutional clause that states that private property, including land, must serve a social function. Land that does not generate sufficient employment or meet defined rates of agricultural production may legally be expropriated from landowners by the government for the purpose of agrarian reform.

Today the MST is organized in 23 of Brazil's 27 states. At the MST's recent 25th year celebration, cofounder and national coordinator João Pedro Stédile stated that the movement has forced the expropriation of 35 million acres of land (larger than the country of Uruguay) and assisted 370,000 families gain titles to land. The MST has built hundreds of public schools, taught tens of thousands of its members to read and write, and has founded over 400 cooperatives. The MST has become a global symbol of resistance, has played a major role in the organization of Via Campesina, and has pioneered the theory and practice of food sovereignty.

These accomplishments come with some hard lessons. The MST's initial approach to production was industrialized agriculture. Eventually, this path provoked major economic collapses for the families on the MST's agrarian reform settlements. Many families sold their lots and returned to city slums. The MST realized it had to provide families with an alternative agricultural model.

In the mid-1990s, the MST's participation in Via Campesina put its leaders in contact with indigenous and campesino movements from other regions of Latin America that were already practicing agroecology. Agroecology is aligned with the MST's mission and vision because it develops small-scale, sustainable, food-oriented and regional agricultural systems; recuperates traditional, indigenous knowledge of sustainable agriculture; and incorporates a political ideology that emphasizes the liberation of campesino families from the destruction and oppression of agribusiness corporations—all essential to forging food sovereignty. At its fourth national congress in 2000, the MST decided to adopt agroecology as national policy to orient production on its settlements.

Via Campesina in Brazil is composed of eight organizations: the Movement of the Landless Rural Workers (MST), Movement of Small Farmers (MPA), Movement of the Dam Affected (MAB), Movement of Campesina Women (MMC), Movement of Pastoral Youth (PRJ), the Pastoral Land Commission (CPT), the Federation of Agronomy Students of Brazil (FEAB) and the Indigenous Missionary Council (CIMI). Today, the eight organizations that participate in Via Campesina-Brasil have all adopted agroecology as an official policy.

To spread agroecology and counter the power of industrial agriculture, the MST and Via Campesina-Brasil have founded 11 secondary schools and introduced university courses in agroecology. These schools have the mission to engage and train the movements' youth to provide technical assistance in agroecology to campesino families in rural areas. The formation of these schools places Via Campesina-Brasil at the vanguard of rural development policy in Brazil, and is testament to the movements' capacity to advance agroecological policies at state and federal levels.

The Latin American School for Agroecology (ELAA) was conceived during the 2005 World Social Forum in Porto Alegre, when representatives of Via Campesina-International, the federal governments of Brazil and Venezuela, the state government of Paraná and the Federal University of Paraná (UFPR) signed a protocol of cooperation for the Latin American countryside. The protocol proposes actions for the strengthening of campesino resistance to industrial agriculture, including the promotion of agroecology through the training of technicians at schools such as ELAA. The first university course for agroecology in Brazil, ELAA is accredited by UFPR, which organizes the school in conjunction with the Latin American Institute for Agroecology, Education and Research for Campesina Agriculture (ICA), composed of members of Via Campesina-Brasil. ELAA was inaugurated on August 27, 2005, on the MST settlement Contestado, in the municipality of Lapa, in Paraná.

In 2008, 88 students from 18 states of Brazil and two from Paraguay were matriculated into two terms at ELAA, both of which were scheduled to graduate in 2009. All of ELAA's students are "militants," or activists, from the social movements in Via Campesina. Women represent about 40% of the student body. The average age of students is 20, and the age range is between 18 and 54.

Each class studies for two semesters per year for three-and-a-half years. The two terms alternate every three months between "school time" and "community time," when the students put into practice in their communities what they are learning at ELAA. School time semesters last 65 days, during which the students live at ELAA and maintain a daily schedule of six hours of theoretical classes, work in agricultural production, management, agricultural experiments, lectures, domestic work (food preparation, cleaning), experiential exchanges, sports, and a cultural night every Saturday. Since the course began, the students have been organized into 20 groups during school time. These develop work and training in agroecological technical assistance with 20 of the 108 families on the Contestado settlement. During community time, each student develops the same work with five families in their home communities.

ELAA's teachers are professionals with high academic qualifications (usually a PhD or masters degree), many of them from public universities and other research institutions in Brazil. These professors work primarily as volunteers.

Despite its progress, three years after it began operating, ELAA continues to function precariously due to lack of funding and support from federal and state government agencies. One semester was cancelled due to lack of funds, and the physical infrastructure of the school remains inadequate. The only classroom remains the *casarão*, the property's original farmhouse, built by slaves in the 1880s, which also holds the library, with only 160 books and 30 titles, and the telecenter, with six computers connected to the Internet. While the *casarão* serves as a symbolic reminder of the MST's contribution to the struggle against historic land and income inequality, it is inadequate for the scientific lab work necessary for the students' learning.

The government's reluctance to provide funding stems from the strong political backlash against the schools for agroecology—from powerful corporations and large landowners vested in Brazil's agro-industrial boom. In an era of rising food prices and increasing global demand for Brazilian ethanol—especially from the US—it is unlikely that the government will increase support to Via Campesina's schools for agroecology in the future.

into a "New Myth" that ignores this accumulated scientific work and regards as "common knowledge" the claim that yields from sustainable agriculture are insufficient to feed the human population. Skepticism is a vital and healthy part of science and public debate, but it must be moderated by even-handed evaluations of available information.

So what does the available information on organic agriculture say? Are organic yields sufficient to feed us?

Ecological agriculture and the global food supply

A study in the June 2007 issue of the *Journal of Renewable Agriculture and Food Systems* looked at 293 examples comparing alternative and conventional agriculture from 91 studies (Badgley et al. 2007). The University of Michigan researchers who carried out the study were able to demonstrate that current scientific knowledge simply does not support the idea that a switch to organic and sustainable agriculture would drastically lower food production and lead to hunger. Instead, they found that current knowledge implies that, even under conservative estimates, organic agriculture could provide almost as much food on average at a global level as is produced today (2,641 as opposed to 2,786 kilocalories per person per day after losses). In what these researchers considered a more realistic estimation, ecological agriculture could actually increase global food production by as much as 50%—to 4,381 kcal per person per day.

The University of Michigan study synthesized as much of the current scientific literature on the subject as possible, gathering 160 cases comparing production from sustainable/organic methods to conventional production, and 133 cases comparing sustainable/organic production to local, low-intensity methods (i.e., subsistence farming or other non-industrialized practices). The research team determined the average ratio of yield from organic production to yield from conventional/low-intensity production. They then took data from the FAO and calculated the amount of food theoretically available on a caloric basis if all agriculture were organically produced.

The study found large differences in yield ratios between developed and developing countries. From the production estimate based on the 160 cases in developed countries, organic production could theoretically generate an amount of food equal to 92% of the current caloric availability (or a yield ratio of 0.92). This ratio is close to that found in a previous study. However, looking at the 133 examples from the developing world, the University of Michigan team estimated food production equivalent to an overall yield ratio of 1.80—or 180% of current production in the developing world.

In the "conservative case" set out by the researchers, the yield ratio for developed countries was used to develop a picture of potential yields from an all-organic global food system. Under this scenario, production would drop slightly, from 2,786 kcal per person per day to 2,641 kcal, a level still above the suggested intake of healthy adults.

BOX 23

Ecological Agriculture

by Roland Bunch

The conventional, high-input agriculture which has dominated agricultural development practice for the last half century has shown itself largely unable to meet the needs of resource-poor smallholders. This is because resource-poor farmers can't afford it, nor do they have access to the infra-structure (irrigation, roads, inputs, credit and markets, etc.) necessary to make it work. Furthermore, many smallholders who have been using small amounts of chemical fertilizers and pesticides have allowed their soils to deteriorate to the point that the use of such fertilizers has become only marginally profitable at best. And recent increases in the price of fertilizers could easily force many smallholders out of the fertilizer market, thereby sharply decreasing their productivity once again.

At the same time, ecological agriculture is rapidly becoming an impor-tant alternative in the developing world to both conventional, high-input agriculture on the one hand and traditional low-yield agriculture on the other. Very frequently, by using small amounts of external inputs, plus large amounts of internal inputs and improved management, smallholders can achieve very good yields, often three to five times traditional levels of productivity (Uphoff 2000; Bunch 1999). Some 3% of all developing world small-scale farmers are already using program-introduced ecological agri-culture technologies, and virtually all of this adoption has occurred within the last decade (Pretty et al. 2006). Small-farmer adoption of such tech-nologies, independent of outside programs, is very likely at least as great, if not several times more extensive. And the investment in spreading these technologies has been very small compared to that invested in high-input agriculture.

For over 25 years, the Consultative Group on International Agricultural Research (CGIAR) has focused on high-input chemical agriculture and on plant genetics. Instead of serving as a network for exchanging ideas generated by farmers, NGOs and others, it tries to develop all the basic technology itself because of an obsolete, top-down, the-scientist-knows-best paradigm. Furthermore, the CGIAR system is largely organized around commodity lines, an approach not at all well suited to the complex, diverse systems of small farmers. Other problems include the CGIAR sys-tem's inability to respond quickly to farmers' needs, its almost exclusively technological approach to farmers' problems and its consistent under-estimation of the negative ecological impact on future productivity of chemical-based technology. These factors make it unlikely that the CGIAR system will respond effectively to farmers' needs in the realm of ecological agriculture. In addition, the limited potential of a largely chemical-based Green Revolution approach was shown clearly in the almost total failure of the Sasakawa/Borlaug effort to introduce the Green Revolution into West Africa in the 1990s. The program blamed this failure on farmers' reactions to a temporary market problem, but to assume subsistence farmers will not adopt a learned technology once prices have readjusted is to assume traditional farmers are incredibly dumb, which they are not. Furthermore, farmer interviews have confirmed that the temporary market problem was not the reason for the program's failure.

Technologically, and in terms of its credibility, ecological agriculture has finally come of age. Over 4.4 million farmers have adopted these practices on 3.5 million hectares. As a result, their harvests increased by an average of 73% (Pretty and Hine 2000).

Extensionists and researchers alike are finding that tremendous, previously unheard of potential exists for achieving sustainably productive agriculture even on soils regarded as "low potential" soils. It turns out that crops' growth does not depend primarily on the total amount of nutrients in the soil, but rather on the constant availability of nutrients, even if they are present in very small concentrations (Primavesi 1980; Bunch 1999). Furthermore, crops can be fed through mulches (or even a nutrient solution of water, as in hydroponics) just as well as through the soil. Therefore, the natural fertility of the soil, or its "cation exchange capacity," even if very low, does not need to affect to any great extent the productivity of the land. Well-managed land, even of close to the poorest quality, can be very productive.

Equally important for the poor, this can be done at very low costs. With an investment of only $0.25 to buy a handful of velvet bean or jack bean seed, a little patience and a willingness to learn a different way of managing the soil, a farmer can increase his or her yields by 200% and even 300% in most cases.

These soils are kept covered at all times, are never or only rarely ploughed, and the crops are fed largely through the mulch, or litter layer (Primavesi 1980; Bunch and Lopez 1995). This sort of soil management, in fact, mimics the rainforest itself, which follows every one of the above rules of thumb (Bunch 1999). And since rainforests have produced prodigious amounts of biomass for thousands of years, we have reason to believe that farmers will be able to maintain high levels of productivity over the long haul.

Such potential has now been proven in case after case (Pretty et al. 2006). Probably the most spectacular case is that of the System of Rice Intensification developed in Madagascar. Scientists at the International Rice Research Institute, the CGIAR center that developed miracle rice, have for many years maintained that the traditional rice plant is genetically capable of producing a maximum of less than 10 tons per hectare of grain. A typical example is the statement that "yields for multiple varieties peak out at about 8 tons per hectare, even with high nitrogen applications, up to 200 kilograms per hectare" (Ladha et al. 1998). Nevertheless, farmers in Madagascar, on some of the most depleted, acidic soils in the world, have been achieving yields of 5-10 tons per hectare, and occasionally even 15 tons per hectare (Uphoff 2000). And they are achieving these yields with no use of chemical fertilizer.

A whole series of interesting and potentially revolutionary technologies are surfacing around the world, among non-governmental organizations and even among the farmers themselves.

These technologies are sometimes similar to conventional technologies, and other times approach being both strange and wonderful. They go by names such as "water harvesting," "dispersed trees," "green manure/cover crops," "home-made foliar sprays," "improved fallows," "contour vegetative barriers," "natural pest control," "hand-hoe precision planting," etc.

In most cases, the yield increases achieved by one of these technologies will compound those achieved by others. For instance, in the case of a program in San Martin Jilotepeque, Guatemala, from 1972 through 1979, a study done in 1994 found that the average farmer studied (among all those who participated in the program from four villages within the target area) had increased his maize yields from 400 kilograms per hecatre in 1971 to 4,500 kilograms per hectare in 1994. And this increase was achieved almost entirely with ecological agriculture technology, even though many of today's best technologies were unknown in 1979 (Bunch 1995).

Bunch, Roland. 1999. More Productivity with Fewer External Inputs: Central American Case Studies of Agroecological Development and their Broader Implications. *Environment, Development and Sustainability* 1 (3/4):219-33.

Bunch, Roland and Gabino Lopez. 1995. *Soil Recuperation in Central America: Sustaining Innovation after Intervention*. London: Sustainable Agriculture Programme, International Institute for Environment and Development.

Ladha, J.K., G.J.D. Kirk, J. Bennett, S. Peng, C.K. Reddy and U. Singh. 1998. Opportunities for Increased Nitrogen-use Effciency from Improved Lowland Rice Germplasm. *Field Crops Research* 56:41-71.

Pretty, J, A.D. Noble, D. Bossio, J. Dixon, R.E. Hine, F.W.T. Penning de Vries and J.I.L. Morison. 2006. Resource-conserving Agriculture Increases Yields in Developing Countries. *Environmental Science & Technology* 40 (4):1114-1119.

Pretty, J. and R. Hine. 2000. *Feeding the World with Sustainable Agriculture: a Summary of New Evidence*. Final Report from SAFE-World Research Project. Colchester, UK: University of Essex.

Primavesi, Ana. 1980. *O manejo ecológico do solo: a agricultura em regiões tropicais*. Sao Paulo: Nobel.

Uphoff, Norman. 2000. Agroecological Implications of the System of Rice Intensification (SRI) in Madagascar. *Environment, Development and Sustainability* 1 (3/4).

Under more realistic assumptions—that a switch to organic agriculture would mean the relatively lower developed world yield ratios would apply to production in the developed world and the relatively higher developing world yield ratios would apply to production in the developing world—the result was an astounding 4,381 kcal per person per day, a caloric availability more than sufficient for today's population. Indeed, it would be more than enough to support an estimated population peak of around 10–11 billion people by the year 2100.

Another frequent claim by critics of organic agriculture is that organic agriculture requires more land. This requirement, they say, is because of lower yields and the use of green manure—nutrients from cover crops planted in between food crop rotations—instead of synthetic nitrogen.

This point was tested in the Michigan study as well, which evaluated the nitrogen availability generated solely by green manure as opposed to nitrogen from synthetic sources. Based on 77 studies, they found that, assuming green manures could be planted on the current agricultural land base in between food crops, during winter fallow, or as a relay crop, 140 million metric tons of nitrogen could be fixed by green manures each year. In comparison, the global use of synthetic nitrogen fertilizers in 2001 was 82 million metric tons, or 58 million metric tons less than the theoretical production of green manures.

These results suggest that, in principle, no additional land is required to obtain enough useful nitrogen to replace the current use of synthetic nitrogen fertilizers. Other organically acceptable sources of nitrogen, including intercropping, alley cropping with leguminous trees, reintegration of livestock and annual crops, and inoculation of soil with free-living nitrogen fixers, were not included in the analysis. In other words, similar to the findings around yields from organic production, their estimate is a conservative one. There may be significant potential in such alternative nitrogen sources that could be realized if research resources were devoted to them on the scale of the effort that has supported the Green Revolution.

The Michigan study shows that (notwithstanding future research) the answer to whether organic agriculture can provide enough food for the world is an unambiguous yes.

Smallholders: Leading the Practice of Sustainable Agriculture

We know ecologically managed farms can be at least as productive as conventional farms, but can this approach avoid the social and environmental pitfalls of the Green Revolution? The functions performed by small ecological farming systems spread widely across Africa, Asia and the Americas comprise a social and ecological asset for humankind. In an era of escalating and increasingly volatile fuel, input and food costs, the unpredictability of climate change, the accelerating degradation of the environment, the spread of GMO contamination and the concentration of corporate-controlled food systems, small and medium-sized, biodiverse, ecologically managed farms are the most viable form of agriculture capable of feeding the world and reducing ecological and economic stress.

There are five main reasons:[9]

1. Small farmers are key for the world's food security

While 91% of the planet's 1.5 billion hectares of agricultural land are increasingly being devoted to agro-export crops, agrofuels and transgenic soybean to feed cars and livestock, some 450 million farms (85%) measuring less than two hectares still produce most of the staple crops needed to feed the planet's rural and urban populations. In Latin America, about 17 million peasant farmers farming more than 60 million hectares (over one-third of the total cultivated land), with average farm sizes of about 1.8 hectares, produce 51% of the maize, 77% of the beans, and 61% of the potatoes for domestic consumption (Ortega 1986; Altieri 1999). Africa has approximately 33 million small farms, representing 80% of all farms on the continent (Nagayets 2005). Despite the fact that Africa now imports huge amounts of cereals, the majority of African farmers (mostly women) farm less than two hectares (Nagayets 2005) and are responsible for 90% of the continent's agricultural production (Spencer 2002). In Asia, some 200 million rice farmers cultivate two hectares of rice, providing the bulk of the rice produced by Asian farmers. Small increases in yields on these small farms that produce most of the world's staple crops will have far more impact on food availability at the local and regional levels than the doubtful increases predicted for large genetically modified monocultures.

2. Small farms are more productive and resource conserving than large-scale monocultures

Although the conventional wisdom is that small family farms are backward and unproductive, research shows that under the same conditions—if total output is considered rather than yield from a single crop—small farms are much more productive than large farms. In terms of kilograms per hectare, integrated farming systems in which the small-scale farmer produces grains, fruits, vegetables, fodder, and animal products can produce four to ten times more than single crop monocultures on large-scale farms (Rosset 1999). The productivity of small farms producing polycultures of beans, squash, potato and fodder is higher in terms of harvestable products per unit area than farms growing just one crop with the same level of management. Yield advantages for polycultures (called "over-yielding") range from 20% to 60%, because polycultures reduce losses due to weeds, insects and diseases, and make

A farmer from the Center for Indigenous Peasant Development, an indigenous organisation that promotes sustainable agriculture in Oaxaca, Mexico.

Leonor Hurtado

BOX 24

Campesino a Campesino: Latin America's Farmers' Movement for Sustainable Agriculture

Farmers helping their brothers, so that they can help themselves... to find solutions and not be dependent on a technician or on the bank. That is Campesino a Campesino.

Argelio González, Santa Lucía, Nicaragua, 1991

This is the farmers' definition of Latin America's 30-year-old farmer-led movement for sustainable agriculture. El Movimiento Campesino a Campesino, or the Farmer-to-Farmer Movement is one of the continent's most successful, extensive and remarkable experiences in sustainable agriculture.

Campesino a Campesino began among the smallholders of the ecologically fragile hillsides and forest perimeters of the Mesoamerican tropics. Using relatively simple methods of small-scale experimentation combined with farmer-led workshops in agroecology, soil and water conservation, seed selection, crop diversification, integrated pest management (IPM), and biological weed control, these farmers found ways to raise yields, conserve the environment and improve their livelihoods, farmer-to-farmer. Through the work of thousands of volunteer and part-time farmer-technicians, or *promotores*, and the support of hundreds of technicians and professionals from local development organizations, the *promotores* of Campesino a Campesino have spread their movement to hundreds of thousands of smallholders throughout the Americas.

Promotores lead by example, inspiring their neighbors and others to experiment, innovate and try new alternatives. The Campesino a Campesino movement can be credited not only with spreading agroecological management, but also for pioneering farmer-led experimentation and farmer-to-farmer development methodologies across Latin America (Brot fur die Welt 2006). One of the most dramatic examples of this has been Cuba, where—thanks to strong government support for farmer-led development—the movement grew to over 100,000 smallholders in just eight years (Holt-Giménez 2006).

Roland Bunch, then of World Neighbors (Bunch 1982), originally described the basic principles for what became farmer-led development as follows:

- Motivate and teach farmers to experiment
- Attain and utilize rapid, recognizable success
- Use appropriate technologies
- Start with just a few, well-chosen technologies
- Train villagers as extensionists.

Bunch saw the development of local capabilities as an inverted pyramid in which farmer-extensionists experimented with one or two new technologies every year. If these were successful, they encouraged other farmers to experiment with the same technologies, and to teach others. In this way, human capacities and the technology base grew at compatible rates and were mutually reinforcing. The focus was on campesino innovation and the sharing of technology.

The Campesino a Campesino Movement is a grassroots response to the technical, ecological and institutional failures of the Green Revolution in Latin America. Many Green Revolution programs hoping to achieve higher rates of farmer participation in their extension programs have since adopted the farmer-to-farmer methodology. The participatory plant breeding now popular among agricultural research centers is an example of this. But Campesino a Campesino is about smallholders' control over their own agroecosystems more than it is about methodologies to extend new seeds. In fact, the farmer-led nature of Campesino a Campesino turns the question of participation on its head. Rather than asking, "How do we get farmers to participate in agricultural development schemes?" the movement challenges professionals to ask how they can best participate in farmer-led processes for agricultural development.

The Campesino a Campesino Movement is actually a movement for social change. Based on principles of agroecology, solidarity, and innovation, the movement resists the ecologically degrading and socially destructive commodification of soil, water, and genetic diversity and asserts the rights of smallholders to determine an equitable, sustainable course for agricultural development. The enthusiasm and commitment of the men and women in the Campesino a Campesino Movement ring clear in the words of promoter José Jesús Mendoza:

> If there is anything that truly satisfies a person, it is helping others; to collaborate so others improve; collaborate so others overcome obstacles; collaborate so that others can live differently all those things one suffers from in the countryside. I have felt such beautiful things through these experiences even though I never had any schooling. When someone wanted to teach me something, I was ashamed because I thought I wouldn't be able to understand them. But with Campesino a Campesino, the Mexicans came to give us a workshop here in Santa Lucía, and everything changed. Before, when technicians came to give workshops, I never understood what they were talking about. But when the Mexicans came, I understood everything because I understood their experience. This filled me with enthusiasm to keep learning about organic agriculture, the alternative for those that love the land and love nature. For me it was like opening a book, a book without letters, a book that says very deep things; immense, great, glorious, marvelous dreams come true! This

is the book of life. It has taught me many things and given me things I never thought I would have. Campesinos came and gave us workshops and I liked what they taught because they taught what they practiced. That was the main thing: do to be able to teach. This has been my mission, to do things in order to teach them to others, which is the best way to improve life in the countryside. That was in 1987. It has been seventeen years and I can see the fruit of the dreams I had when I went to my first workshop. I never imagined the setbacks I would have, but I have been able to assimilate their lessons. Each day the school of life teaches us new things, beautiful things, precious things. Above all, when a dreamer has positive, concrete things that lift him up, criticism is not important. Campesino a Campesino is one of the most glorious experiences of my life. Some might ask, "What have you done?" They don't want to see these marvelous things, or see that one can live better with everything that nature gives us. But I feel fulfilled because I have been able to help many people healthily, purely, without prejudice.

(Holt-Giménez 2006)

Brot fur die Welt. 2006. *Campesino a Campesino: Construyendo procesos*. Stuttgart: Brot fur die Welt.

Bunch, R. 1982. *Two Ears of Corn*. Oklahoma City: World Neighbors.

Holt-Giménez, E. 2006. *Campesino a Campesino: Voices from Latin America's Farmer to Farmer Movement for Sustainable Agriculture*. Oakland: Food First Books.

more efficient use of the available resources of space, water, light and nutrients (Beets 1982; Gliessman 1998). In overall output, the small, diversified farm produces much more food, even if measured in dollars. In the US, data shows that the smallest two-hectare farms produced $15,104 per hectare and netted about $2,902 per hectare. The largest farms, averaging 15,581 hectares, yielded $249 per hectare and netted about $52 per hectare (USDA 2002). Not only do small- to medium-sized farms exhibit higher yields than conventional farms, but when farmed agroecologically, they reduce negative impact and can even have a positive impact on the environment. Small farms are multifunctional, more productive, more efficient, and contribute more to economic development than do large farms. Communities surrounded by many small farms have healthier economies and more food security than do communities surrounded by depopulated, large mechanized farms (Goldschmidt 1978). Because their livelihoods depend on healthy, on-farm ecosystem functions, small-scale ecological farmers also take better care of natural resources, reduce soil erosion and conserve biodiversity (Holt-Giménez 2001; Rosset 1999).

The inverse relationship between farm size and output can be attributed to the more efficient use of land, water, biodiversity, labor and other agricultural resources by small farmers. So in terms of converting inputs into outputs, society would be better off with small-scale farmers. Building strong rural economies in the global South based on productive small-scale farming will provide employment and allow the people of the South to remain with their families, stemming the painful tide of migration. As the worlds' population continues to grow and the amount of farmland and water available to each person continues to shrink, a small farm structure will become even more central to feeding the planet.

3. Small, traditional and biodiverse farms are models of sustainability

Despite the onslaught of industrial farming, the persistence of more than three million agricultural hectares under ancient, traditional management in the form of raised fields, terraces, polycultures and diverse agroforestry systems is proof of successful indigenous agricultural strategies and a tribute to the ingenuity of traditional farmers. These microcosms of traditional agriculture that have stood the test of time, and that can still be found almost untouched after 4,000 years of cultivation in the Andes, Mesoamerica, Southeast Asia and parts of Africa, offer promising lessons for sustainability because they maintain biodiversity, thrive without agrochemicals, and sustain year-round yields even under marginal environmental conditions. The local knowledge and wisdom accumulated during centuries of farming comprise a Neolithic legacy of fundamental value for the future of humankind.

Recent research suggests that many small farmers cope and even prepare for climate change, minimizing crop failure through increased use of drought-tolerant local varieties, water harvesting, mixed cropping, opportunistic weeding, agroforestry and a series of other traditional techniques. Surveys conducted on hillside farms after Hurricane Mitch in Central America showed that farmers using sustainable practices such as "velvet bean" leguminous cover crops, intercropping, and agroforestry suffered less hurricane damage than their conventional farm neighbors. The study, spanning 360

BOX 25

Las Chinampas: Testament to Indigenous Science

The traditional floating gardens called *chinampas* of Mexico produced maize yields in the mid-1950s of 3.5-6.3 tons per hectare (Sanders 1957). At that time, these were the highest long-term yields achieved anywhere in Mexico, and were nearly double the average yields in the United States. Each hectare of *chinampa* could produce enough food for 15-20 persons per year at modern subsistence levels. Recent research has indicated that each *chinampero* can work about three-quarters of a hectare of *chinampa* per year (Jimenez-Osornio and del Amo 1986), meaning that each farmer can support 12-15 people sustainably, and without expensive inputs.

Jimenez-Osornio, J. and S. del Amo. 1986. *An Intensive Mexican Traditional Agroecosystem: The Chinampa*. Paper read at 6th International Scientific Conference IFOAM, at Santa Cruz CA.

Sanders, W.T. 1957. Tierra y agua: A Study of the Ecological Factors in the Development of Meso-American Civilizations. PhD dissertation, Harvard University.

communities and 24 departments in Nicaragua, Honduras and Guatemala, showed that diversified plots had 20% to 40% more topsoil, greater soil moisture, less erosion, and experienced lower economic losses than their conventional neighbors (Holt-Giménez 2002).

Undoubtedly, the ensemble of traditional crop management practices used by many resource-poor farmers represent a rich resource for modern development workers seeking to create novel agroecosystems well adapted to the local ecological and socioeconomic circumstances of peasants. Peasants use a diversity of techniques, many of which fit well to local conditions. The techniques tend to be knowledge intensive rather than input intensive, but clearly not all are effective or applicable, therefore modifications, adaptations, and agroecological innovation are constantly occurring. The challenge is to ground the foundations of such changes in farmers' agroecological knowledge.

4. Small farms represent a sanctuary of agrobiodiversity

In general, traditional and small-scale farmers grow a wide variety of cultivars. Many of these plants are landraces grown from seed passed down from generation to generation, and are more genetically heterogeneous than modern cultivars. This reduces farm vulnerability and enhances harvest security in the face of diseases, pests, droughts and other stresses. In a worldwide survey of crop varietal diversity on farms involving 27 crops, scientists found that considerable crop genetic diversity continues to be maintained on farms in the form of traditional crop varieties, especially of major staple crops (Jarvis et al. 2008). In most cases, farmers maintain diversity as insurance in the face of social, economic and environmental unpredictability. Many researchers have concluded that this varietal richness enhances productivity and reduces overall yield variability. For example, studies by plant pathologists provide evidence that mixing of crop species and/or varieties can delay the onset of diseases by reducing the spread of disease-carrying spores, and by modifying environmental conditions so that they are less favorable to the spread of certain pathogens (Altieri 2004). Recent research in China found that four different mixtures of rice varieties grown by farmers from 15 different townships over 3,000 hectares suffered 44% less blast incidence and exhibited 89% greater yield than homogeneous fields—without the need to use chemicals (Zhu et al. 2000).

Transgenic crops are already contaminating the world's centers of genetic diversity, putting the planet at tremendous ecological risk (Quist and Chapela 2001). It is crucial to maintain areas of peasant agriculture free of contamination from crops with genetically modified organisms (GMO), as traits important to indigenous farmers (resistance to drought, food or fodder quality, maturity, competitive ability, performance on intercrops, storage quality, taste or cooking properties, compatibility with household labor conditions, etc.) could be eliminated by GMOs whose transgenic qualities (e.g. herbicide resistance) are of no importance to farmers who don't use agrochemicals. Under this scenario, risk will increase and farmers will lose their ability to produce relatively stable yields with a minimum of external inputs under changing biophysical environments. The social impacts of local crop shortfalls, resulting from changes in the genetic integrity of local varieties due to genetic contamination, is already underway in the global South.

Maintaining pools of genetic diversity that are geographically isolated from any possibility of cross fertilization or genetic pollution from uniform transgenic crops will create "islands" of intact germplasm which will act as safeguards against future ecological failure brought on by the spread of GMO crops. These islands of genetic sanctuary will serve as the source for the GMO-free seeds that will be needed to repopulate the ecological farms in the North inevitably contaminated by the advance of transgenic agriculture. The small farmers and indigenous communities of the global South, with the help of scientists and NGOs, can continue to create and safeguard the biological and genetic diversity that strengthens and enriches agriculture on the planet.

BOX 26

Back to the Future: From *Frijol Tapado* to Green Manures

The *frijol tapado* is an ancient system used to produce beans in mid-elevation areas of Central America on steep slopes with high amounts of rainfall where most beans in the region are grown. To begin the process, farmers choose a fallow field that is two to three years old so that the woody vegetation dominates the grasses. If the fallow period is less than two years, then the grasses will be able to out-compete the emerging bean plants and soil fertility will not have been fully restored since the last harvest. Next, paths are cut through the field with machetes. Then bean seeds are broadcasted into the fallow. Finally, the fallow vegetation with bean seed is cut down into a mulch that is allowed to decay and provide nutrients to the maturing bean seedling. Approximately 12 weeks after broadcasting, a harvest is made. In Costa Rica, the estimate is that 60%-70% of the beans in the country are produced by *frijol tapado*. Compared to other more intensive methods of bean production, the *tapado* system has a higher rate of return because of lower costs. Soil erosion is minimized, there is no need for expensive and toxic agriculture chemicals and the system requires relatively little labor (Buckles et al. 1998).

By understanding the rationale of *frijol tapado*, a contemporary discovery, the use of "green manures," has provided an ecological pathway to the intensification of maize in areas where long fallows are not possible anymore due to population growth or conversion of forest to pasture. After the maize is harvested, the field is sown with *Mucuna pruriens* or "velvet bean," leaving a thick mulch layer year-round. One of the main effects of the velvet bean-mulch layer is improved mineral nutrition in the maize crop, cumulative soil fertility and reduced soil erosion (Altieri 2004).

5. Small farms cool the climate

Industrial agriculture is directly responsible for 13.5% of global greenhouse gases through emissions of carbon dioxide (CO_2), methane (CH_4), and nitrous oxide (N_2O — a gas with 296 times the warming power of CO_2) (IPCC 2007; Crutzen 2007). These result from extensive cultivation, large cattle operations, and the production and application of synthetic fertilizers. Fifty percent of all fertilizer applied to the soil ends up in the atmosphere or in local waterways. Deforestation, largely for industrial agriculture, constitutes another 18% of global emissions (Stern Review 2007).

Climate change poses enormous threats to food production. One

---

Experiences in Central America show that *Mucuna*-based maize systems are stable, allowing respectable yields every year. In particular, the system appears to greatly diminish drought stress because the mulch layer helps conserve water in the soil profile. With enough water around, nutrients are made readily available, in good synchronization with major crop uptake. In addition, the *Mucuna* suppresses weeds, either because velvet bean physically prevents them from germinating and emerging, or from surviving very long during the velvet bean cycle, or because a shallow rooting of weeds in the litter layer-soil interface makes them easier to control. Most important for the tropics, *Mucuna* helps neutralize pH in the mulch-soil interface, thus helping plants avoid the aluminum toxicity that plagues many acid soils in the tropics. Data shows that this system, grounded in farmers' knowledge and involving the continuous annual rotation of velvet bean and maize, can be sustained for at least 15 years at a reasonably high level of productivity, without any apparent decline in the natural resource base (Flores 1989). As illustrated with the *Mucuna* system, an increased understanding of the agroecology and ethnoecology of traditional farming systems is necessary to continue developing contemporary systems. This can only result from integrative studies that determine the myriad of factors that condition how farmers perceive their environment and subsequently how they modify it to later translate such information to modern scientific terms.

Altieri, Miguel. 2004. Linking Ecologists and Traditional Farmers in the Search for Sustainable Agriculture. *Frontiers in Ecology and Environment* 2:35-42.

Buckles, D., B. Triomphe and G. Sain. 1998. *Cover Crops in Hillside Agriculture: Farmer Innovation with Mucuna.* Ottawa, Canada: International Development Research Center.

Flores, M. 1989. Velvetbeans: an Alternative to Improve Small Farmers' Agriculture. *ILEIA Newsletter* 5:8-9.

Figure 7 Projected Impact of Climate Change

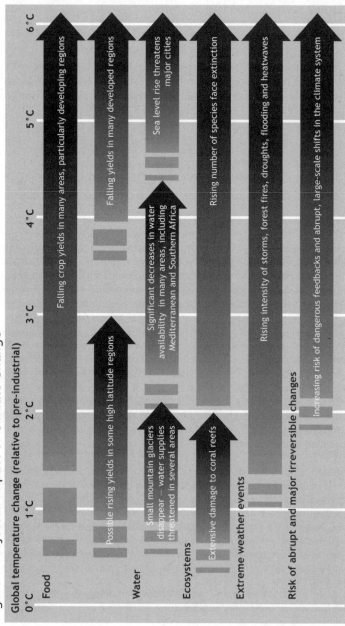

IAASTD. 2009. Summary for Decision Makers of the Global Report. Island Press, Washington DC. Source: The Economics of Climate Change: The Stern Review, 2007. Design: UNEP/GRID-Arendal, Ketill Berger.

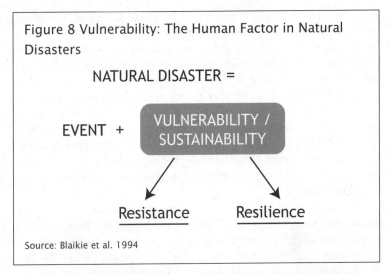

Figure 8 Vulnerability: The Human Factor in Natural Disasters

NATURAL DISASTER =

EVENT + **VULNERABILITY / SUSTAINABILITY**

Resistance   Resilience

Source: Blaikie et al. 1994

to two degrees centigrade increases in average global temperatures will likely cause crop yields to fall in many underdeveloped areas of the global South. According to the UN Intergovernmental Panel on Climate Change (IPCC), large areas of Africa could be stricken by yield decreases of over 50% by the year 2020 as a result of an increasingly hotter and drier climate. Small mountain glaciers will disappear, threatening water supplies, and there will be extensive damage to coral reefs. When average global temperatures rise by three, four and five degrees centigrade, we can expect major declines in productivity in northern regions, severe crop losses, widespread water shortages in the Mediterranean and southern Africa, species extinctions, and a devastating rise in sea level.

Vulnerability: the human side of disaster

Severe climate-induced events are called "hazards." Even at low increases in global temperature hazards can occur in the form of intense storms and droughts, heat waves, freezing spells, and forest fires. The higher the average global temperature change, the higher the likelihood that global climatic changes become irreversible, making agriculture so hazard ridden that in many parts of the world it may become impossible to sustain farm livelihoods.

Unstable weather and extreme weather hazards are already increasing worldwide and are especially dangerous for rain-fed agriculture, farmers on steep, fragile hillsides, farms with shallow soils and agriculture in the low-lying delta regions—in other words, for the smallholders that make up the majority of the world's farmers. Whether or not an extreme weather hazard is disastrous depends not only on the intensity of the hazard itself, but also on the level of vulnerability of the people who experience it. If the level of vulnerability is high, even a low-intensity hazard can result in a climate disaster. When farmers are poor and hungry, have too little agricultural land, farm unprotected soils with poor water access and low agrobiodiversity, even a low-intensity hazard—like a heat wave, cold snap, or a three-week delay in the rainy season—can have devastating consequences.

It is important to realize that the vulnerability of people to climate disasters is socially produced: that is, pushing the world's farmers to precarious farming conditions is the result of decisions taken in the market, in government, and in the global institutions. The fact that these decisions have put nearly half of the world's food production and three-fifths of the world's poor at risk of disaster is tragic and needs to be immediately reversed. The good news is that, just as vulnerability is socially produced, so is sustainability the result of human decisions. We can decide to build resiliency, equity, and sustainability into our agricultural systems.

Will genetic engineering save us? Unfortunately, the high likelihood of multiple, overlapping, unpredictable hazards precludes the ability of a single, transgenic "drought-resistant" or "virus-resistant" crop to protect agriculture from the destructive impacts of climate change. A drought-resistant variety might save a crop in the unusual year in which only drought limits production. But when drought is accompanied by some combination of floods, heat waves, cold snaps or new pest outbreaks, these "climate-ready" seeds will not be able to stabilize production. Studies carried out by the Australian government even indicate that the new "drought-resistant" seeds from the Center for Maize and Wheat Improvement (CIMMYT) underproduce local varieties in good years.[10]

In the long run, "one problem-one gene" technologies are a poor mitigation option because it will be impossible to find, isolate and insert all the genes needed to deal with the multiple hazards resulting from climate change. It will also be impossible to insert climate-ready genes into all of farmers' crops. If one or two "climate-ready" seeds begin dominating production it will reduce agrobiodiversity and undermine whatever existing agroecological resiliency farmers had to climate hazards in the first place. What is urgently needed is not a few designer seeds, but integrated agro-ecosystem management that builds in environmental resilience in the face of complex and unpredictable climate hazards.

Coping with climate change

Helping farmers cope with climate change will require action in three main areas: remediation, mitigation and adaptation. Remediation addresses the causes of climate change by reducing agriculture's impacts on the climate. Mitigation measures must reduce impacts of climate change on agriculture. Adaptation strategies are designed to improve farmer's ability to respond to climate change. When formulating coping strategies to address agriculture and climate change, we need to ask some very basic questions:

How will the strategy or technology *remediate* the problem? Does it actively reduce agriculture's contribution to global warming by reducing carbon and nitrous oxide emissions (e.g. by building soil and biomass reserves and by maintaining low levels of petroleum consumption)?

Will it *mitigate* the impact of climate events on agriculture? Does it reduce farmers' vulnerability in social, economic and environmental terms? Will it increase their environmental resistance to the impacts of climate events? Will it increase their ability to recover (resilience) from the event? Does it enhance and protect their agrobiodiversity, ensure their rights over seeds and protect their access to land and water? Will it increase their market power?

How will the approach reinforce farmers' capacity to quickly and constantly *adapt* to unpredictable changes in climate, weather, and agro-ecosystem functions? Does it develop a dependence on expensive, hard to get or slow to develop inputs? Or does it strengthen quick, flexible, independent responses? Does it enhance local management practices for agrobiodiversity and ecosystem buffering?

Small, biodiverse, ecological farms have a positive effect on climate remediation because small farmers usually amend their soils with organic materials that absorb and sequester carbon better than soils that are farmed with conventional fertilizers. Around four tons of carbon per hectare is stored in organically managed soils (LaSalle and Hepperly 2008). Researchers have suggested that the conversion of 10,000 small- to medium-sized farms to organic production would store carbon in the soil equivalent to taking 1,174,400 cars off the road (Sayre 2003).

Further climate contributions by small farms accrue from the fact that most use significantly less fossil fuel in comparison to conventional agriculture. This is mainly due to a reduction of chemical fertilizer and pesticide use, relying instead on organic manures, legume-based rotations, and habitat diversity practices designed to enhance the populations of beneficial insects. Farmers who live in rural communities near cities and towns and are linked to local markets avoid the energy wasted and the gas emissions associated with transporting food hundreds and even thousands of miles.

There is much to learn about mitigation from indigenous modes of production. These systems have a strong ecological basis, maintain valuable genetic diversity, and lead to regeneration and preservation of biodiversity and natural resources. Traditional methods are particularly instructive because they provide a long-term perspective on successful agricultural management under conditions of climatic variability.

The great advantage of small farming systems is their high levels of agrobiodiversity arranged in the form of variety mixtures, polycultures, crop-livestock combinations and/or agroforestry patterns. Modeling new agro-ecosystems using such diversified designs are extremely valuable to farmers whose systems are collapsing due to debt, pesticide use, transgenic treadmills, price volatility, or climate change. Such diverse buffers are highly adaptive systems against natural or human-induced hazards.

A comparison of the "one problem-one gene" approach being pushed by biotechnology industry and Green Revolution advocates, with the smallholder-based agroecological approach reveals that the former *potentially* addresses only mitigation (drought-resistant GMOs are still an uncertain 5–10 years away from being released). However, agroecological approaches are already helping smallholders remediate, mitigate and adapt to climate change.

Agroecological smallholders are the planet's safeguards against the looming agricultural collapse being provoked by industrial agricultural systems. Institutions in the North can play a major role by supporting small biodiverse farms as the basis for strong rural economies in the global South. Such economies will not only provide sustainable production of healthy, agroecologically produced, accessible food for all, it will help cope with and reverse climate change. It will also ensure that indigenous peoples and small farmers continue their millennial work of building and conserving the agricultural and natural biodiversity on which we all depend, now and in the future.

The International Assessment of Agricultural Knowledge, Science and Technology for Development[11]

> The way the world grows its food will have to change radically to better serve the poor and hungry if the world is to cope with a growing population and climate change while avoiding social breakdown and environmental collapse.
>
> (IAASTD 2008)

The importance of agroecological smallholder agriculture was finally gaining official recognition just as the world food crisis hit. While "emergency responses" like the *Comprehensive Framework for Action* were being hastily cobbled together by high-level task forces, 61 nations met in Johannesburg, South Africa in April of 2008 to adopt a ground-breaking United Nations report on agriculture (IAASTD 2008). A joint initiative of the World Bank, the UNDP, the FAO and other institutions, the International Assessment of Agricultural Knowledge, Science and Technology for Development (IAASTD) was designed as a hybrid consultation model based on the Intergovernmental Panel on Climate Change and the Millennium Ecosystem Assessment. The report took four years and consultations with over 400 scientists to complete.

Considering that the IAASTD grew from discussions initiated by agribusiness corporations with then-president of the World Bank James Wolfenson, the report's findings are surprisingly radical—calling for a thorough, bottom–up transformation of the global food system.

Applauded by farmer organizations and civil society groups, shunned by agribusiness monopolies, shelved by the World Bank, yet quietly approved by 61 governments (excluding US, Canada and Australia), the IAASTD advocates reducing the vulnerability of the global food system through *locally based* innovations. It calls for redistributing productive land to the rural poor. According to co-author Marcia Ishii-Eitemann, in sum the IAASTD found that:

> Agriculture involves more than yields: it has multiple social, political, cultural, institutional and environmental impacts and

can equally harm or support the planet's ecosystem functions on which human life depends.

The future of agriculture lies in biodiverse, agroecologically based farming and can be supported by "triple-bottom-line" business practices that meet social, environmental and economic goals.

Reliance on resource-extractive industrial agriculture is unsustainable, particularly in the face of worsening climate, energy and water crises; expensive, short-term technical fixes—including transgenic crops—do not adequately address the complex challenges of the agricultural sector and often exacerbate social and environmental harms.

Achieving food security and sustainable livelihoods for people now in chronic poverty requires ensuring access to and control of resources by small-scale farmers.

Fair local, regional and global trading regimes can build local economies, reduce poverty and improve livelihoods.

Strengthening the human and ecological resilience of agricultural systems improves our capacity to respond to changing environmental and social stresses. Indigenous knowledge and community-based innovations are an invaluable part of the solution.

Good decision making requires building better governance mechanisms and ensuring democratic participation by the full range of stakeholders.

(for full conclusions see IAASTD 2008)

IAASTD's four-year analytical exercise started with a collective framing of the core problems of hunger and environmental destruction. Scientists then identified and evaluated the most appropriate actions and solutions to these problems, locally, nationally and internationally.

The IAASTD team found that the limiting factors to production, equitable distribution and environmental sustainability were overwhelmingly social, rather than technological in nature. Further, many proven agroecological practices for sustainable production increases were already widespread across the global South, but unable to scale up because they lacked a supportive trade, policy, and institutional environment. This is why IAASTD recommends improving the conditions for sustainable agriculture, rather than just coming up with technological fixes.

Unsurprisingly, even though the idea of a world-wide agricultural assessment originally came from the biotechnology industry, when it became clear that genetically modified seeds were not to be hailed as the solution to the food crisis, both Syngenta and Monsanto abandoned the IAASTD process, and refused to endorse the final report "because of its failure to recognize the role modern plant sciences, including plant biotechnology and crop protection, can play in increasing agricultural crop productivity" (CropLife 2008). While IAASTD found multiple and flexible answers to complex agricultural problems, the corporations wielding the biotechnology hammer could not keep from seeing Southern agriculture as one big nail.

This industrial ire may be one reason why the FAO and the World Bank chose not to refer to IAASTD at the food crisis summits in Rome and Madrid. None of the institutional responses to the food crisis (the High-Level Task Force, the *Comprehensive Framework for Action*, World Bank, FAO, World Food Program) dare address the IAASTD's call for trade reform, land reform, and investment in low-input, sustainable agricultural management technologies. Nonetheless, because the IAASTD's conclusions are very compatible with the calls from grassroots food and farming groups for food sovereignty, the report has created a rare political opening for alternatives and the social movements that promote them. While the "official" solutions to the food crisis garner only weak support, social movements working to advance agroecological alternatives are using the IAASTD as a national and international policy tool to open up the public debate on the future of agriculture.

8

Africa and the End of Hunger

Africa is central to any lasting solution to hunger on the planet. When poverty and hunger are eliminated in Africa, all of the world's poor will be better off. Whatever happens in Africa—or doesn't happen—will have a profound effect on the world's food systems.

What is happening in Africa to address the food crisis is in many ways emblematic of global events. Successes or failures in Africa reflect the potential or the limitations of the global food systems to serve the interests of the world's poor majorities. If the system doesn't work in Africa, then it doesn't work for the world. In this sense, ending hunger in Africa is not simply a "global challenge" for the world's governments. Just as the persistence of poverty in Africa is a challenge for the global economic system, the food crisis is a challenge to the dysfunctional global food system. The stakes on the continent are high in human, environmental and geopolitical terms.

In many ways, of course, Africa's recent history is one of conquest by and resistance to foreign economic and geopolitical interests. The carving up of the continent at the 1884 Berlin Conference sealed the first "Scramble for Africa." Countries that missed the opportunity to profit from Africa in the 19th century had plenty of chances in the 20th and even more in the 21st century. Africa was the continent most consistently pushed towards extreme structural adjustment policies. As Walden Bello has observed, the continent was a net food exporter in the 1960s, "averaging 1.3 million tons a year between 1966–70. Today, the continent imports 25% of its food, with almost every country being a net food importer" (Bello 2008).

A corollary of this import dependence has been an opening up of the continent's resources to the highest, and in some cases most unscrupulous, bidder. Thus US businessman Philippe Heilberg has claimed 4,000 square kilometers of fertile land by the Nile in a deal with a Sudanese warlord (Blas and Walls 2009), and the Korean Daewoo corporation attempted to lease 1.3 million hectares of land in Madagascar (Jung-a and Oliver 2008). While there are other high profile land grabs involving foreign powers, notably from Europe, North America, India and China, the inequities of land distribution in some parts of Africa have been merely exacerbated by neoliberal agricultural policy. Under the 'willing buyer, willing seller' models of land reform promoted by the World Bank in South Africa, less than 5% of the land has been redistributed from white to black owners since the end of apartheid (Zigomo 2008). Yet social movements in Africa are vital and active, working on concrete solutions in the fields and concrete policy changes for governments—to bring about food sovereignty. Central to these efforts have been the work of women and women's organizations—women grow the majority of the food on the continent, yet they shoulder the triple burden of needing to work for a wage, build community, and feed their family. It is no surprise, then, that at the 2008 Via Campesina 5th international conference in Maputo, Mozambique, one of the loudest calls was for the recognition of food sovereignty as an end to violence against women.

It is important to realize that just as there is a world-wide diversity of people-driven food systems struggling to emerge from under the weight of the agrifoods monopolies, there is also a continent-wide diversity of grassroots initiatives to end hunger in Africa. Collectively, these life-affirming initiatives cover more area and reach more people than official, more centralized efforts. Their organizational and technological approaches tend to be grounded in a people-first, noncorporate perspective. They employ more agroecological and democratic means for improving smallholder agriculture as a strategy to end hunger. These African alternatives were not given a seat at the table at the *Comprehensive Framework for Action* (CFA), nor were they considered in the planning of the new Green Revolution in Africa. However, because extreme hunger is so widespread, it is hard to imagine how any effort to end hunger in Africa could be successful without them. Whether or not official and grassroots efforts can work together to end hunger is the question facing not just Africa, but the entire world.

Africa's Agrarian Question

Because the majority of sub-Saharan Africa's hungry people come from poor farming families cultivating two hectares or less—and because over 80% of the continent is still rural—the challenge of ending hunger and poverty on the continent is necessarily an agrarian question. Africa's agrarian questions concern land, labor, markets, technology and politics at local, regional, national and international scales. These concerns are not just about feeding people, but also about changing the present conditions of production that keep the rural poor from feeding themselves. Africa's agrarian questions are not adequately addressed by simply asking, "What is the role of African smallholders?" Because of the great diversity of smallholder agroecosystems on the African continent, we also need to ask what kinds of technologies, markets, resource use and ownership rights will suit Africa's diverse agricultural transformations. And, we need to ask, who will lead these transformations? This last question is especially important because, as the result of decisions regarding the food, fuel, and economic crises, Africa's smallholders are increasingly falling victim to new grabs for land, water, markets, and genetic resources. Will the food crisis usher in a new era of rural debt, contract farming, and agricultural exports for foreign food and energy needs? Or will the crisis provide an opportunity for new agrarian models of development and food sovereignty? In Africa, the struggle to eliminate hunger is the struggle for the future of agriculture.

There are many parallels between the continent's historic movements for independence and today's struggles for food sovereignty. Though sub-Saharan Africa is a region rich in minerals and natural resources, over 450 million live on less than $2 a day and over a third of the population suffers from malnutrition (Faurès and Santini 2008). Proposals to end poverty and hunger on the African continent must come to grips with the fact that since colonial times, Africa's food systems and natural resources have been relentlessly appropriated by foreign capital, frequently in collusion with national elites. Even today, at the height of the food crisis, some African governments are negotiating the sale and long-term lease of agricultural land to foreign governments and corporations. Others are providing forests, brushland and pastureland to foreign agrofuel corporations.

The struggles for food sovereignty in Africa are widespread, and are especially difficult because the continent not only continues to be a major source of natural resources for the industrial North, but, in a time of shrinking global markets, the food crisis actually makes Africa's poor farmers a prime target for major seed, biotechnology and fertilizer companies desperate for new consumers. While each poor farmer may not have much money to spend, taken as a whole these farmers constitute a big and lucrative market, particularly if foreign aid and African governments provide conditions for market expansion with infrastructure, research, and investment incentives.

Of course, African governments must increase aid to agriculture. Encouragingly, in 2003 at the African Union summit in Maputo, Mozambique, African leaders endorsed the Comprehensive African Agriculture Development Program (CAADP), in which they promised to increase government agricultural support to 10% by 2015.[12] The private sector has an important role to play in ending hunger, and in these times of crisis has a social responsibility to serve the public good. However—especially in Africa—care must be taken to ensure that the benefits from improvements in agriculture accrue primarily to poor farmers, not state farms, agro-export farms, sovereign wealth funds or transnational corporations.

Who improves African agriculture, how, under what agreements and by what means, will determine whether the efforts to end hunger in Africa succeed or fail. Lack of attention to these issues runs the risk that the long-overdue support to African agriculture will be used as a prop for a flawed global food system when what is needed is a thorough transformation of agriculture.

Tensions between top–down and bottom–up approaches to solve the food crisis in Africa are being played out in a transnational "development arena" where official discourses of "partnerships" frequently accompany less altruistic political or commercial agendas, and often mask the real exclusion of farmers from participating in the substantive decisions that affect their lives. The future of Africa's food systems and the fate of millions of smallholders and hungry people hinge on the outcomes emanating from this arena. Informed public debate, institutional transparency and accountability, and amplifying the diverse voices of farmers' organizations and *their* proposals are essential for finding a sustainable and equitable path through the food crisis. The challenge is to diversify and democratize initiatives for agricultural development and at the same time respond quickly and effectively to the crisis on the ground.

The difficulty in doing all of this is especially evident in the rift between official calls for a new Green Revolution in Africa and the continent's grassroots movements for African agroecological alternatives.

BOX 27

A Return to the Roots? Or Fertilizing the Money Tree?

Boosting Food Production in Africa's Breadbasket Areas: An unprecedented partnership among key players in agricultural development aims to significantly boost food production in Africa's "breadbasket regions," link local food production to food needs, and work across Africa's major agricultural growing areas—or agroecological zones—to create opportunities for smallholder farmers.

This upbeat byline announced the new "Memorandum of Understanding" signed by the Alliance for a Green Revolution in Africa (AGRA), the Food and Agriculture Organization of the United Nations (FAO), the International Fund for Agricultural Development, and the World Food Program at the FAO High-Level Conference on World Food Security in Rome, June1-4, 2008 (AGRA 2008).

The memorandum not only signaled the renewal of the Green Revolution as a solution to food crises, it marked the return of the Green Revolution to its strategic roots. Over 50 years ago, when the Rockefeller Foundation began funding research for the industrial transformation of agriculture (Jennings 1988; Rockefeller Foundation 2007), researchers introduced high-yielding varieties (HYVs) of wheat, maize, and rice on prime, irrigated cropland in the Philippines, Mexico and India, leading to impressive yield increases among the farmers able to afford the inputs required for HYVs to deliver their high-yielding traits (Toenniessen 2008). The Green Revolution rode a wave of "development decades" from the 1960s into the 1980s (Rapley 1996), and was instrumental in establishing the dominance of Northern agribusiness in Latin America and Asia (Burbach and Flynn 1980; Patel 2007; Janvry 1981). During that period, developing countries were awash with foreign aid and experiencing impressive economic growth. They built roads, extended subsidies, established price supports, provided cheap credit, and built national agricultural research systems to spread the HYVs being produced by international crop breeders. This led to a worldwide explosion of grain production (Evanson and Gollin 2003).

The germplasm collected from peasants by Green Revolution scientists contributed $10.2 billion a year to US corn and soy production in the 1970s-80s. Heavy US government subsidies led to a surplus of cheap grain that was dumped in Southern countries, destroying local markets and help-ing major corporations—Cargill and Archer Daniels Midland (ADM)—capture three-quarters of the world grain trade (Vorley 2003). Fully one-third of the seed produced by the International Center for Maize and Wheat Improvement was appropriated by private Northern companies, including

Pioneer Hy-Brid, and Cargill (*Ecologist* 1996). The expansion of biotechnology in the 1990s helped consolidate these global monopolies. Bayer Crop Science, Syngenta, and BASF control half of the total agrochemical market (UNCTAD 2006).

In the 1990s, fallout from the Green Revolution's environmental degradation and the increasingly poor performance of its high-yielding varieties led to a 21% drop in donor support, provoking a "silent crisis" in the CGIAR research system. Under a conditional bailout from the World Bank, the CGIAR diversified operations with a "thrice green" revolution in an attempt to bring the Green Revolution's externalities under control, raise yields, and attract more funding (CGIAR 1996).

For five decades the Green Revolution has tried to eliminate hunger by increasing productivity through genetic crop improvement. Now focused on biotechnology, genetic improvement continues to eclipse all other agricultural research and development activities (CGIAR 1996; WorldBank 2008).

AGRA. 2008. *Boosting Food Production in Africa's "Breadbasket Areas": New Collaboration Among Rome-based UN Agencies and AGRA*. Alliance for a Green Revolution in Africa. http://www.agra-alliance.org/content/news/detail/633/ (accessed April 2, 2009).

Burbach, Roger and Patricia Flynn. 1980. *Agribusiness in the Americas*. New York: Monthly Review.

CGIAR. 1996. *CGIAR Annual Report: CGIAR 25 Years, 1971-1996*. Washington DC: Consultative Group on International Agricultural Research.

Ecologist, The. 1996. CGIAR Agricultural Research for Whom? *The Ecologist* Nov/Dec, 259-70.

Evanson, R.E. and D. Gollin. 2003. Assessing the Impact of the Green Revolution, 1960 to 2000. *Science* 300 (5620):78-82.

Janvry, Alain de. 1981. *The Agrarian Question and Reformism in Latin America*. Baltimore: John Hopkins University Press.

Jennings, Bruce H. 1988. *Foundations of International Agricultural Research: Sciences and Politics in Mexican Agriculture*. Boulder: Westview Press.

Patel, Raj. 2007. *Stuffed and Starved*. London: Portobello Books.

Rapley, J. 1996. *Understanding Development: Theory and Practice in the Third World*. Boulder and London: Lynne Rienner Publishers.

Rockefeller Foundation. 2007. *Africa's Turn: A New Green Revolution for the Twenty-first Century*. The Rockefeller Foundation. http://www.rockfound.org/library/africas_turn.pdf (accessed August 15, 2008).

Toenniessen, Gary H., Joseph de Vries and Eric Holt-Giménez. 2008. *Replenishing the Breadbasket: Food and Philanthropy. A World of Possibilities*. http://www.aworldofpossibilities.com/details.cfm?id=336 (accessed July 10, 2008).

UNCTAD. 2006. *Tracking the Trend Towards Market Concentration: The Case of the Agricultural Input Industry*. United Nations Conference on Trade and Development. http://www.unctad.org/en/docs/ditccom200516_en.pdf (accessed October 14, 2008).

Vorley, Billy. 2003. *Food Inc.: Corporate Concentration From Farm to Consumer*. United Kingdom Food Group. http://www.ukfg.org.uk/docs/UKFG-Foodinc-Nov03.pdf (accessed July 15, 2008).

World Bank. 2008. *World Bank Launches $1.2 Billion Fast-Track Facility for Food Crisis*. World Bank. http://web.worldbank.org/WBSITE/EXTERNAL/NEWS/0, ,contentMDK:21783685~pagePK:64257043~piPK:437376~theSitePK:4607,00. html (accessed November 11, 2008).

The Green Revolution Returns[13]

For two and a half decades the Consultative Group on International Agricultural Research (CGIAR) invested 40%–45% of their $350 million a year budget in an unsuccessful effort to spread the Green Revolution across Africa (World Bank 2004). Supporters of the Green Revolution offer multiple explanations for its failure to raise yields on the continent, among them Africa's exhausted soils, inadequate infrastructure, poor governance and declining support for African agriculture (Evanson and Gollin 2003). They claim the Green Revolution "bypassed" Africa, and the CGIAR's failure to eradicate hunger on the continent is due to lack of proper implementation of the Green Revolution model (Rockefeller Foundation 2007). Critics of the Green Revolution maintain that Africa can't be blamed for its actual conditions, and that the failure is with the Green Revolution's model itself (see Food First www.foodfirst.org; ETC Group http://www.etcgroup. org; and GRAIN http://www.grain.org).

There is some basis for claims that Africa was bypassed by the Green Revolution. Prior to the oil shocks of the 1970s, many African governments moved decisively to increase food production by enacting land reform, implementing rural development projects, providing producer subsidies, establishing marketing boards and price guarantees, and increasing investments in rural infrastructure. National agricultural research systems were established to test and distribute packets of seeds and fertilizer. Under these conditions, the Green Revolution did begin to raise yields in basic grains in some places, leading many to believe that the "Asian miracle" could be replicated in Africa (Havnevik et al. 2007).

However, following the oil shocks and the debt crisis of the 1970s, and the World Bank/IMF structural adjustment programs of the 1980s, African governments were forced to reduce state services, dismantle marketing boards, close development projects and end subsidies and price guarantees. Government research and extension vanished. As market-led approaches to economic development replaced state-led approaches, agriculture fell off the development agenda and the Green Revolution ground to a halt (Havnevik et al. 2007).

In the 1990s there were multiple high-profile unsuccessful attempts to score victories in Africa, notably by former US presidents Jimmy Carter and Bill Clinton, and philanthropist Ryoicho Sasakawa with the "father" of the Green Revolution, Nobel laureate Norman Borlaug. The repeated failures of the Green Revolution in Africa also coincided with the Green Revolution's overall global slump (see Box 27 "A Return to the Roots?"). Notwithstanding, at the 2004 African Union summit, then secretary-general of the United Nations Kofi Annan called for a "uniquely African Green Revolution."

Renewed alliances for the Green Revolution

In 1997 then newly appointed president of the Rockefeller Foundation Gordon Conway published *The Doubly Green Revolution: Food for All in the 21st Century,* in which he called for a new, high-yielding Green Revolution based on equity and sustainability. Rockefeller's attempt to re-launch the Green Revolution in Africa in 1999 made little headway until June 2006, when it cosponsored the African Fertilizer Summit with the New Partnership for Africa's Development (NEPAD) in Abuja, Nigeria. Representatives from 40 African governments, African and multilateral development banks, the CGIAR, and agribusiness executives discussed strategies for modernizing African agriculture. A month later, the foundation rolled out its strategy in *Africa's Turn: The New Green Revolution for the 21st Century.* It included:

- Promotion of hybrid and genetically engineered seeds and chemical fertilizers
- Training of African agricultural scientists for crop improvement
- Market development
- Local agrodealer distribution networks
- Infrastructure investments
- Agricultural policy reforms.

Two months later, the Rockefeller Foundation partnered with the Bill and Melinda Gates Foundation to launch the Alliance for a Green Revolution for Africa (AGRA)—the non-governmental organization

BOX 28

Like Living Software: AGRA's Strategy for Agricultural Development

The Bill and Melinda Gates Foundation is spending billions on its Alliance for a Green Revolution in Africa. The vast majority of those dollars are going into new technologies for African agriculture. Likening plants to software, the foundation is attempting to build a new technological infrastructure.

AGRA's grants tend to focus in four key areas: technological research and development; soil fertility (mostly through increasing the use of chemical fertilizers); increasing access to seed and inputs; and creating policy environments favorable to market driven, export-oriented agriculture.

Program for Africa's Seed Systems (PASS)

In order to address a perceived deficiency in improved seed, AGRA plans to release 1,000 new crop varieties in the next 10 years through partnerships with the CGIAR, private seed companies, and public extension. The technological development program uses genetic engineering as well as conventional breeding, and focuses on enhancing stress tolerance, yield and nutrient content. The program will also fund the education of master's and PhD level scientists and plant breeders, as well as training programs for thousands of students and technical graduates in agribusiness leadership. Under this program falls AGRA's Agro-dealer Development Program, which seeks to build a network of agro-input dealers to be the primary conduit by which improved seed and fertilizer reach rural communities (and through which surplus is extracted). A $13.2 million grant from this program to set up agro-input dealers in Tanzania, Kenya and Malawi comes at a time when the government of Malawi is using an IMF loan to subsidize the price of fertilizer by up to 90% (Gates Foundation 2008).

AGRA Soil Health Program

The foundation aims to improve soil fertility, largely by increasing fertilizer use in Africa 400% to 30 kilograms per hectare (Gates Foundation 2008). AGRA is negotiating with Yara Fertilizer on concessionary pricing and with the African Development Bank and the World Bank on a potential Fertilizer Financing Mechanism.

Policy Advocacy

AGRA seems to subscribe to the minimalist state, market dependent theory of development (Moyo et al. 2008), and is actively advocating for pro-industry policies in Africa. At a recent private sector forum, AGRA called for

Summary of Projects Implemented Under PASS

AGRA's sub-program	Total amounts (US$)	Participating countries
Agrodealer Development	$24,824,032	Kenya, Malawi, Tanzania, Mali, Nigeria, Zambia
Education for African Crop Improvement	$15,685,943	Ghana, Uganda, South Africa, sub-Saharan Africa
Fund for the Improvement and Adoption of African Crops	$5,516,366	Ghana, Kenya, Malawi, Mali, Nigeria, Ethiopia, South Africa, Tanzania, Uganda, sub-Saharan Africa
Seed Production for Africa	$3,754,003	Ghana, Nigeria, Burkina Faso, Kenya, Malawi, Mali, Mozambique, Rwanda, Tanzanian, Uganda, South Africa, sub-Saharan Africa
Total	$49,780,344	

Source: Moyo, Chambati and Murisa. 2008.

regulatory frameworks to approve new seed technologies (i.e., GM crops), facilitate the privatization of national seed industries, and reduce barriers to national and international trade (AGRA 2008).

Gates and AGRA are generously funding the institutions that brought about the first Green Revolution—the CGIAR system, the International Rice Research Institute, the International Maize and Wheat Improvement Center (CIMMYT)—and government agriculture ministries, as well as national research centers and public universities in Africa. However, one major departure from the model of the first Green Revolution is the heavy participation of private industry. Partners in the private sector include Monsanto, Syngenta, DuPont, Yara Fertilizer, and several national seed companies. Though AGRA claims it is not currently funding the development of GM crops, the Gates Foundation is, and AGRA's partners, such as the African Agricultural Technology Foundation, are actively advocating for their legalization.

AGRA. 2008. Private Sector Forum on African Agricultural Development. Alliance for a Green Revolution in Africa. http://www.agra-alliance.org/content/news/detail/823 (accessed January 3, 2009).

Gates Foundation. 2008. *Agricultural Development Strategy 2008-2011*. Seattle: Bill and Melinda Gates Foundation.

Moyo, S., W. Chambati and T. Murisa. 2008. *An Audit of the Alliance for a Green Revolution in Africa*. Nairobi, Kenya: Action Aid International.

designed to implement the ideas of the *Doubly Green Revolution* and the strategies in *Africa's Turn*. The Bill and Melinda Gates Foundation's $38.7 billion philanthropy put up $100 million of AGRA's initial $150 million budget.

The alliance quickly formed the Program for a Green Revolution in Africa (ProAGRA) to implement AGRA. Most of the board members of both AGRA and ProAGRA were employees of the Gates and Rockefeller Foundations (Daño 2007).

AGRA: recycling the Green Revolution?

While AGRA adopted the Green Revolution's technological paradigm—prioritizing genetic crop improvement and fertilizer applications as the central pillar of their strategy for agricultural improvement—it also added variations that reflect new developments within the CGIAR, the seed and chemical industries, and the global finance

BOX 29

Gates' Gene Revolution

The Gates Foundation is using the vast majority of its agricultural development funds to develop new seeds for African agriculture. While some of this development is taking place through conventional crop breeding, Gates' programs invest heavily in biotechnology.

One example is the foundation's partnership with the African Agricultural Technology Foundation (AATF). AATF has received $43 million from Gates to develop genetically engineered "water efficient maize for Africa." New lines of genetically engineered maize are slated to be completed by 2010, with field trials scheduled for 2013. The AATF will manage the funds in collaboration with the International Maize and Wheat Improvement Center (CIMMYT) and the Monsanto Corporation. Monsanto is providing the project proprietary genetic material, expertise, and their nascent drought-tolerant transgenes. CIMMYT is providing high-yielding maize varieties adapted to "African conditions" and AATF will distribute the seed to local dealers.

The Gates Foundation is also funding a project of the AATF in partnership with University of California Berkeley, the International Crops Research Institute for the Semi-Arid Tropics, and DuPont to develop a sorghum variety with increased lysine and vitamin A (ISSAA 2008). The International Potato Center is working on a Gates-funded vitamin A enriched sweet potato, while Harvest Plus, a program of the CGIAR (also with foundation money), is

sector. This time a broader array of traditional African food crops will be included in the technological mix. Microfinance, and loan guarantees to state and commercial banks will provide credit. The project is establishing a powerful advocacy arm to influence the policies of African governments. AGRA is making a special effort to reach women—both as farmers and as researchers. Its "integrated soil fertility program" will use "smart subsidies" to increase the application of chemical fertilizers of four million farmers by 400% to 30 kilogram per hectare per year (Gates Foundation 2008). This is to be accompanied by instruction on how to build up and conserve soil organic matter. While AGRA's Program for Africa's Seed Systems (PASS) is not now distributing genetically engineered seeds, AGRA has made it known that it will consider introducing GMOs in the future when regulations are in place. Meanwhile, AGRA's training programs are steadily preparing African crop scientists in

---

working on biofortification of several crops including maize, cassava, rice, wheat, and sweet potato.

Drought, climate change, and biofortification offer a public relations "Trojan Horse" for the biotechnology industry, especially in Africa. The new so-called, climate-ready (drought tolerant) transgenics are by most estimations years away, but the industry is not waiting. Syngenta, BASF and Monsanto have already filed patent applications on nearly two-thirds of climate-related genes at patent offices worldwide (ETC Group 2008). Although the AATF promises to release their new water-efficient crops royalty free, just who will own the seeds, who will sell them, and how long the magnanimity of the foundation's corporate partners will last is yet to be seen.

Even if the biofortified and water-efficient crops are distributed royalty free forever, the industry still stands to profit enormously. Biofortified and water-efficient crops, posing as a development strategy, will open African markets to biotechnology in general. The prying open of this massive new market to biotech products explains the "donation" of the industry's intellectual property.

ETC Group. 2008. *Patenting the Climate Genes and Capturing the Climate Agenda*. ETC Group. http://www.etcgroup.org/upload/publication/pdf_file/687 (accessed September 25, 2008).

ISSAA. 2008. *South Africa Approves Biofortified Sorghum Trials*. International Association for the Acquisition of Agri-Biotech Applications, September 19. http://www.isaaa.org/kc/cropbiotechupdate/online/default.asp?Date=9/19/2008#3141 (accessed January 5, 2009).

BOX 30

Opening Africa to the Biotech Industry

Until 2008, South Africa was the only African nation commercially growing genetically modified crops, but the landscape for transgenics is rapidly changing. The biotech industry is fiercely marketing their products as a "development strategy" in Africa. In a clever act of double-speak, the Syngenta Foundation has been lobbying for the legalization of Bt corn in Kenya under the banner of a "development project" called "Insect Resistant Maize for Africa." The African Agricultural Technology Foundation, a public-private partnership between the Gates and Rockefeller Foundations, AGRA, the CGIAR system, and biotechnology firms Monsanto, Syngenta, and DuPont, is developing new GM crops for Africa and advocating pro-biotech policies. With support from Gates and AGRA, biotechnology is being marketed as Africa's only way to end cycles of hunger, drought, and poverty, and to deal with the impacts of climate change.

All told, 2008 was a milestone year for the industry's project of "development" in Africa. Egypt and Burkina Faso became the second and third African nations to commercialize GM crops. Egypt approved a Monsanto Bt corn variety (MON810) and Burkina Faso allowed the planting of Bt cotton. Kenya, Uganda, Mali and Malawi initially approved biosafety laws that will likely pave the way to commercialization of GM crops in those countries. Meanwhile field trials of GM crops are planned or underway in Zimbabwe, Tanzania, Ghana, Nigeria, Tunisia, Morocco, Mali, and Mauritania.

The pipeline for biotech crops specifically marketed to Africa is long, and again, is being created largely under the banner of "development."

A peek into Africa's transgenic future:

- GM bananas—Researchers at Cornell University's Agricultural Biotechnology Support Project II (funded by USAID) are developing a transgenic variety of East African highland banana resistant to both nematodes and the black Sigatoka fungus. Field trials are underway in Uganda (Shotkoski 2006a).
- GM tomatoes—Also through USAID and Cornell, a new GM tomato resistant to yellow leaf curl virus is being tested in Mali (Shotkoski 2006b).
- GM potato—South Africa has been asked to approve plantings of a GM potato developed at Michigan State University resistant to the potato tuber moth. The moth is a post-harvest pest that attacks potatoes in

storage and shipping. The potato is being marketed toward small-scale farmers (Swanby 2008; Matloga 2008).

- "Water Efficient Maize for Africa"—Joint project of the Gates Foundation, AGRA, Monsanto, and the CGIAR system, transgenic varieties of maize that supposedly confer drought resistance are under development and may be released as early as 2013.

- High nitrogen use efficiency rice—US based Arcadia Biosciences is partnering with the AATF to bring rice with better nitrogen use efficiency to Africa (Arcadia Biosciences 2008a). Arcadia received funding from USAID and has partnerships with affiliates of DuPont and Monsanto for commercializing its technology (Reuters 2008; Arcadia Biosciences 2008b).

Arcadia Biosciences. 2008a. *Arcadia Biosciences and the African Agricultural Technology Foundation Enter into Agreement for Development of Improved African Rice*. Press release, December 2. http://www.arcadiabio.com/pr_0032.php (accessed December 8, 2008).

Arcadia Biosciences. 2008b. *Arcadia Biosciences Receives $3.6 Million USAID Grant to Develop Improved Crops in India*. Press release, December 2. http://www.arcadiabio.com/pr_0031.php (acessed December 8, 2008).

Matloga, Polelo. 2008. *New GM Potato Book: Executive Summary*. African Center for Biosafety. http://www.biosafetyafrica.net/portal/index.php?option=com_content&task=view&id=174&Itemid=35 (accessed December 8, 2008).

Reuters. 2008. *DuPont and Arcadia Biosciences Collaborate to Improve Nitrogen Use Efficiency in Corn*. March 12. http://www.reuters.com/article/pressRelease/idUS165580+12-Mar-2008+PRN20080312 (accessed December 8, 2008).

Shotkoski, Frank. 2006a. *East African Highland Banana Resistant to Black Sigatoka and Nematodes. Single-Project Report*. Cornell Univeristy. http://www.absp2.cornell.edu/projects/project.cfm?productid=23 (accessed December 8, 2008).

Shotkoski, Frank. 2006b. *Tomato Virus Resistance for West Africa. Single-Project Report*. Cornell University. http://www.absp2.cornell.edu/projects/project.cfm?productid=26 (accessed December 8, 2008).

Swanby, Haidee. 2008. *GMO's in South Africa: Overview of Current Status 2008*. African Centre for Biosafety. http://www.biosafetyafrica.net/portal/index.php?option=com_content&task=view&id=246&Itemid=63 (accessed December 8, 2008).

biotechnology (Agra-Alliance 2008). Further, AGRA's main benefactor, the Bill and Melinda Gates Foundation, along with the Yara, Monsanto, and Syngenta Foundations, support African biotechnology institutions such as the African Harvest Biotech Foundation, the African Agricultural Technology Foundation (AATF), and the International Service for Acquisition of Agricultural Biotechnology Applications, in a concerted push for GMO research and promotion (Daño 2007). This work focuses on genetically engineering crops for high vitamin content, pest resistance, drought, and weed tolerance. Within the larger Green Revolution scheme, these projects and AGRA are mutually reinforcing: as one prepares the scientists, the other prepares the biotechnology; as one establishes seed distribution networks, the other releases GMOs.

Strategically, AGRA signifies a substantive shift for the Green Revolution. In the absence of the 1960s' African "development state" that provided funding for credit, research, infrastructure and marketing services, supporters of the new Green Revolution are hoping that this time public–private philanthropy partnerships will step in to take up the slack. While there may not be large profits to be made at first, "recognition is a proxy" until profits can be obtained (Gates 2008). Given the reluctance of the private sector to invest in infrastructure and services for the poor, this is clearly a big gamble. Africa needs some $15 billion a year in agricultural investment. If Northern governments are backtracking on their promises for increasing aid, how can we be sure the private sector will make up the difference? The Green Revolution requires major social investment in order to be successful (even on its own terms).

Structurally, however, AGRA appears to reproduce the same commercial bias of former Green Revolutions and reinforces the World Bank's antagonistic position against smallholder agriculture. For all its claims to independence, AGRA is considered by the Bill and Melinda Gates Foundation to be the "African face and voice for our work." AGRA's benefactor clearly spells out its function in the Gates Foundation's theory of change:

> In order to transition agriculture from the current situation of low investment, low productivity and low returns to a market-oriented, highly-productive system, it is essential that supply (productivity) and demand (market access) expand together and that production systems use natural resources efficiently and help farmers man-

age their risks... [this] involves market-oriented farmers operating profitable farms that generate enough income to sustain their rise out of poverty. Over time, this will require some degree of land mobility and a lower percentage of total employment involved in direct agricultural production... We are uniquely focused... on 150 [million] smallholder households in Sub-Saharan Africa... that have the potential to transform agriculture at scale. We consider these farmers, most of whom are women, our customers and their needs and realities guide our work.

(Gates Foundation 2008)

AGRA will follow the market-driven development strategies of the World Bank designed to open Africa's smallholder sector to the volatile world market and push the "least efficient" African farmers out of agriculture. When combined with the same social and technological paradigm that has driven the Green Revolution for four decades, and given the present economic and political limitations of many weakened African states, potential for a renewed structural violence against poor rural communities is great.

Will it work?

AGRA appears to be having some successes in reviving the Green Revolution. Government agricultural ministries in seven countries and national agricultural research centers like the Kenya Agricultural Research Institute, the National Agricultural Research Organization of Uganda, the University of Ghana, and the University of KwaZulu Natal—all strapped for cash—have flocked to AGRA in the hopes of resurrecting their abandoned agricultural programs. Over 550 African scientists are being trained in biotechnology and crop breeding. National and international non-governmental organizations are accessing resources directly and indirectly by participating in AGRA projects. Even the international agricultural research centers, including the International Potato Center, the International Maize and Wheat Improvement Center, and the International Rice Research Institute, are benefiting from new research funding for biotechnology. International agribusiness corporations, while not stampeding into the continent, are making exploratory investments in seed and fertilizer markets, positioning themselves for future opportunities. (For example, Yara, the Norwegian fertilizer giant, is willing to take lower returns on their investments in order to establish their dominance in the African market.) For those convinced that a new Green

Revolution is the answer to Africa's problem of hunger, AGRA must seem like a long-awaited miracle.

Whether or not AGRA will be able to revive and re-fit the Green Revolution and whether or not this solves the problem of hunger in Africa is another story. The effort, the largest in over three decades, raises a number of questions:

- Why did the Green Revolution not consider the successful, already existing agroecological alternatives when formulating its strategy for Africa?
- Why were farmers' organizations never consulted? Why are individual farmers being consulted after the program has already been designed?
- How will the Green Revolution protect the agroecological biodiversity of smallholders? How will it avoid the old Green Revolution's "monoculture trap?"
- How will the Green Revolution protect farmer's rights to their native seeds? How will it ensure a robust, *in situ* conservation of these seeds and the knowledge of how to cultivate them?
- If credit is only available for commercial seeds and fertilizers— which are bought and sold as commodities—how will the Green Revolution ensure the sustainable restoration of those aspects of healthy agroecosystems that are *not* commodities, like soil organic matter, agrobiodiversity, non-commercial and non-food crops, and refuges for beneficial insects?
- How will the Green Revolution ensure the democratic representation of farmers' organizations in agricultural development, especially key projects like AGRA?
- How will the Green Revolution empower farmers and farmers' organizations to advance their own agendas for agrarian reform and agricultural development?
- Beyond national self-sufficiency in grains, how will the Green Revolution strengthen farmers' food sovereignty, i.e., ensure the democratization of the food system in favor of the poor?
- What are the Green Revolution principles and mechanisms for social and environmental safeguards? For public accountability and transparency? What role will farmers play in establishing these principles and using these mechanisms?
- How will the Green Revolution address climate justice and the remediation, mitigation and adaptation to climate change? How

will it help farmers roll back "land grabbing" for agrofuels and food export?

These are just a few of the complex concerns that can't be answered on a program website under "Frequently Asked Questions." They must be addressed socially, in open dialogue and in public debate at local, national and regional levels. Addressing these questions—and opening up the debate to agroecological alternatives to the Green Revolution—is a necessary step in a larger, democratic, problem-solving process of social learning that allows for trial and error, change and adjustment on the basis of broad-based consent.

The fact that AGRA brings together the same social and techno-logical assumptions, research institutions and corporate interests from the world's first Green Revolution to re-launch a new Green Revolution in Africa cannot be welcomed as good news. Despite claims that Africa's new Green Revolution will now benefit women and conserve soils, if the same paradigms and structures of the old Green Revolution remain intact, the biggest unanswered question is: How will AGRA avoid reproducing the devastating structural vio-lence of the first Green Revolution?

African Agroecological Solutions

There has been no lack of agroecological solutions to the Green Revolution in Africa (Asenso-Okyere 1997; Mortimore and Adams 2001; Reij et al. 1996). The system of rice intensification (SRI) devel-oped in Madagascar has raised yields as high as eight tons per hec-tare and spread to a million farmers in over two dozen countries (Uphoff 1999). A survey of 45 sustainable agriculture projects in 17 African countries, covering some 730,000 households, revealed that agroecological approaches substantially improved food production and household food security. In 95% of these projects, cereal yields improved by 50% to 100% (Pretty et al. 2003). A study of organic agri-culture on the continent (See Box 31 Organic Agriculture in Africa) showed that small-scale, modern, organic agriculture was wide-spread in sub-Saharan Africa, contributing significantly to improved yields, incomes and environmental services (Pretty et al. 2008).

Over 170 African organizations from nine countries in East and Southern Africa belong to the Participatory Land Use Management (PELUM) network, which has been sharing agroecological knowledge

BOX 31

Organic Agriculture in Africa

In 2008 the United Nations Conference on Trade and Development in conjunction with the United Nations Environment Programme (UNEP-UNCTAD capacity-building Task Force on Trade, Environment and Development) released a study entitled *Organic Agriculture and Food Security in Africa*. The study, prepared by Rachel Hine and Jules Pretty (University of Essex) and Sophia Twarog (UNCTAD), begins by acknowledging that "[d]espite global pledges... the number of people suffering from hunger has increased every year since 1996." Through the analysis of 15 programs promoting and implementing the transition to sustainable organic farming in East Africa, the study shows that, in the words of Supachai Panitchpakdi, secretary-general of UNCTAD and Achim Steiner, executive director of UNEP, "organic agriculture can be more conducive to food security in Africa than most conventional production systems, and... it is more likely to be sustainable in the long term" (Pretty et al. 2008).

In every case examined, access to food was enhanced by the transition to organic farming. In spite of the widespread association of organic agriculture with lower yields, the study found that the conversion from traditional low-chemical input farming to organic practices did not result in any loss of productivity. In fact, as the farms became more established, productivity well exceeded that of traditional farms and even matched that of high-input modern farms. Farming household food security was enhanced not only by increased quantities of readily available calories, but also by the income generated through sale of the surplus produce resulting from the conversion to organic. Local communities also experienced direct benefit from the increased supply of fresh organic products.

Not surprisingly, the transition to organic farming practices has an overwhelmingly positive effect on the natural environment. The programs studied promoted a highly sustainable and ecologically integrated model rather than a simple substitution of chemical inputs with organic fertilizers. By harnessing natural biological and ecological processes to increase production, 93% of the case studies showed "benefits to soil fertility, water supply, flood control and biodiversity." The organic soil fertility management practices which were employed minimize or eliminate the use of non-renewable chemical fertilizers and pesticides, reduce soil erosion, increase soil water retention and bring the water table closer to the surface. This affords farmers a longer growing season and greater resilience to natural fluctuations in weather. Organic farms benefit from increased biodiversity, which provides habitat for predacious insects and pollinators as well as nutrient complementary plant associations. The increased health and diversity of the farm ecology creates a more secure system overall, which promotes stability in the regional food supply.

The factors that contribute to the success of organic agriculture in addressing the problems of food insecurity are intricately interwoven with the very processes of production on a regionally adapted organic farm. Whereas conventional high-input agriculture relies on costly technologies and chemicals, the shift to successful organic farming depends more on the enhancement of local environmental and social resources. For example, the organic farmer is compelled to form closer connections and alliances with neighbors in order to effectively safeguard their common water and land resources. These stronger community ties lead to a variety of positive results such as the formation of farmers' advocacy groups, cooperatives for collective credit, mutually supportive work arrangements that lower overhead and the sharing of skills and innovations. These enhanced social connections were considered by 93% of the participants to be critical to the success of their projects.

The majority of the estimated 200 million people in sub-Saharan Africa who lack consistent access to adequate amounts of food are small-scale farmers. The challenge then is to enhance marginalized farmers' ability to feed themselves. Because organic agriculture relies on locally available resources rather than costly chemical fertilizers and pesticides, it offers a viable solution. The case study of Manor House Agricultural Center in Kitale, Kenya, cited in the UN report, describes the experience of the 3,000 farmers who have learned and implemented the bio-intensive methods that are taught and promoted by the center. The adoption of double digging and integrated pest management increased (sometimes doubling) the vegetable yields of the farmers. Participating farmers were not only able to grow more food for themselves, they also saved money by abandoning the use of chemical inputs. The organic farm systems are less energy dependent and therefore resilient even in the face of rising fuel prices that can be crippling to the high-input dependent farm.

Pretty, Jules, Rachel Hine and Sophia Twarog. 2008. *Organic Agriculture and Food Security in Africa, UNEP-UNCTAD Capacity-building Task Force on Trade*. New York and Geneva: United Nations Conference on Trade and Development/ United Nations Environment Program.

in West Africa for 13 years.[14] For 20 years, the Center for Information on Low External Input and Sustainable Agriculture (LEISA), has documented hundreds of agroecological solutions that successfully overcome many of the limiting factors in African agriculture.[15] Elsewhere, these practices have proven to increase farmers' agroecological resistance and resilience to climate-related hazards (Holt-Gimenez 2002).

A growing number of Africans have other ideas about the future of their food systems. Repeatedly, at the World Social Forum in Nairobi (2006), the Food Sovereignty Forum (February 2007) and the Conference on African Agroecological Alternatives (November 2007) in Selingue, Mali, African researchers, technicians, civil society organizations, and farmers organizations rejected the new Green Revolution and demanded transparency and accountability from AGRA. They also called for debate, public engagement and democratic solutions to the African food crises (Food First 2007).

Sustaining sustainability

To be successful, efforts to improve agriculture and end hunger in Africa must be able to inspire and mobilize millions of farmers. To be sustainable, these efforts need to be based on smallholders' capacity for innovation and solidarity. This way, a continuous stream of agroecological innovations can be spread across the continent quickly and effectively. This is possible if the process for agricultural improvement cultivates farmers' enthusiasm. Roland Bunch, author of the development classic *Two Ears of Corn*, says:

> Technologies that fail to arouse people's enthusiasm will spread only as far as the paid extensionists personally take them, whereas those that do create enthusiasm will "spread with phenomenal rapidity from one individual to another with very little outside stimulus." In terms of program efficiency, the former situation is untenable. If a technology does not spread beyond the range of contact of the program's paid personnel, whether they are agronomists or not, the program must find a more appropriate technology. We simply do not have the financial resources to use paid personnel alone to spread new technologies around the world.
>
> (Bunch 1982)

The last 20 years of successful farmer-led movements for sustainable agriculture indicate that the seeds of enthusiasm are planted in the beginning stages of the technological innovation process. When farmers identify problems and select, test and innovate possible solutions they later enthusiastically share these innovations. Farmers who lead the innovation process are capable of spreading methods for agricultural improvement farmer-to-farmer, over wide geographic areas. With minimal support they have also effectively shared their knowledge with farmers of other countries (Holt-Giménez 2006). The many African agroecological alternatives spreading across the sub-Sahara are an example of this. If the new Green Revolution techniques are to succeed where past crop-breeding attempts have failed, its advocates will need to meet with the farmer-led agoecological farmer organizations who are actually transforming agriculture on the ground in Africa. Otherwise, despite the unprecedented philanthropic injections of cash, Africa's new Green Revolution will not be able to take agricultural improvement very far, or sustain its effort for very long.[16]

Beyond the impasse: transparency, accountability and public debate

It is important to recognize the ways in which AGRA and the movements for African agroecological solutions agree, coincide or are complimentary. In the best scenarios, these areas provide potential common ground and ideally could lead to important synergies needed to overcome the food crisis. In the worst of scenarios, they can co-opt and dilute currently successful and independent efforts at agroecological development.

It is just as important to recognize where and when the differences between AGRA and African agroecological alternatives prevent these two from working together. If these differences are great, they may even prevent convergence in those areas where the Green Revolution and African social movements actually agree. These conflicts can end up weakening the positive aspects of both approaches and lead to a failure to end hunger and poverty—an option that no one would wish for.

The largest area of agreement between the approaches is the focus on smallholders, which for some governments and institutions is long overdue. AGRA's commitment to African food production and their stated desire to help smallholders to capture more of the food value chain are also important areas of common ground. No one disputes the necessity of grounding a transformation of African agriculture on the needs of women farmers.

However, there is a large gray area of discourse in which AGRA's interpretations and plans for implementation are unclear and raise

BOX 32

The Tigray Project

In Northern Ethiopia, a region severely affected by drought, famine, soil erosion, and poverty, a small sustainable agriculture project has helped farmers nearly double their yields while reducing chemical fertilizer use by almost a third (Edwards et al. 2007). The Tigray Project started in 1996 in just four communities. It has since spread to 65 districts. The farming system, according to a report by the Swedish Society for Nature Conservation (SSNC 2008) "is based more on biological diversity—particularly the rich knowledge and agrobiodiversity of the farmers—and ecosystem services than on fossil fuel."

Since 1996 the Third World Network along with the Institute for Sustainable Development, the Bureau of Agriculture and Rural Development in Tigray, the Mekelle University, the Ethiopian Environmental Protection Authority, the UN Development Program, and the Swedish Society for Nature Conservation have worked with local communities to improve the output and resilience of farms by enhancing the health of the surrounding natural environment. Many of the solutions that the project promotes are adaptations of traditional farming techniques that have been employed in the region for thousands of years. Composting, interplanting and crop rotation are the cornerstones of managing soil fertility in the program. A variety of techniques, including check dams, contour ditches, selective grazing and re-propagation of native grasses are used to decrease soil erosion and retain water. In some cases the creative management of water resources, through catchments and diversion of runoff, is allowing farmers to grow two crops annually, one rain fed, and the other irrigated. Rather than planting one or two staple crops, the farmers spread their risk and increase the overall resilience of the farm by using diverse traditional crop varieties and regionally adapted seeds (SSNC 2008).

The Tigray project has not only been successful in increasing yields of the farms themselves, it has also created new opportunities as a result of

---

many doubts among ecological farmers and social movements. Just how AGRA understands and acts on terms like "agroecology," "land rights," "biodiversity," and "fair markets" will determine whether or not its programs compliment or undermine agroecological practices and peasant demands.[17]

There are two important, interrelated areas in which AGRA and African agroecological movements fundamentally differ. The first is technical and the second is sociopolitical.

Technically, AGRA has fully adopted the Green Revolution's con-

better ecosystem services provided by a well managed commons. Gebre Mikael, a farmer in the region who also keeps over 30 bee hives, has watched the regional production of honey increase over the years as a result of the reforestation and insectiary plantings, which provide forage for bees (SSNC 2008). A nursery set up in 2004 has provided more than 50,000 saplings to the communities in Northern Ethiopia. The varieties are carefully selected to be multifunctional—stabilizing soil, fixing nitrogen, shading the under story and providing animal forage. The project has also created opportunity for women. Fruit trees from the nursery have become an important source of income for many women, who are traditionally barred from plowing fields or using work animals. Women farmers are encouraged to pre-germinate seed for vegetable seedlings and tend to nurseries for plants that require a longer growing season (SSNC 2008).

Dr. Tewolde Berhan Gebre Egziabher, "the godfather of the Tigray Project" and the force behind its inception, believes that sustainable agriculture is the future not just in Ethiopia, but also in the world. "Organic farming, I am sure, will feed the world. I am also sure that unless organic farming re-expands, the human component of the world will eventually shrink" (Moberg and Lundberg 2007).

Edwards, Sue, Arefayne Asmelash, Hailu Araya, and Tewolde Berhan Gebre Egziabher. 2007. *Impact of Compost Use on Crop Yields in Tigray, Ethiopia*. Rome: Natural Resources Management and Environment Department, Food and Agriculture Organization of the United Nations.

Moberg, Fredrik and Jakob Lundberg. 2007. Ecosystem Services-Based Farming in Ethiopia Increases Crop Yields and Empowers Women. *Sustainable Development Update* 7 (6).

SSNC. 2008. *Ecological in Ethiopia—Farming with Nature Increases Profitability and Reduces Vulnerability*. Stockholm: Swedish Society for Nature Conservation. www.naturskyddsforeningen.se/upload/Foreningsdokument/Rapporter/engelska/Report_international_Ethiopia.pdf (accessed February 2, 2009).

ventional Northern paradigm of seeing crop genetics as the main road to agricultural improvement. The institutional and political mutualism between AGRA's crop breeding work and the Gates Foundation's support for transgenic crops is a potential "deal breaker" for ecological farmers, many NGOs, smallholder organizations and peasant movements in Africa. As long as the Gates Foundation continues to view agricultural "science" in the narrow terms of genetic manipulation, it is unlikely that AGRA will gain the trust needed for significant collaboration with African smallholder movements.

Despite claims that it will employ well-known "participatory crop breeding" methodologies, AGRA's technical paradigm still centers the locus of agricultural innovation in the laboratory under the direction of crop scientists, rather than in the field under the direction of farmers. This effectively prioritizes crop science over agroecology. It also undermines the potential for agroecological innovation and keeps control over development in the hands of scientists rather than farmers. In order to respond to constantly changing local conditions, ecological agriculture needs strong support for constant, widespread, and decentralized agroecological innovation. This kind of support has the added benefit of cultivating the capacity for agroecological innovation among farmers rather than depending on new seeds from a relatively small cadre of experts. The tremendous potential for widespread farmer-led agroecological innovation is not well supported by AGRA's expert-led crop breeding model, and it is highly unlikely that AGRA's expert knowledge will ever reach or keep up with the 150 million smallholders it targets as clients.

Socially, AGRA claims to be a farmer-led, African initiative. However, AGRA's design comes from the US-based Rockefeller Foundation. During its first year, before Kofi Annan was invited to be chairman of the board, Rockefeller program officer Gary Toenneissen ran AGRA. While most of the AGRA board and 90% of its staff are now from Africa, its scientific direction comes from Joseph De Vries, director of the Program for African Seed Systems.

Since its inception AGRA has given the primary decision-making power over problem-framing and strategic design, i.e., *what* is to be done, to the experts working within the Green Revolution's institutional structures, with input from the corporate heads of the transnational seed, chemical and fertilizer monopolies. Secondary decision-making power, i.e., concerning *how* to implement AGRA, is being allocated to AGRA experts and government officials. A select group of NGOs have been invited to participate in civil society consultations on AGRA.

Stung by widespread criticism over its Green Revolution approach, AGRA representatives have begun participating in public consultations with NGOs and African farm leaders. While this dialogue is a very important step in the right direction, African farm leaders are understandably unhappy about being the last ones consulted. At a recent AGRA dialogue called by the UN special rapporteur on the right to food, Simon Mwamba of the East African Small-Scale Farmers' Federation expressed this frustration in no-nonsense terms:

You come. You buy the land. You make a plan. You build a house. Now you ask me, what color do I want to paint the kitchen? This is not participation!

The problem with consulting Africa's farm organizations after all the major program decisions have already been made and all the powerful institutional relationships established is more than an unfortunate oversight. The lack of early consultation with Africa's farm organizations precludes substantive questioning of the way the problems of hunger and smallholder agriculture were defined. This has limited AGRA's awareness and selection of potential solutions. The lack of early consultation has also influenced AGRA's ideas regarding farmer participation. Presently, farmers will be allowed to provide information to AGRA scientists regarding their preferences for crop varieties through participatory methodologies in crop breeding. However, AGRA's strategies and positions on key issues that concern farmers—such as land reform, agroecology, global markets, and GMOs—have all been formulated without any input from Africa's farmers or their organizations. These omissions reflect a limited understanding of African agrarian struggles and a lack of recognition or appreciation of the dynamism of Africa's farmers' movements and ecological farmers. Sadly, the architects of AGRA seem to have missed, undervalued, or simply ignored the tremendous potential of the already existing and truly African-led experiences in ecological agriculture that over the last 20 years—in the wake of the first Green Revolution's failures—have been steadily spreading across Africa.

Not including the principal beneficiaries from the very beginning of such a major effort is a grave strategic error that, given AGRA's institutional momentum, will not be easy to rectify. The lack of mechanisms to ensure transparency, accountability, and substantive input on major strategic decisions will hinder AGRA's ability to partner with African social movements. This squanders an opportunity to unleash the tremendous transformative power of the grassroots. Distributing money and grants to governments and NGOs may improve conditions as far and as long as the money is flowing, but it is unlikely to spark the widespread social transformations needed to save African agriculture.

Can this change? Of course it can. The question is whether or not the helmsmen of Africa's new Green Revolution have the political will to make these changes. A positive first step would be for AGRA and the rest of the Green Revolution's institutions to open up to informed public debate on the problem, the means, and the ends of eradicating hunger on the continent.

Africa's Lessons

Africa has much to teach us about ending hunger: the importance of creating favorable conditions for sustainable smallholder agriculture, and the potential dangers of relying on technological or philanthropic "megafixes." It also shows us that the potential for turning the food crisis into a transformative moment exists even in the most desperate circumstances. In the face of the food crisis, African

BOX 33

Cuba's Urban Agricultural Transformation

In 1997 Miguel Salcines, a mid-level agronomist, got permission to use a 3.7 hectare plot of "waste land" on the outskirts of Havana for an *organoponico*, an intensive vegetable garden. Salcines and four others, including a carpenter and a chemist, began the process of founding the Organoponico Vivero Alamar. What happened in the intervening years surpassed all expectation. Vivero Almar has seen its production jump from 20 to 240 tons of vegetables and its cooperative grow from 5 to 147 members, all on a little over 11 hectares. Lettuce, swiss chard, cucumber, tomato, cabbage, beets, carrots, green beans, celery, okra (ladies' fingers), eggplant (aubergines), peppers, and pot herbs are produced for local markets and schools. Vivero Almar is committed to spreading the perception that the co-op's work is based on science and technology. Fifty members have either engineering degrees or mid-level technical training—and the group does much of their own research and development. The group is experimenting with different interplantings, biocontrol, and biologically based pesticides, all of which helps develop not only valuable technologies, but a sense of dignity and pride in agricultural work. According to one author, "Gone are the days where agriculture is seen as backbreaking work undertaken by backward farmers toiling from sunup to sundown" (Koont 2009).

Across the city, the patio garden of Dr. Raul Gil is lush with fruit trees, vegetables, and medicinal herbs. Dr. Gil asked the government for permission to turn a local dump site adjacent to his backyard into a patio garden in 1995. Now every Saturday morning children gather on the patio for classes on gardening and environmental issues. The abundant patio garden—one of some 60,000 in Havana—produces only for the household

agroecological alternatives are spreading, despite the lack of official support. African farm organizations, civil society groups, and their converging demands for food sovereignty are growing stronger—in the face of opposition from multinational agribusiness corporations. The possibility for a quantitative and qualitative leap in Africa's capacity to feed itself is embedded in the continent's capacity for social transformation. To end hunger we need social change.

Much of the developing world has large pockets of hunger driven by the same kind of blinding poverty, environmental degradation, and exploitation of people and resources. These countries are home to similar struggles for justice, food sovereignty and survival. They are also the theater for major aid and development efforts. To solve the

---

and neighbors, but still receives free organic material, seeds, and technical assistance from the government.

The experience of individual gardeners like Dr. Gil and co-ops like Vivero Alamar are the backbone of Cuba's urban agricultural success story. The reasons for Cuba's journey to its seat as world leader in sustainable and urban agriculture are well known. After the Soviet Union collapsed, diesel fuel, gasoline, spare parts, agricultural machinery, synthetic fertilizers, and pesticides virtually disappeared from the island. This "Special Period" forced the government to undertake a massive, rapid shift to ecological and urban production. However, what is less well known is that Cuba had been preparing at least to some degree, for the potential of a complete blockade of the island. *Organoponicos* began showing up on armed forces compounds in the late 1980s and the Department of Defense had been sponsoring research into self-sufficiency in agriculture since the 1970s. At the launch of the "Special Period," Cuba had the "necessity," the "possibility," and the "will" to make a profound change in the food system.

The resulting programs were swift and successful. In 1994 the government established an organization to oversee the introduction of *organoponicos* like Vivero Almar. Instead of the traditional state-owned or collective models, land was distributed partly in parcels to individual farmers, often organized in credit and services co-ops. Three years later that organization became the Urban Agriculture National Movement. Since then, the Cuban economy has added 350,000 new jobs in agriculture and its production of vegetables and herbs increased 1000%. But Cuba's stunning success in this department comes not in simply adding jobs or increasing production. The program has also played an enormous role in community development, environmental quality, and building a healthier city.

Adapted from Sinan Koont, The Urban Agriculture of Havana, *Monthly Review*, vol.60, no. 8, 2009.

food crisis, the experience, needs and demands of smallholders, and the resources of official aid efforts, will need to come together to overcome the structural violence, racism and injustices that cause hunger.

The breathtakingly successful urban agriculture program in Havana, Cuba—now producing over four million tons a year of the city's food—has transformed Cuba's urban food systems (See Box 33 Cuba's Urban Agricultural Transformation). The architects of this transformation affirm that the key ingredients for success were "necessity, possibility, and will" (Koont 2009). Those suffering from the injustices that cause hunger and poverty have a great supply of the first two. The third ingredient—will—is fundamentally political. Unfortunately, it is not clear that governments, official development programs, the private sector and large philanthropies have the political will to transform (rather than prop up) the current dysfunctional and inequitable global food system. The good news is that the "will for transformation" has taken root in the world's smallholder and food justice movements—and, it is growing. If the *social* will of farmers, communities and their movements bubbles up into governments, development programs and business to express itself as *political* will, it can unleash the tremendous transformative forces of smallholders and communities worldwide. The power of people demanding political change is not the only resource needed for solving the food crisis, but hunger can't be ended without it.

9

The Challenge of Food Sovereignty in Northern Countries

Fixing the US Food System

As in the rest of the world, the global food crisis hit the US's 50 million poor and near poor the hardest. Low-income, and historically marginalized communities already disproportionately suffered from diet-related disease and food insecurity. These communities have taken the lead in food justice struggles nationwide.

> Food justice asserts that no one should live without enough food because of economic constraints or social inequalities. Food justice reframes the lack of healthy food sources in poor communities as a human rights issue. Food justice also draws off of historical grassroots movements and organizing traditions such as those developed by the civil rights movement and the environmental justice movement. The food justice movement is a different approach to a community's needs that seeks to truly advance self reliance and social justice by placing communities in leadership of their own solutions and providing them with the tools to address the disparities within our food systems and within society at large.
>
> **Brahm Ahmadi, People's Grocery, Oakland, California**

While Uncle Sam's food and farm bill continues to subsidize bad food, overproduction and the dumping of commodities in the food systems in the global South, a broad-based, home-grown food movement led by youth, underserved communities, community groups, and family farm and labor organizations, is steadily taking back control over the food system. The actors in the US food movement range from inner-city food justice advocates and food banks working in the nation's food deserts; to family farm organizations lobbying for price floors, grain reserves, fair trade rules and support for young farmers and farmers of color; to the diet and environment-conscious "foodies"

BOX 34

Structural Racism in the US Food System

by Brahm Ahmadi, People's Grocery

The modern industrial food system has left millions of poor people without access to basic healthy foods. This is the one of the leading causes of the disproportionately high levels of chronic, diet-related diseases in low-income communities of people of color. Research shows that there are far fewer supermarkets located in these communities than in middle class or affluent ones. The University of Connecticut's Food Marketing Policy Center examined census and grocery store information for 21 major metropolitan areas across the United States. They found there were 30% fewer super-markets in low-income areas than in higher-income areas, and these low-income areas had 55% less grocery store square footage than their wealthier counterparts. The study also found that the levels of unmet food demand in these communities were as high as 70% (Cotterill and Franklin 1995).

The modern food system began failing inner city neighborhoods with the explosion of suburban growth in the 1940s and 1950s, when many middle class and upwardly mobile white families moved to newly emerging subur-ban communities. This "white flight," combined with the growing poverty of those left behind, weakened the buying power of poor neighborhoods in the inner cities. This economic decline was compounded by the practice of "redlining," in which banks refused to invest in neighborhoods of color. Supermarkets stopped investing in improvements or expansion, and sales dropped. The greater buying power of suburbanites and a nationwide trend towards larger stores were important "pull" factors favoring investment in the suburbs. With the emergence of the "big-box" retail format—targeted at buyers with autos—chain stores rolled out larger and larger stores to capture the growing suburban market. At the same time, older inner-city stores with smaller floor areas became relatively less important to these chains' success. Ultimately, the inner city was virtually abandoned by the leading supermarket chains.

Today, in many urban communities of color it is easier to purchase a gun than it is to buy a fresh tomato. Because of the lack of access to healthy foods, as well as a lack of knowledge about healthier food choices, the diets of many people of color are typically higher in sugar, salt, fat, and refined carbohydrates. The modern food system has turned entire communities of color into unhealthy "food deserts," leading to charges of structural racism and "food apartheid." In the United States today, the prevalence of virtu-ally every diet-related disease is highest among people of color. Women of color are about 50% more likely to be obese than their white counterparts. In West Oakland, California, a predominantly African-American community, the diabetes rate is four times greater than the diabetes rate of the surrounding Alameda County.

Given the magnitude of problems in the modern industrial food system, many people are encouraged by the growing food movement in the United States. This movement emerged from the back-to-the-land movements of the 1960s and 1970s, and has achieved notable successes in the proliferation of farmers markets, community supported agriculture (CSA) and a high-end organic food industry. However, these developments have not significantly improved food access for low-income urban communities of color or addressed the needs of our nation's underserved and vulnerable populations.

Because they do not confront the problems of racism and classism inherent in the industrial food system, the sustainable agriculture and organic food movements share some of the same social failures of the system they propose changing. Their alternatives fail to address the urgent food, health and livelihood needs of low-income and underserved communities of color and often end up reproducing the same political and economic disenfranchisement inherent in the industrial food system. This does nothing to heal the profound physical and psychological disconnect many people of color have to healthy food systems or to break the dangerous cycle of dependency between these vulnerable communities and the food system presently ruining their health.

In order to dismantle the structural racism within our food systems we must make a determined effort to cultivate and increase the leadership, voice, perspectives and demands of low-income communities of color within the food movement. These communities have a central role to play in building a food system that meets their specific needs. Indeed, a healthy food system can and should be a powerful engine for local economic development and political empowerment in low-income and underserved communities.

The massive demographic shifts underway in the United States indicate that people of color will soon be the majority in many states. The food movement won't be able to build the social, economic and political will to transform our inequitable and unsustainable food system without the strong participation from the majority. In turn, this participation hinges on strong leadership coming from communities of color. Prioritizing the participation and leadership of people of color in the food movement is not simply a humanistic exercise—it is a prerequisite for the democratization and liberation of the food system.

Cotterill, R.W. and A.W. Franklin. 1995. The Urban Grocery Store Gap. *Food Marketing Policy* 8. Food Marketing Policy Center, University of Connecticut.

BOX 35

The Next Generation of the Food Justice Movement

by Anim Steel, The Food Project, Boston, Massachusetts

Something unusual happens on Tuesday afternoons at the corner of Dudley Street and Blue Hill Avenue in one of Boston's poorest neighborhoods. A group of teenagers set up tents and signs. They unload a van filled with vegetables from a farm just down the street, and soon a market is in full swing.

These young people, who work with The Food Project, are part of a growing movement to make local, healthy, fair, and sustainable food the norm in their communities—rather than the exception. That's a tall order given both the conceptual and political obstacles. It's hard for most people to grasp the food system let alone a different kind of food system. Our food system, controlled by one of the most powerful lobbies in the world, is not easily changed.

But what's happening on this street corner is also powerful. Indeed, whether or not we change the food system may ultimately depend on these youth and their peers across America.

Beginning in the early 1990s with The Food Project in Boston and Growing Power in Milwaukee, hundreds of programs have introduced thousands of young people in every region of the country to the simple power of growing their own food. Today, these projects stretch from Hawaii to Philadelphia; they produce mangoes and kale; they run CSAs and nutrition classes. As the movement grew, they took root in colleges and started to tackle school food policies.

These programs could pave the way for even bigger changes over the next decade. As we enter a new phase of the food justice movement—one punctuated by a new administration in 2009 and a new Farm Bill around 2012—the things that matter increasingly match the strengths and inclinations of the generation currently in their teens, twenties, and thirties.

In this new phase of the movement, for instance, targeted pressure on key lawmakers will matter, particularly in the lead-up to the next Farm Bill. To win more policy victories than it did last time around, the movement will need its own "surge" of citizens to call, write, and lobby legislators. A mobilized group of high school and college students—even a fraction of the US's 34 million—could make the crucial difference.

Over the next several years, public opinion will also matter—much more than it did to when the movement was younger and its goals more modest. To amplify the targeted pressure, the movement needs to build a groundswell of public support. As drivers of popular culture and as early adopters of new media (e.g., MySpace, Facebook), young people may be key to spreading the message beyond the choir.

Something else that will matter in the next phase of the movement is collective action and the ability to work across differences. I have often found young people more willing to take risks, think differently, and embrace a more expansive view of the movement than their older counterparts—not universally or exclusively so, but with enough force that they are likely to cement crucial connections between local food and fair trade, urban agriculture and green jobs, foodies and farm workers. The more we understand what the essential ingredients of change are, the more we appreciate how important young people are.

It's not just theory. History shows that young people often play a critical role in social movements, especially in the later stages. In April 1960, 300 college students gathered in Raleigh, NC to determine how they could build on the success of their sit-ins. The organization that emerged, the Student Nonviolent Coordinating Committee (SNCC) was instrumental in creating the climate of crisis that paved the way for the Civil Rights Act of 1964. In fact, it's almost impossible to imagine the civil rights movement—from SNCC to the Freedom Rides to the Little Rock Nine—without the organized energy of youth. (Martin Luther King himself was just 26 when he was drafted into the movement in the early 1950s.)

Even more to the point, young people are already beginning to flex their political and economic muscle. The Student Farmworker Alliance, working in solidarity with the Coalition of Immokalee Workers, forced the fast food industry to the negotiating table for the first time in 30 years. The Real Food Challenge is taking aim at $4 billion worth of college food spending; in effect, getting schools to divest from industrial agriculture and invest in a fair, green food economy. And a new generation of leaders—nurtured by the Rooted in Community network, the Michael Fields Agricultural Institute's internships, United Students for Fair Trade, the Black Water Mesa Coalition, and others—is poised to take on even bigger targets.

If they seize the opportunity, an organized group of young people could inject this movement with some vital energy. United across lines of race, class, and geography, they could be the force that gets us to a tipping point. What's more, if they are sufficiently organized, they may be the best guard against one of our biggest obstacles: the "green-washing" of the agrifood industry with unjustified and confusing claims about nutrition, the environment, and social responsibility.

Not only could young people play a critical role, they should. They have the greatest stake in the future. As Josh Viertel told Slow Food's International Congress in 2007, "There is bad news and good news about the youth of America. The bad news is that this is the first generation in America to have a shorter life expectancy than its parents. The good news is that there is a group of young people who are determined to change that."

The market on Dudley Street winds down around seven o'clock. Any produce that's left over either goes home with the teens or is donated to hunger relief organizations. The day began with an early harvest, so it's been a long one. But the sense of satisfaction that comes with a hard job well done is palpable. I think this is a key point. The Food Project and its kindred programs around the country are powerful not just for their potential and for the immediate need they address, but because they satisfy a deep desire in all people to be useful, to produce—not just consume—and to be connected to the earth. They tap into something deep that was lost as most people moved off farms and teenagers became just a market segment.

Here is cause for hope. Though the movement may be relatively young and small, its roots are very old—they stem from the deepest truths of nature and the best aspects of human nature. We will grow.

---

and well heeled *gourmands* of the Slow Food movement, who want everyone to enjoy the pleasure of fresh, locally grown food.

The socioeconomic realities and political strategies of these actors and organizations are diverse, and have sometimes led to tensions and work at cross-purposes. However, with the food and financial crises, their demands are converging, and point to a powerful consensus: people want a food system that provides real, healthy food; good, green jobs; and that leads to a fair, sustainable future. Globalizing "from below," advocates and practitioners in the food movement are reaching out to their international counterparts, drawing the links between food justice, sustainability, equity, food sovereignty and the right to food at home and abroad. These international similarities are widespread (Halweil 2004).

In the US, where only 2% of people are farmers and most people are two or three generations and many miles away from the farm, the national food movement tends to draw most of its numbers from consumer and rights-based organizations. Youth activism—a growing force nationwide—injects new energy, diversity, ideas and forward-searching visions into the movement.

Initiatives that make not just food, but healthy, culturally-appropriate food accessible to all, that bring grocery stores back to inner-city neighborhoods, use the food system to bring jobs to young people and revitalize local economies, and promote social justice are emerging from the scorched earth of the industrial agrifoods complex in America. Most of these initiatives are local in scale, but taken together they reveal a rising tide of change. The number of community supported agriculture (CSA) farms has more than doubled in the past ten years. In a CSA, consumers purchase a "share" of the farmer's harvest each season and receive regular deliveries of produce directly from the farmer. In 2008 the USDA counted 4,865 "official" farmers markets—nearly twice as many as a decade ago (USDA 2008d). Thousands more informal direct market channels go uncounted. Many CSAs have adopted a sliding scale to make fresh produce more accessible to low-income residents; many farmers markets now accept food stamps and are expanding into "food deserts"—neighborhoods, often in the inner city, without supermarkets or other places to buy healthy food.

Urban agriculture is taking off as well. Programs like The Food Project in Boston, Grub in Olympia, Washington, the Growing Youth Project in Alameda, California and countless others are employing youth in sustainable agriculture and food distribution, giving teenagers meaningful work and bringing healthy food to local communities. Shortening the distance between consumers and the farm gate to a matter of feet, start-up businesses in backyard farming have taken

Local products being sold in a farmers market at Point Reyes, California

Leonor Hurtado

BOX 36

Food Crisis Solutions: Urban Food Gardens

The growing awareness of the industrial food system's negative social, environmental and health impacts is forcing reform from the bottom-up. Recent years have seen a massive resurgence of interest in small-scale urban food gardening as a direct and self-empowering way of reasserting control over our basic right to healthy, affordable food. While buying organic and locally grown foods offer improvements over fast and processed foods, it is difficult for even the most dedicated urban dweller to entirely avoid participation in the unjust and ecologically devastating systems that currently feed us. Growing our own food is perhaps the most direct and transparent means of creating the food delivery system that is based on human need rather than corporate profit. Even a few potted tomatoes on a balcony represent an act of resistance to the industrial agrifoods complex.

Community gardens and urban farming programs also unite neighborhoods, provide much needed green space and offer hands-on opportunities for land-based education. Urban farming is not only beginning to make a real contribution to local food access, it has also become an integral arena for social justice, reinvigorating communities and shifting consciousness towards a deeper connection with the earth and the natural processes upon which we depend. Although the amount of food produced within cities represents a small percentage of the calories consumed, the positive effects of these efforts can lead to exponential changes on a personal as well as societal level.

The non-profit Growing Power is an example of using urban food production in the service of greater social justice. The organization enhances local food security by linking a collective (Rainbow Farmer's Collective) of over 300 family farms to residents of Milwaukee, Madison and Chicago via their "Farm-to-City Market Basket Program." They also create employment and professional training opportunities for low-income youth at their urban farm sites, which furnish produce for CSA boxes. The garden tours Growing Power provides are an inspiration to over 3,500 people annually. Workshops and professional training offer practical gardening and farming "know-how" on a diversity of cutting-edge food production processes such as organic gardening, bee keeping, aquaculture and animal husbandry, which can be adapted to small urban spaces.[i]

The People's Grocery, in Oakland, California, is another grassroots organization that interweaves programs for food sovereignty with food justice. With "30,000 residents, 53 liquor stores, 17 fast food restaurants and 0 grocery stores," West Oakland sports a rate of hospitalization for diabetes that is four times higher than the national average. The People's Grocery is focused on improving the health of their underserved local community by providing better access to nutritional education as well as sources of fresh organic produce. Three urban plots together with a two-acre farm, located half an hour outside the city, grow food for their CSA program, which delivers low-cost, top-quality produce to West Oakland residents with a tiered pricing system. The farm, urban food gardens and green-house also create jobs and training while supporting a variety of other local food growing organizations. An ambitious project is underway to open a grocery store which will stock locally grown produce and value-added food products, as well as provide a range of community services. By keeping the food production and distribution chain within a single neighborhood, jobs and profits can re-circulate within the local economy. One of their partner organizations, City Slicker, operates an innovative back yard food garden program, which provides installation and upkeep mentoring for West Oakland residents interested in growing their own food. The success of these and other such programs has been dependent on embracing and respecting racial and cultural diversity by working with a model that involves community collaboration on every level.[ii]

In Spain, the collective Bajo el Asfalto Esta la Huerta (BAH) represents a powerful social mobilization against the established agro-industrial system. BAH translates as "Under the concrete is the garden." The collective reclaims abandoned parcels in and around Madrid and installs high-diversity organic food gardens. The group focuses significant attention on maintaining an entirely horizontally structure which directly links over 250 families to the seven "partner" growers. Decisions are made democratically through a system of consumer sub-groups which send a speaker to the monthly meetings and more directly by attending the general open assemblies that take place every three months. The collective serves as an ecological education forum and catalyses political organization on various food and justice issues.[iii]

Growing food from within the city walls is not only a phenomenon of the global North. Supplementing food sources with small urban plots has long been an economic necessity for impoverished residents of overcrowded cities in the global South. Increasing food security through enhancing the potential of urban food production is beginning to be promoted more seriously. In 2007 the UN FAO launched its "Food for the Cities" urban farming program, which has projects in a number of countries throughout Africa and South America including the Democratic Republic of the Congo, Senegal, Gabon, Mozambique, Botswana, South Africa, Namibia, Egypt, Mali and Columbia. The programs advocate large numbers of small-scale gardens adapted to the special constraints of each particular urban situation. In the Democratic Republic of Congo, the FAO is working with city planners on the ambitious goal of providing food and extra income for 16,000 families by converting 800 hectares of urban land into allotment gardens. The program in Bogota and Medellin, Columbia works specifically with internally displaced people living in slums. Food is grown in whatever space is available using planters made from salvaged containers such as old tires. According to the FAO: "Every month, each family's 'garden' yields some 25 kg of produce including lettuce, beans, tomatoes and onions. Any surpluses are sold off for cash to neighbors or through a cooperative set up under the project" (FAO 2007).

i. See http://www.growingpower.org/.
ii. See http://www.peoplesgrocery.org/ and http://www.cityslickerfarms.org/.
iii. See http://bah.ourproject.org/article.php3?id_article=57.

FAO. 2007. *Urban Farming Against Hunger*. FAO Newsroom. 1 February. http://www.fao.org/newsroom/en/news/2007/1000484/index.html (accessed January 3, 2009).

root in Portland and San Francisco. And in a nation with only 5% of its farmers under the age of 35, a quiet renaissance of young, small-scale farmers are going back to the land.

Farm-to-school programs, farm-to-college programs, and institutional purchasing policies that prioritize local farmers are becoming easier to implement. Food banks are partnering with farmers to glean produce that normally gets left in the field. Citizen-led food policy councils are helping local governments support local food systems. In times of global food and financial crises, they see the local food system as a potential engine for local economic growth.

Taken together, this outpouring of practical initiatives reflects one of the necessary conditions for transforming the food system: alternatives that work. This is not a sufficient condition, however. We will never end hunger or tackle the structural issues at the root of the food crisis by dint of a linear increase in the numbers of projects and initiatives. Giving these alternatives a fair chance also requires changing the laws and regulations that are currently holding them back.

Industry is well aware of the political side of the food system and works tirelessly to prevent any changes that might benefit small farmers and local communities. Aside from campaign contributions (and other, less ethical means), corporations operate a three-way "revolving door" (boardroom–congressional committee–lobbying firm) to maintain insider networks and build favorable political will for deregulation, subsidies, tax breaks, bailouts—whatever is needed to ensure corporate profits and strengthen their market power.

Political will is not constructed by money and insider networks alone. In democracies, political will also requires building a broad social consensus. Changing the social consensus regarding our food system will occur when people change the way they think about food and demand changes in the food system. Political will can then be constructed by applying widespread social pressure that is too strong for politicians to safely ignore. This kind of pressure comes from strong social movements whose political demands both resonate with the majority and activate the minority.

In 2008 a coalition of over 50 anti-hunger, labor, religious, farm, and food advocates released a policy brief on the US food crisis and launched a Call to Action to end hunger on World Food Day. This was followed by a declaration of the US Working Group on the Food Crisis that reflects the perspectives of thousands of grassroots organizations working to transform the food system and end hunger worldwide (see Appendix 7: US Call to Action).

These demands call on the US government to stop catering to the interests of corporate lobbyists and to end hunger by supporting a food system that protects the environment and provides healthy food. Like the IAASTD, these groups seek support for locally controlled, sustainable food systems as a strategy to end hunger and poverty.

Topping the list are demands to remove the volatility in food prices. Re-regulating the international finance sector's investment in food commodities and overturning the Commodities Futures Modernization Act of 2000 would help take food prices out of the hands of speculators. Resurrecting publicly owned, strategic grain reserves and a guaranteed minimum loan rate to farmers would maintain an effective price floor for agricultural commodities by regulating supply, and would create an effective price ceiling to protect consumers from food price inflation.

United States food and agriculture policies—especially the US Farm Bill—are in large part, food system policies for the world. Food and farm advocates are calling for changes to US food aid so that the World Food Program can purchase food locally and regionally from small-scale farmers at fair prices for distribution to those in need, rather than putting these farmers out of business by dumping US subsidized surpluses.

Currently, the US agrofuels sector receives over three-quarters of all tax credits and two-thirds of renewable energy subsidies—dwarfing the money spent on wind and solar (EWG 2009). By 2010 ethanol

BOX 37

Food Policy Councils

Across the US people aren't waiting for policy change to come from the top. Local food policy councils are beginning to tackle food system issues at the local level. Food policy councils (FPCs) study the way their local food system works and recommend policies to make the system more equitable and sustainable. No two FPCs are exactly alike—some work at the state level, others at the city, or even neighborhood level.

The first food policy council, created in Knoxville, Tennessee in 1982, emerged as a response to a study about food access which argued for comprehensive food policy planning within the city (Wilson et al. 2004). The proposed council model provided a safe and healthy way for communities to address city policies, and coordinate and ensure better access to healthy food in the city. From public transportation to grocery stores and school nutrition programs, the changes in Knoxville were incremental. But the potential for innovative and creative problem solving immediately appealed to a wide range of political and social activists. Since Knoxville's groundbreaking experiment, support for food policy councils has grown exponentially.

Throughout the 1980s, local food policy activism gained traction: the Hartford Food System nonprofit, Rodale's Cornucopia Project and Cornell's Center for Local Food and Agriculture were founded; a Food Systems Council emerged in Onondaga County NY; a Philadelphia Food Task Force was commissioned; and the US Conference of Mayors initiated a five-city project to develop food policy councils (Clancy 1997). In the 1990s, the USDA began funding food policy councils through Community Food Projects Competitive Grants, and by 2007 the American Planning Association wrote its first ever policy guide on community and regional food planning. Now there are almost 50 official councils in the US (Community Food Security Coalition 2009), and stakeholders from across the food system are increasingly collaborating with one another to create win-win solutions connecting resources across food sectors.

Food policy councils have had some big successes. Some examples of these success stories are:

- New Mexico: Thanks to the New Mexico Food Policy Council, the state committed to providing an additional two servings per week of fresh fruits and vegetables in school meals with first preference given to New Mexico-grown produce when available (NMFAPC 2009).
- Toronto: In Toronto, the food policy council there helped to create a peer nutrition program which gives educational programs in more than

32 languages around the city. Sixteen peer facilitators, called community nutrition assistants, study under professional nutritionists and then share their knowledge in their communities (Moscovitch 2006). The council also initiated a buy local campaign to increase the amount of fresh food local hospitals purchase from county farmers, expanded community gardens, and launched Canada's first food access grants program to help schools and social organizations buy kitchen equipment.

- Connecticut: Food policy councils can also help hold their cities and states accountable. In Connecticut, the state's goal to preserve 130,000 acres of farmland lost momentum over several years, culminating in an entire year (1999) in which no farmland was preserved at all. The food policy council there partnered with the Working Lands Alliance and the Save the Land Conference to secure development rights to 12 farms in 2000, totaling 1,350 acres—more than the total preserved during the prior six years (CFPC 2007).

Building on this success, food policy councils are widening their reach. The nascent Food Policy Council in Oakland, California hopes to strengthen the local food system, capturing more of the $50 million spent on food in the city each year within the local economy, creating jobs and encouraging local ownership of food-related businesses. Ultimately, the Oakland Food Policy Council hopes to ensure access to healthy, affordable food within walking distance of every Oakland resident, and source at least 30% of the city's food needs from within the city and immediate region.

CFPC. 2007. *Farmland*. Connecticut Food Policy Council. http://www.foodpc. state.ct.us/farmland_preservation.htm (accessed January 31, 2009).

Clancy, Kate. 1997. A Timeline of Local Food Systems Planning. In *Strategies, Policy Approaches, and Resources for Local Food System Planning and Organizing*, edited by K. C. Kenneth A. Dahlberg, Robert L. Wilson, Jan O'Donnell. http://homepages.wmich.edu/~dahlberg/ResourceGuide.html (accessed May 11, 2009).

Community Food Security Coalition. 2009. *Council List*. http://www.foodsecurity.org/FPC/council.html (accessed January 31, 2009).

Moscovitch, Arlene. 2006. *Peer Nutrition Program: Developing a Model for Peer-Based Programs Aimed at Diverse Communities Prepared for Toronto Public Health and Health Canada*. http://www.toronto.ca/health/pn/pdf/pn_evaluation_report.pdf (accesed January 31, 2009).

NMFAPC. 2009. *History and Outcomes*. New Mexico Food and Agriculture Policy Council. http://www.farmtotablenm.org/policy/history-and-outcomes/ (accessed January 31, 2009).

Wilson, L.C., A. Alexander and M. Lumbers. 2004. Food Access and Dietary Variety Among Older People. *International Journal of Retail & Distribution Management* 32 (2).

BOX 38

Fighting for Fair Food: The Coalition of Immokalee Workers

As the Coalition of Immokalee Workers (CIW) knows, when it comes to the fast food industry, "image is everything." Behind the McDonald's million dollar advertising budget and Taco Bell's cheery TV ads is a tomato field in Florida where seven cases of modern day slavery involving over 1,000 victims have been prosecuted in the past 11 years (Heuvel 2008). In addition to outright forced labor, Florida's tomato industry has some of the worst working conditions and poorest pay in the nation. Farm workers receive just $50 for harvesting two tons of tomatoes in a day (CIW 2009).

The CIW began organizing for better working conditions in 1993. In 2001, the coalition set their sights high in a Campaign for Fair Food, and went after Yum Brands, the parent company of Taco Bell, KFC, and Pizza Hut. After a four-year sustained boycott involving hundreds of student and church groups, "Boot the Bell" campaigns on 350 college and high school campuses, and a "Truth Tour" of farm workers around the country, Yum Brands became the first corporation to bargain directly with workers—committing to a penny-per-pound increase in the price of tomatoes to go directly to worker pay raises, and fair labor standards for its suppliers. A penny-a-pound may not sound like much, but that single cent amounts to a 75% wage increase—from $10,000 to $17,000 a year (Heuvel 2008).

The CIW set their sights on McDonald's next, and by 2007, days before the CIW's "Truth Tour" was due at company headquarters in Chicago, McDonald's had agreed to the penny-per-pound increase as well as a collaborative third-party system for investigating abuse in the fields. In 2008 Burger King agreed not only to the penny-per-pound increase, but to compensate growers for payroll tax increases due to the pay raises, and a zero tolerance policy that requires the company to immediately terminate contracts with growers involved in unlawful activity such as forced labor.

Subway, the largest fast-food buyer of Florida tomatoes, signed on in

---

will cost taxpayers more than $5 billion a year—more than is spent on all US Department of Agriculture conservation programs to protect soil, water and wildlife habitat (EWG 2009). This is even though corn ethanol produces *more* greenhouse gases than it captures and will never supply more than a fraction of our national fuel needs. Without a guaranteed fair price for their corn, farm lobbies have supported the agrofuels agenda because they see these fuel crops as a way to end low prices. Establishing a fair price to farmers would render both agrofuels

December 2008, and Whole Foods voluntarily agreed to meet the CIW's standards before the campaign could even focus on their chain.

The CIW continues to struggle for better working conditions. On the heels of the Subway victory, four members of an Immokalee family were convicted of modern-day slavery, beating their former employees, chaining workers by the leg, locking them in trucks, and forcing workers into the fields. In response to the case, Florida agriculture spokesman Terrence McElroy dismissed the systematic instances of slavery in Florida saying, "but you're talking about maybe a case a year." CIW launched an immediate campaign in response, saying in an open letter to Florida's governor:

> Tolerating a little modern-day slavery is like tolerating a little murder or accepting a little child abuse; in moral terms, it makes Mr. McElroy an apologist for what is recognized as one of the most heinous crimes of any kind. In the same breath as he trivializes the severity and frequency of modern-day slavery, Mr. McElroy is quick to defend Florida growers who have, for too long, prospered through willful ignorance of conditions in their own fields.
>
> (CIW 2008)

Saying "the fast-food industry has spoken," the CIW is turning their sights to the supermarket and food service industries. In 2009 the Campaign for Fair Food will be targeting companies like Publix, Safeway, WalMart, Sodexo and Aramark, to demand the same higher standards (CIW 2009).

CIW. 2008. *An Open Letter to Charlie Crist*. Coalition of Immokalee Workers. http://ciw-online.org/Open_letter_to_Crist.html (accessed December 17, 2008).
CIW. 2009. *Coalition of Immokalee Workers Online Headquarters*. http://ciw-online.org/ (accessed February 1, 2009).
Heuvel, Katrina Vanden. 2008. In the Trenches and Fighting Slavery. *The Nation*. December 28. http://www.thenation.com/blogs/edcut/391546/in_the_trenches_and_fighting_slavery?rel=hp_blogs_box (accessed January 31, 2009).

and the US's massive grain subsidies irrelevant and superfluous. Demands for a freeze or an immediate repeal of biofuels mandates in the US, and a suspension of international agrofuels trade and investment, need to be coupled with demands for a fair market price to farmers and a demand that any tax incentives and subsidies for fuel crops go only to small-scale, decentralized, farmer-owned refineries.

It is time to close the revolving door between agribusiness, lobby groups and government by reforming campaign finance and lobbying laws. Just as the finance sector needs to be re-regulated, agri-foods monopolies need to be dismantled and regulated with stronger enforcement of antitrust laws to ensure fair competition in the food system. These demands join those to ensure local control and access to land, water and seeds at fair prices worldwide, and ensure that farmers keep their right to save seeds.

There is no social, biological or economic reason why agroecological farming practices can't become the standard worldwide. The US should approve and endorse the findings of the 2008 International Assessment of Agricultural Knowledge, Science and Technology for Development (IAASTD), and implement the options for agroecological development domestically and internationally through the US Farm Bill and USAID. The government should support biodiverse, sustainable small- and mid-scale food production and urban farming by independent family farmers and small- to medium-sized cooperative businesses. This will require redirecting state, national and international agricultural policies, research, education and investments towards sustainable agroecological farming and independent community-based food businesses.

Food systems need to be based on social and economic justice as well as the right to healthy food. This requires ensuring full labor rights for farmworkers and other wage earners in the US food system—including no exemptions to the National Labor Relations Act, and minimum wage increases to ensure a living wage so that everyone (including farmworkers, food processing workers, food service workers and consumers) can afford good, healthy food.

The US must change its vote in the UN to uphold the human right to food. When grounded in that fundamental right, governments are obliged to protect people from laws, regulations and business ventures that undermine the right to food—such as free trade agreements and the unregulated spread of GMOs. It also would require the US to shore-up the national social safety-net for low-income people by raising benefits high enough so they can purchase fresh, healthy food.

The food movements in the United States are working toward an economy that puts compassion and care for one another ahead of short-term corporate profits. They are not waiting for the big issues to be resolved to start fixing the food system. Communities and organizations are already hard at work laying the foundation for a world where the food system is a source of abundance, health, and justice for all.

"Algo se mueve"—Something's Moving in Europe[18]

The growing impossibility of a dignified livelihood in the European countryside has provoked a widespread and active social response on the part of Europeans unwilling to sacrifice their society and environment to corporate greed. Farmers' unions, environmental organizations, consumers' groups, fair trade organizations, and economic solidarity networks, among many others, have begun to work throughout Europe to denounce the impact of the EU's agricultural policies and call for alternatives.

Responses have varied by country according to the character of local organizations, but all are creating and strengthening alliances between the different social sectors that are negatively affected by the agrifood policies of the EU's neoliberal Common Agricultural Policy. Together, they are creating a host of alternative practices and policies for sustainable production, distribution, and consumption.

For example, in France solidarity networks are being forged between producers and consumers through Associations for the Maintenance of Smallholder Agriculture (AMAPs). Like community supported agriculture, the AMAPs establish solidarity contracts between groups of consumers and local agroecological farmers. The group pays in advance for produce that the farmer provides weekly. The first AMAP was created in 2001 between a group of consumers in Aubagne and a farm in the Olivades region of Provence. Today, there are 750 AMAPs serving 30,000 families throughout France.

These experiences in Europe date back to the 1960s, when Germany, Austria and Switzerland began to develop similar initiatives in response to growing agricultural industrialization. In Geneva, Les Jardins de Cocagne, a cooperative of producers and consumers of organic vegetables, now serves some 400 homes. In Britain, CSAs or "vegetable box schemes" began in the 1990s. At the beginning of 2007, there were some 600 CSA initiatives, up 53% from 2006. There are an equal number of farmers' markets in the country (Soil Association 2005). In Belgium, where these alternatives have appeared more recently, some 200 homes periodically receive fresh fruit and vegetables through the solidarity purchasing groups called GASAP (Groupes d'Achat Solidaires de l'Agriculture Paysanne). In Spain, an AMAP-style initiative of agroecological cooperatives called Bajo el Asfalto Esta la Huerta ("Under the Asphalt lies the Garden") operates in Madrid and environs. Ecoconsum Coordination reports more than 70 similar cooperatives exist in Cataluña. Similar initiatives have existed in Andalucía since the 1990s.

All these experiences show it is possible to produce, distribute and consume food based on ecological practices and social justice principles, maintaining a direct relationship between farmer and consumer. Similar initiatives rapidly spreading across Europe in the last few years include farmers' markets, direct distribution, participatory certification models, and urban gardens.

These food networks are joining forces to politically roll back the EU's neoliberal policies. In France, Minga, a grouping of 800 associations working on fair local and international trade, now coordinates with the Confédération Paysanne (farmers' union) and other consumer, farmer, and agroecological organizations.

In Spain, the Plataforma Rural, a diverse, broad-based coalition that brings together farmers, consumers, environmental groups and NGOs, works to create stronger linkages between the rural and urban, to improve rural life, and to promote local, socially responsible, and ecological agriculture. The Plataforma Rural carries out unified campaigns against GMOs, large supermarket chains, the CAP and agrofuels, as well as campaigns in favor of food sovereignty, responsible tourism, and quality public services in rural areas.

In Europe, one of the principal reference networks is the Via Campesina European Coordination, which brings together organizations and farmers' unions from Denmark, Switzerland, France, Italy, the Netherlands, Spain, Greece, Malta, and Turkey. Its objective is to fight the current agricultural policies promoted by the EU within the framework of the CAP, to move toward a diverse, land-based, smallholder agriculture and a more vibrant rural world. The European Coordination of Via Campesina works with other social movements within the European Social Forum and with other unified campaigns against the CAP and GMOs.

One important challenge in Europe is to increase the connections and coordination between the distinct networks that are part of the alternative globalization movement ("Another World is Possible") and those groups working for food sovereignty. The International Food Sovereignty Forum, celebrated in Mali in 2007, in which networks of women, campesinos, fishermen, consumers, and pastoralist organizations all participated, is a good example. Countries including Hungary and Spain are moving in this direction, by holding national forums.

Activists and practitioners in Europe are beginning to coordinate action strategies in favor of food sovereignty at the local, national, and continental levels. As these networks bring in new players, they gather strength. The task is not easy, but food sovereignty movements and anti-globalization movements are steadily building a common front behind a call popularized by La Via Campesina: "Globalize struggle, globalize hope."

10

Epilogue

The food crisis seems to have slipped from the headlines, surfacing only briefly in final statements at high-level meetings, or when droughts, lack of credit, or market volatility lead to renewed fears of food shortages. Worse, these fears are self-fulfilling, because the longer that efforts to end hunger focus on the superficial effects rather than the root causes, the more our food systems are volatile, vulnerable, and subject to crash. Poverty and injustice—not a shortage of food—are still the primary causes of hunger. Unless we transform our food systems to make them more equitable, democratic, and sustainable, they will not be able to withstand the waves of environmental and financial shocks rocking the planet. Our food systems will break down and food will routinely be both expensive and in short supply, putting it increasingly out of reach of the world's poor, leading to more food riots, political and environmental instability, and suffering.

This imminent disaster scenario is completely avoidable. Despite the global financial crisis, the world has more than enough infrastructure, resources, knowledge, and institutional capacity to put a permanent end to hunger. But decades of failed summits and portentous declarations show that all the technology, financing and good intentions in the world cannot solve the food crisis unless they lead to the transformation of the food system.

Unfortunately, the High-Level Ministerial Meeting on Food Security for All held in Madrid, Spain, January 26–27, 2009—a follow-up to the Rome Food Summit just four months earlier—produced no new ideas or further funding commitments. Despite the strong interventions of groups like La Via Campesina, the ETC Group, FIAN and others at Madrid's roundtable discussions, the experts running the meeting focused on the symptoms rather than the causes of the food crisis. The heavily trumpeted "New Global Partnership for Agriculture, Food Security and Nutrition"—a thinly veiled move by agribusiness and the G8 to move the global governance of food and agriculture out of the FAO and into the World Bank—failed to launch because Southern governments refused to approve a partnership upon which they had not been consulted. This is a blessing. It is significant that the human right to food was recognized at the ministerial meeting. However, the human right to food is still not considered as a *means* to address the food crisis. As a result, the right to food is still lacking clear accountability mechanisms to protect smallholders' land rights in the face of land grabs and agrofuel expansion; for protecting the world's half-billion agricultural workers—including women and children—from industrial labor abuse; or for protecting producers and consumers from financial speculation in global commodities markets.

The failed food summits and the weak multilateral responses from governments have resulted in a lack of inter-governmental coordination and a lack of global leadership on the food crisis.

The new Green Revolution's champions are moving quickly to fill the multilateral void by financing high-level policy papers to counter the IAASTD's trenchant findings and transformational proposals. The Bill and Melinda Gates Foundation funded the Chicago Council of Global Affairs to produce a quick, six-month white paper (timed to influence the new Obama administration within its first 100 days) entitled *Renewing American Leadership in the Fight Against Hunger and Poverty: The Chicago Initiative on Global Agricultural Development*. The report was written primarily by Robert Paarlberg, a professor of political science and author of *Starved for Science: How Biotechnology is Being Kept Out of Africa*. Paarlberg is a tireless advocate for the biotechnology industry and fierce opponent of agroecological approaches to food production. The Chicago Initiative's report took just six months and a handful of policy experts to prepare (compared to the IAASTD's four years and 600 scientists). It is a platform for redirecting the US's foreign aid to support the research and extension of genetically engineered crops into Asia and Africa. The report has already been used as a policy blueprint by the Lugar-Casey Global Food Security Act, a policy proposal to the US Congress to "improve the effectiveness and expand the reach of U.S. agriculture assistance to the developing world." The new bill stands to completely overhaul the way the US offers agricultural development and food aid to the developing world. While the bill permits some local purchase, the bill also mandates funding for genetically modified crop research as a major underpinning of its global food security strategy.

The policy strategy to advance the new Green Revolution in Africa and Asia contrasts starkly not only with the more rigorous IAASTD, but also with the fresh initiatives coming out of the global South, such as the sweeping Food Sovereignty Law announced by Ecuador to guarantee "permanent self-sufficiency in healthy, nutritious, and culturally appropriate forms of food for all persons, communities, and peoples." Ecuador's food sovereignty law was discussed and debated for months by representatives from government, academia, industry, farmers' organizations, and civil society groups. It specifically privileges smallholders, agroecology, and redistributive approaches to production, and declares the nation GM-free (future introduction of GM seeds is to be assessed on a case-by-case basis and requires both presidential and full congressional approval). To oversee implementation, the law sets up a permanent Consultative Body for Food Sovereignty made up of six representatives from peasant organizations, indigenous organizations, small and medium producer organizations, and six representatives from the executive branch. To ensure permanent policy discussion, deliberation and debate, the law also establishes a National Conference on Food and Nutritional Sovereignty made up of civil society organizations, consumer groups, universities and polytechnical schools, research centers and producers' organizations.

The contrast between the corporate-driven, GM approach to ending hunger and poverty, and the socially driven food sovereignty approach to ensuring healthy food and sustainable livelihoods could not be more stark. That industry and big philanthropy would enroll government to advance its approach to the food crisis is sadly not new. That peasant, indigenous and civil society groups would reach a social consensus with their democratically elected government to make sure citizens control their own food, is unprecedented and a sign that the global transformation of our food systems is indeed underway.

The transformation of our food system is a reflection of deep social changes coursing through our societies. Our challenge is to cultivate these changes in ways that bring about the transformations we need in time to avert catastrophe and put us firmly on the path to ending hunger. This will only be possible if we unlock the tremendous transformative capacity of people, their movements, their innovations, their solidarity, compassion, creativity, and their ability to work, organize, and mobilize for change.

The transformation of our food system is not limited by a lack of money, technology, or even good will, but by the lack of political will on the part of governments. As long as global leaders address only the proximate rather than the root causes of the crisis, as long as they rely on technical fixes to avoid structural changes and bow to the power of monopolies over the power of people, we will fall farther and farther behind in our efforts to end hunger. Therefore, for every action, declaration, announcement, project and investment we need to ask: Does this build the movement we will need to force politicians to address the root causes of the food crisis? Will this help or hinder the deep transformations we need to make in our food systems? Does this unleash widespread human potential to equitably and sustainably manage our food resources, or does it concentrate power in the hands of an unaccountable corporate elite?

The transformation of our food systems will occur when the desire for change becomes irresistible. As more and more people see alternatives working on the ground, and as more people hear the voices of others demanding and obtaining transparency, accountability, equity and sustainability, hope and action will overcome fear—the root cause of fatalism, cynicism and apathy. They will join the food sovereignty movement, and drag their elected officials with them, along the people's pathway out of poverty and hunger.

Other Food Systems are Possible

Transforming the global food system means changing the way we produce and consume. It also means changing the ways we make decisions. This requires a fundamental shift in the balance of power within the world's food systems so that the diverse interests of the planet's majorities are served first. This shift is already underway, evident in the political spaces where decisions over food are made— and in the physical places where food is produced, processed, distributed and consumed. Food sovereignty represents a substantive shift *away* from the structural violence of the Green Revolution, the social injustice and structural racism of the industrial agrifoods complex, and a shift *towards* democratizing our food systems. This movement is horizontal, decentralizing the power of decision and action by localizing it in favor of the poor and underserved. It is also vertical, shifting our understanding of food systems from the corporate logic of exclusive boardrooms, expert institutions and high-level summits, towards the socially constructed logic of the majority, actively forged from the ground up.

While the logic of the majority is evident in the growing practice of food sovereignty, the diversity of cultures, social contexts, physical environments and economic conditions all put local efforts for food sovereignty at a disadvantage when constructing the political will of the majority. Without political will, calls for sustainable agriculture, fair trade and locally managed food systems—widespread as they may be—will always be dominated by industrial agrifood corporations who are able to buy political will at the centers of power in Washington DC, Chicago, New York, Tokyo, London, Rome, in Davos, and in the capital cities of the global South.

The political will of the majorities can be constructed in many ways and in many spaces: in the community and the market, and inside government and multilateral institutions. Strategies for constructing political will may range from lobbying and informed engagement, to protest and constructive resistance. Historically, the political will of the majorities has always been built on the power of strong social movements. The labor movement, the anti-slavery, and colonial independence movements, the civil rights movements, women's suffrage and liberation, and the anti-globalization movements are notable examples.

Strong social movements can persuade entrepreneurs to invest responsibly in isolated communities; convince politicians to listen to progressive lobbyists; force international finance institutions to stop bad projects; and trump abuses of power. Movements for food sovereignty can open political spaces at many levels to establish supportive institutions, policies, and projects for equitable and sustainable food systems.

The growing convergence in diversity of food sovereignty movements reflects the increasing strength of social justice movements around the globe.[19] Though some people from food security movements might not choose to use the term "food sovereignty," their demands are strikingly similar to food sovereignty movements elsewhere. The demands for political and economic democracy grounding these movements are very close to the demands of many social justice movements worldwide. Indigenous rights, women's rights, workers' rights, immigrants' rights, even the rights of the homeless are all strengthened by food sovereignty because control over one's food is essential to control over one's self. In this sense, the strength and spread of food sovereignty movements will depend on their

Pedro Sanchez explains that the farmer-to-farmer movement walks on the legs of innovation and solidarity, works with the hands of production and protection, has a heart to love the land, eyes for a vision of a sustainable future, and a mouth with which to speak

ability to use the present moment of crisis to both advance practical alternatives locally, and to converge socially — across boundaries and sectors, with other movements.

The women and men of Latin America's Campesino a Campesino Movement describe their movement as a person, a peasant. This peasant-in-movement walks on two legs: one of innovation, the other of solidarity. He and she work with two hands: one to produce food, the other to protect the environment. The movement has a heart that throbs with life and loves family, community, farming, and nature. Two eyes provide a clear vision for a fair and sustainable future in which peasants do not have to choose between starving or exploitation, and are not made to disappear under the wheels of modernization. In this vision they are a respected, integrated part of a world in which progress is measured by the values of all those things one loves. And, they have a voice to speak, to make their demands heard, and to lend their wisdom, opinions, doubts, fears, hopes and dreams to the next chapters in the continuing saga of agriculture and society.

This is a metaphor for food sovereignty as a way of living.

It tells us that sustainability depends on balancing the work of food production with environmental protection. It recognizes that the processes of agroecological innovations critical for adaptation need to coevolve with the social innovations that equitably link producers and consumers. These are a source of great enthusiasm and need to be shared widely in the spirit of solidarity and good will.

Amplifying the voices of the world's smallholders and of underserved communities around the world is fundamental for creating the social force needed to tip the political will of our societies and institutions toward the sustainable transformations we seek.

Finally, the motivation and the vision for these transformations, coming from the heart and searching out new possibilities for a better future, are essential for keeping hope strong in our movements. Hope and enthusiasm are literally priceless. They can't be bought, subsidized, programmed or substituted. No real or lasting change can come about without them. The world's food systems are being transformed from the ground up by people, communities and organizations for whom losing hope is not an option.

The food crisis has brought us together. We can end the injustices that cause hunger. There has never been a better time.

Appendix 1

Civil Society Statement on the World Food Emergency

No More "Failures-as-Usual"!

Historic, systemic failures of governments and international institutions are responsible.

National governments that will meet at the FAO Food Crisis Summit in Rome must begin by accepting their responsibility for today's food emergency.

At the World Food Summit in 1996, when there were an estimated 830 million hungry people, governments pledged to halve the number by 2015. Many now predict that the number will instead increase by 50% to 1.2 billion, further threatened by unpredictable climate chaos and the additional pressures of agrofuel production.

In the midst of collapsing farm and fish stocks, skyrocketing food and fuel prices, new policies, practices and structures are required to resolve the current food emergency and to prevent future—and greater—tragedies. Governments, including those in the global South, and intergovernmental organisations must now recognize their part in implementing policies that have undermined agricultural productivity and destroyed national food security. For these reasons, they have lost legitimacy and confidence of the world's peoples that they can make the real, substantial changes necessary to end the present food crisis; to safeguard peoples' food availability and livelihoods; and to address the challenges of climate change.

The emergency today has its roots in the food crisis of the 1970s when some opportunistic OECD governments, pursuing neoliberal policies, dismantled the international institutional architecture for food and agriculture. This food crisis is the result of the long standing refusal of governments and intergovernmental organisations to respect, protect and fulfil the right to food, and of the total impunity for the systematic violations of this right among others. They adopted short-term political strategies that engineered the neglect of food and agriculture and set the stage for the current food emergency.

As a consequence, the UN agencies and programmes and other international institutions, dominated by a small group of donor countries, are badly governed, grossly inefficient, competitive rather than cooperative and incapable of fulfilling their (conflicting) mandates. The structural adjustment policies imposed by the World Bank and the IMF, the WTO Agreement on Agriculture and the free trade paradigm have undermined local and national economies, eroded the environment and damaged local food systems leading to today's food crisis. It has facilitated the development of corporate oligopolies and break-neck corporate concentration along the entire food chain; allowed predatory commodity speculation and financial market adventurism; and enabled international finance institutions and bilateral aid programmes to devastate sustainable food production and livelihood systems.

Social movements and other civil society organisations have joined together to determine a new approach to the dysfunctional global food system. We are developing the following global plan of action for food and agriculture and would be willing to discuss this plan with governments and intergovernmental organisations that will be attending the Rome Food Summit—the "High-Level Conference on World Food Security: the Challenges of Climate Change and Bioenergy."

We are prepared to work with committed governments and United Nations organisations that share our concerns and are dedicated to end the food emergency and develop food sovereignty.

We declare a <u>People's State of Emergency</u> for the ongoing food crisis. In a State of Emergency, people and governments can suspend any legislative or regulatory measures that could imperil the Right to Food and can also abolish any private arrangements considered damaging to Food Sovereignty. Any public or private measures that might restrict the ability of peasant and small-producers to get domestic food to market can be cancelled. Debt cancellation is urgently needed if the global South is to address the immediate and ongoing food emergency. We believe the current food emergency and the ongoing threat of climate change are sufficient grounds for declaring a State of Emergency.

- **We call on the Human Rights Council and the International Court of Justice to investigate the contribution of agribusiness, including grain traders and commodity speculators, to violations of the right to food and to the food emergency.** High production input costs and food prices during the current food emergency are in some measure due to historic agribusiness profits and the actions of commodity market speculators. The oligopolies and speculators, who operate throughout the food chain, must be investigated and suspected criminal behaviour must be brought to justice. The UN Human Rights Council should undertake the necessary investigations. National governments should not hesitate, wherever other governments have failed in their international obligations, to challenge abuses through the International Court of Justice. At the national level, anti cartel and monopoly laws should be strengthened. The Human Rights Council should support governments to guarantee that their public policies respect, protect and promote the right to adequate food, in the context of the indivisibility of rights.
- **We demand an immediate halt to the development of land for producing industrial agrofuels for cars, planes and energy production in power stations, including the use of so-called biomass "waste."** The sudden sharp increase in large scale industrial agrofuel production threatens local and global food security, destroys livelihoods, damages the environment and is a significant factor in the steep rise in food prices. This new enclosure movement—converting arable, pastoral, and forest lands to fuel production—must be rejected. The Rome Food Summit should endorse the proposal of the UN Special Rapporteur on the Right to Food for a five year moratorium on the expansion of large scale industrial production of agrofuel in order to resolve conflicts with food production, develop rules for agrofuel production and to evaluate proposed agrofuel technologies.
- We call for a new and truly cooperative global initiative in which we are full participants in the process of policy change and institutional correction. We will not stand aside to watch the rich and the incompetent destroy our lives and our earth. We will fight for food sovereignty including the right to food, for sustainable food production and for a healthy biologically-diverse environment. To achieve this:

1. **We call for the establishment of a UN Commission on Food Production, Consumption and Trade**. This Commission must have a significant and substantive representation of small-scale food producers and marginalized consumers. The Secretary-General's recently convened Task Force offers a clear and welcome political signal that the food emergency transcends individual institutions and demands urgent global action. However, the Task Force is dominated by the failed institutions whose negligence and neoliberal policies created the crisis. Those whom the governmental and intergovernmental systems have damaged—those we must feed and those who must feed us—are once again, excluded. The Task Force should end its work at the conclusion of the Rome Food Summit and the new, inclusive, Commission must begin its work immediately thereafter.

   Membership: The Commission should expand upon the format established by the Brundtland Commission 20 years ago which opened the way for the environmental summits that followed. In forming the Commission, the Secretary-General should be mindful of the findings of the International Assessment of Agricultural Knowledge, Science and Technology for Development (IAASTD) whose recently completed report was approved by nearly 60 governments, as well as the outcomes of FAO agrarian reform (ICARRD) conference and process.

   Mandate: The mandate of the new Commission must include all forms of—and constraints to—food production; all aspects of—and barriers to—safe, adequate, affordable and culturally appropriate food; and a full analysis of the entire food chain in consideration of changing climatic conditions. The Commission should provide an interim report to the UN General Assembly and the governing bodies of FAO, IFAD and WFP by the end of 2008 and provide a final report, with recommendations, to these organisations in the final quarter of 2009.

2. **We must fundamentally restructure the multilateral organisations involved in food and agriculture.** Several food-related multilateral institutions have been criticised for their governance and program failures. Notably, Independent External Evaluations (IEE) of FAO and IFAD have exposed serious systemic shortcomings. In particular, the IEE of FAO shows that the senior management of FAO—while recognizing the urgent need for change—does not believe that the governments or the institution is capable of

substantive changes. The evaluation of CGIAR is ongoing and is exposing major governance failures that cannot be resolved within the CGIAR framework. Last year, the World Bank undertook an internal evaluation of its agricultural work in Africa and was deeply and appropriately self-critical. It is because of this that civil society is convinced that the Secretary-General's Task Force must evolve into the wider Commission outlined above. In order to facilitate the Commission's work, civil society recommends three immediate decisions:

- The Rome Food Summit should agree to undertake a meta-evaluation of the major food and agricultural institutions (FAO, IFAD, WFP and CGIAR) by the end of 2008.
- Based on this meta-evaluation, FAO's biennial budget for regional conferences should be adjusted to allow the convening of regional food and agricultural conferences, equally involving all the major multilateral institutions, in the first half of 2009. These meetings must ensure the full and active participation of representatives of peasant and small-scale farmers, pastoralists and fisherfolk.
- Building from the meta-evaluation and regional conferences, the Commission—by the end of 2009—must submit its report including a new architecture for the UN's food and agricultural work.
  Without prescribing the integrity of the process described above, we are convinced that responsibility for international policies and practices related to food and agriculture must reside with a single agency within the community of agencies of the United Nations where the principle of "one nation—one vote" must prevail.

3. **We call for a local and global paradigm-shift towards Food Sovereignty.** Food production and consumption are fundamentally based upon local considerations. The answer to current and future food crises is only possible with a paradigm-shift toward comprehensive food sovereignty. Small-scale farmers, pastoralists, fisherfolk, indigenous peoples and others have defined a food system based on the human right to adequate food and food production policies that increase democracy in localised food systems and ensure maximisation of sustainable natural resource use. Food Sovereignty addresses all of the continuing issues identified by the 1974 World Food Conference. It focuses on food for people; values food providers; localises food systems; assures community and collective control over land, water and genetic diversity; honors and builds local knowledge and skills; and works with

nature. Food sovereignty is substantially different from existing neoliberal trade and aid policies purporting to address world 'food security.' These policies are exclusionary; insensitive to those who produce food; silent on where and how it is grown or consumed; and have—since the 1970s—been proven failures. Governments and international institutions must respect and adopt food sovereignty.

4. **We believe that the Right to Food prevails over trade agreements and other international policies. In the current food emergency, trade negotiations related to food and agriculture must halt and work should begin on a new trade dialogue under UN auspices.** The structural adjustment policies imposed by the World Bank and the IMF, the WTO Agreement on Agriculture and the free trade paradigm have undermined local and national economies, eroded the environment and damaged local food systems leading to today's food crisis. Neoliberal trade policies have also strengthened multinational agribusinesses and encouraged windfall profiteering. Food dumping and artificially low-priced food exports have also destroyed local systems and must end. The international finance institutions and the WTO have forced the global South to close marketing boards and shutdown mechanisms for market stabilisation and price guaranties for food producers. Governments have been forced to abolish food reserves and eliminate import controls. Yet, state intervention in the market is necessary to fulfill the right to food, secure food production and the economy of small scale food producers. Therefore, FTA, EPA and WTO negotiations on the Agreement on Agriculture must be ended. These negotiations are hurting the vast majority of food producers. A new approach to international food and agricultural trade is urgently needed. This approach must be based on the right of countries to decide their level of self sufficiency and support for sustainable food production for domestic consumption. Discussions leading to a new trade regime based on the diverse needs of people and societies and the preservation of the environment should take place within the UN system.

5. **We insist that the right of governments to intervene and regulate in order to achieve food sovereignty, be reinstated.** National governments have to take up their responsibility, control and push back elites and make food production for domestic consumption their priority. Countries have to raise their level of self sufficiency

in food as far as possible and to achieve this the following measures must be taken:
- Respect, protect and fulfil the right to adequate food, among other rights;
- Increase the budget support of peasant based food production;
- Implement genuine agrarian reform to give landless and other vulnerable groups access to land and other productive resources;
- Guarantee credit access to peasants and other small-scale food producers;
- Abolish all barriers preventing peasants and small-scale farmers from saving and exchanging seeds between communities, countries and continents;
- Strengthen peasant led research and support autonomous capacity building;
- Improve infrastructure so that peasants and small-scale producers can reach local markets;
- Develop strategies with peasant and other appropriate organisations to manage specific hazards and emergencies;
- Guarantee marginalised consumers access to domestic food and — if not available — to food brought in from adjacent surplus regions.
6. **We reject the Green Revolution models. Technocratic techno-fixes are no answer to sustainable food production and rural development.** Industrialised agriculture and fisheries are not sustainable. The International Assessment of Agricultural Knowledge, Science and Technology for Development (IAASTD) clearly shows the need for a major change in the current research and development model. This report shows that governments (South and North) have wilfully and tragically neglected agriculture and rural development, especially small scale farming and artisanal fisheries since the last global food crisis. This attitude appears to be changing as the current emergency unfolds. However, the new interest in agriculture remains fundamentally flawed as private US foundations partner with global agribusiness to press national governments and international research systems to pursue a so-called "green revolution" in Africa and elsewhere based upon technological quick-fixes and failed market policies rather than social policy decisions. Governments, research institutions and other donors must learn from this study; change direction; and support small scale sustainable crop and livestock production and fisheries based on the expressed needs of local communities.

The farmer/fisher-led programs will lead to local and national self-reliance. Specifically, governments attending the Third High-Level Forum on Aid-Effectiveness in Ghana in September [2008] should reject the philanthro-capitalist directed models for a new green revolution and should reaffirm the central role of people and governments in setting the policy and practical framework for development.

7. **We support an inclusive strategy for the conservation and sustainable use of agricultural biodiversity that prioritises the participation of small-scale farmers, pastoralists and fisherfolk.** Biological diversity in agriculture is a prerequisite for securing food supplies. The huge loss in diversity, the use of GMOs and the patenting of seeds and genes make food production vulnerable. To support small-scale farmers that develop resilient, biodiverse production systems, we must work together to safeguard agro-ecosystems, species and genetic diversity that can adapt on-farm to new threats such as climate change. The Rome Food Summit should challenge governments, FAO, the UN Convention on Biological Diversity and the Global Crop Diversity Trust to provide massive and immediate financial support for in situ and on-farm conservation through farmer-led crop and livestock conservation and improvement.

8. **We will participate in the development of a comprehensive local/global strategy to respond to climate change.** Climate change is already causing major losses in food production and is devastating the lives of millions of people including those of migrants. The future is uncertain but most studies assume that climate change will be more damaging to people and food systems in tropical and subtropical countries than those in temperate zones. There is an urgent need to cut greenhouse gas emission by at least 80 per cent by 2030. This is primarily the responsibility of the industrialised countries. The global South must also adopt different policies and practices for energy production. In agriculture, the high input fossil fuel-driven industrial model for production and transport is a major cause of CO_2 emissions. The development of peasant led sustainable food production, based on the sustainable use of local resources is a key solution to reduce these emissions. In addition, however, the polluting industrial countries must accept responsibility for the destruction of our environment and food systems and must pay reparations at levels, not less than 1 per cent of their

annual GDP, that will help to alleviate damage and further development of sustainable and adaptable food and energy systems.

Social movements and other civil society organisations who are prepared actively to pursue the agenda we have described, at local, national and global levels, are invited to sign up to this statement.

For more information and to sign up, see www.nyeleni.eu/foodemergency.

This statement was prepared by members of the IPC, the International Planning Committee for Food Sovereignty. The IPC is a facilitating network in which key international social movements and organisations collaborate around the issue of food sovereignty: these include ROPPA, WFFP, WFF, La Via Campesina, and many movements and NGOs in all regions (see: www.foodsovereignty.org/new/focalpoints.php). The IPC is coordinating a Parallel Forum to the FAO Food Summit in Rome.

Further details

The International Planning Committee for Food Sovereignty (IPC) includes organisations that represent small farmers, fisherfolk, Indigenous Peoples, pastoralists, women, youth, agricultural workers' trade unions and NGOs. www.foodsovereignty.org.new/ (English, Français, Español, Italiano)

La Via Campesina is the international movement of peasants, small and medium sized producers, landless, rural women, indigenous people, rural youth and agricultural workers active in more than 56 countries in Asia, Africa, Europe and the Americas. www.viacampesina.org (English, Français, Español)

ROPPA Le Réseau des orgnisations paysannes et de producteirs de l'Afrique de l'Ouest (ROPPA). www.ropa.info (Français)

Appendix 2

Land, Territory and Dignity Forum, Porto Alegre, March 6–9, 2006

For a New Agrarian Reform based on Food Sovereignty!

Final Declaration

We are representatives of organizations of peasants, family farmers, indigenous peoples, landless peoples, artisanal fisherfolk, rural workers, migrants, pastoralists, forest communities, rural women, rural youth, and defenders of human rights, rural development, the environment, and others. We come from the whole world, to participate in the "Land, Territory and Dignity," to defend our land, our territory, and our dignity.

States and the international system have not been capable of defeating poverty and hunger in the world. We reiterate our call to our governments, to the FAO (with its founding mandate), to the other institutions of the United Nations system, and to the other actors who will be present in the International Conference on Agrarian Reform and Rural Development (ICARRD), and on our societies, to decisively commit themselves to carrying out a New Agrarian Reform based on Food Sovereignty, the Territories and the Dignity of the Peoples, which guarantees us, as rural women, peasants, family farmers, indigenous peoples, communities of artisanal fisherfolk, pastoralists, landless peoples, rural workers, afrodescendents, Dalit communities, unemployed workers and other rural communities, effective access to and control over the natural and productive resources that we need to truly realize our human rights.

We call the International Conference on Agrarian Reform and Rural Development (ICARRD), the States and the FAO to assume a real political will need to eradicate the hunger and poverty that millions of women and men are facing all over the world [sic]. If this Conference fails to recognize the proposals put forward by our Parallel Forum the Conference cannot be considered successful.

Food Sovereignty and Agrarian Reform

The new agrarian reform must recognize the socio-environmental function of land, the sea, and the natural resources, in the context of food sovereignty. We understand that food sovereignty implies policies of redistribution, equitable access and control over natural and productive resources (credit, appropriate technology, etc.), by rural women, peasants, indigenous peoples, communities of artisanal fisherfolk, rural workers, unemployed workers, pastoralists, Dalit communities and other rural communities; rural development policies based on agroecological strategies centered on peasant and family agricultural and artisanal fishing; trade policies against dumping and in favor of peasant and indigenous production for local, regional and national markets; and complementary public sector policies like health care, education and infrastructure for the countryside.

The use of natural resources should primarily be for food production. The new agrarian reform must be a high priority on the public agenda. In the context of food sovereignty, agrarian reform benefits all society, providing healthy, accessible and culturally appropriate food, and social justice. Agrarian reform can put an end to the massive and forced rural exodus from the countryside to the city, which has made cities grow at unsustainable rates and under inhuman conditions; would help provide a life with dignity for all members of our societies; would open the way toward a more broad-based and inclusive local, regional and national economic development, that benefits the majority of the population; and could put an end to unsustainable practices of intensive monoculture that make wasteful use of water and poison our land and water with chemicals, and of industrial fishing that over-exploits and exhausts our fishing grounds. It is necessary new fishing policies that recognize the rights of fishing communities and stop depleting life in the sea [sic]. For all these reasons, agrarian reform is not just needed in the so-called "developing countries," but also in Northern, so-called "developed" countries.

Food sovereignty is based on the human rights to food, to self-determination, on indigenous rights to territory, and on the rights of rural peoples to produce food for local and national markets. Food sovereignty defends an agriculture with farmers, fisheries with artisanal fishing families, forestry with forest communities, and steppes with nomadic pastoralists...

Furthermore, agrarian reform should guarantee rights to education, to healthcare, to housing, to social security and to recreation. Agrarian reform should assure the creation of the spaces where we maintain our culture, to provide a home to children and youth, so that our communities can develop their full diversity and so we can construct a citizenship on the basis of our relationship to the land, the sea, the forests...

Role of the State

The State must play a strong role in policies of agrarian reform and food production. The State must apply policies that recognize rights and democratize access to land, to coastal areas, forests, and so on, especially in cases where access to these resources are concentrated in the hands of a few. Furthermore, the State should guarantee community control over natural resources by peasant, fisherfolk, pastoralist, and forest communities, and by indigenous peoples, such that they can continue to live and work in the countryside and on the coasts, by means of collective and community rights. Agrarian reform should create jobs with dignity and strengthen the rights of rural workers. States have the right and the obligation to define, without external influences, their own agrarian, agricultural, fishing and food policies in such a way as to guarantee the right to food and the other economic, social and cultural rights of the entire population. The small-scale producers must have access to credit at low interest rates and adapted to local conditions, to fair prices and market conditions, and to technical assistance for agro ecological forms of production. Research and systems of support for collection of harvests and distributing them to local and regional markets must have strong state support and must work for the common good.

Recognition of the Concept of Territory

The concept of territory has been historically excluded from agrarian reform policies. No agrarian reform is acceptable if it only aims at the distribution of land. We believe that the new agrarian reform must include the Cosmo visions of territory of communities of peasant, the landless, indigenous peoples, rural workers, fisherfolk, nomadic pastoralists, tribes, afro-descendents, ethnic minorities, and displaced peoples, who base their work on the production of food and who maintain a relationship of respect and harmony with the Mother Earth including the oceans.

All of the original peoples, indigenous peoples, ethnic minorities, tribes, fisherfolk, rural workers, peasants, the landless, nomadic pastoralists and displaced peoples, have the right maintain [sic] their own spiritual and material relationships to their lands; to possess, develop, control, and reconstruct their social structures; to politically and socially administer their lands and territories, including their full environment, the air, water, seas, ice floes, flora, fauna and other resources that they have traditionally possessed, occupied and/or utilized. This implies the recognition of their laws, traditions, customs, tenure systems, and institutions; as well as the recognition of territorial and cultural borders of peoples. This all constitutes the recognition of the self-determination and autonomy of peoples.

The expression of gender and youth in the struggle for agrarian reform

We recognize the fundamental role of women in agriculture and fishing and in the use and management of natural resources. There can be no genuine agrarian reform without gender equity, thus we demand and we commit ourselves to ensuring that women receive full equality of opportunities and rights to land and natural resources that recognize their diversity, and that past discrimination against rural women and the social disadvantages they have faced be redressed. We also recognize that without young people who stay in the countryside there is no future for our societies. The new agrarian reform must give priority both to women's rights and to guaranteeing a future with dignity for today's rural youth.

We demand that governments honor their commitments and obligations that they assumed in various international conferences such as the Beijing Conference and the World Conference on Racism. Their commitments to gender equality and racial diversity that are upheld in the Convention for the Elimination of All Forms of Discrimination Against Women and the Peasant Charta that was adopted in the World Conference On Agrarian Reform and Rural Development. We demand the implementation of a redistributive agrarian reform which will allow women and youth access to and jurisdiction over land and natural resources and guarantee the representation of women and youth in the decision making mechanisms concerning management at all levels, local, national and international. It is indispensable to have adequate financial resources for capacity building and education in sexual and reproductive health.

No to the Privatization of the Seas and the Land, No to the Dominant Model of Production and Development

Together with the privatization of land and coastal areas we are seeing the privation of biodiversity. Life is not a commodity.

We will continue to **resist** the neoliberal policies implemented by our governments and imposed by the World Bank, the WTO and other actors. These destructive policies include so-called land administration, cadastre, delimitation, titling and parceling of lands, and the policies of decollectivization, all with the goal of privatization of land in individual hands; the promotion of markets for buying, selling and renting of lands, "land banks," the end of land distribution programs; the return of reformed lands to former landlords, the reconcentration of land; the privatization of water, the sea, seeds, forests, fishing areas, and other resources, as well as services of extension, credit, transport and marketing, roads, healthcare, education, and so on, and the dismantling of public sector support for peasant production and the marketing of their products. We roundly oppose the introduction of transgenic seeds and the suicide or "terminator" seed technology, that expropriates control over seeds from rural communities and transfers it to a handful of transnational corporations.

The privatization of natural resources and technologies has increased the inequality between men and women, casts [sic], ethnicities, classes and generations. These policies are perpetuating displacement, persecution and criminalization of these already marginalized groups.

By the same token, we will continue to resist the dominant model of production and development, with its processes of neoliberal globalization, the transformation and insertion of farming, fishing and forestry into the production chains of transnational corporations, industrial agriculture, forestry and fisheries (contract production, export monocultures, plantations, big-boat fishing, biofuels, genetic engineering and GMOs, nanotechnology). Investments in mining, agribusiness, biopiracy, green neoliberalism, infrastructure mega projects, are destroying our territories and agriculture, our fisheries and are causing displacement of local people and rootlessness from the countryside and costal areas as "Reconstruction" programs after natural disasters, wars and free trade policies (WTO, FTA, CAP, Farm Bill and so on) are also doing.

Agricultural policies financing the dumping exports of agrarian and fishing products must be replaced by policies realizing food sovereignty which respect the endogenous development of peoples.

We recognize and value initiatives like ALBA for the regional integration and the exercise of food sovereignty. In this context agrarian reform and rural development should be an integral part of these initiatives.

Criminalization and repression of social movements

We reject and condemn the repression that we face, that any person who fights for agrarian reform faces, in almost all countries in the Americas as in Asia, in Europe, in Africa. We denounce the militarization and military occupation in Iraq, South Korea, Palestine that displace our peoples and steal them [sic] their territories; the so-called "war against terrorism" that serves as a pretext to repress us, and the criminalization (labeling us as "criminals") of our movements. To fight for our rights and dignity is an obligation; and it is our human right to do so.

We demand that the States establish mechanisms for protection of life and security of persons who struggle to protect their land, water and natural resources. States must guarantee effective legal mechanisms for punishing those who are guilty of such crimes.

Land Occupations, and the Recovery and Defense of Territories. Social mobilization as a strategy of struggle and construction of proposals

We defend our actions of land occupation and the recuperation and active defense of our land, territories, seeds, forests, fishing grounds, housing, etc., as necessary and legitimate to realize and defend our rights. If our day-by-day experience in the struggle for human dignity has taught us anything, it is that direct actions like land occupations, and recuperations and active defense of territories, are absolutely necessary in order to move governments to fulfill their obligations and implement effective policies and programs of agrarian reform. We pledge to keep carrying out these non-violent actions for as long as is necessary to achieve a world with social justice, which gives each and everyone the real possibility of having a life with dignity. Without the mobilization and full participation of social movements, there will be no genuine agrarian reform.

Food sovereignty is not just a vision but is also a common platform of struggle that allows us to keep building unity in our diversity. We believe that access and control over natural resources, food production, and the increase of decision-making power are three main themes that bring us together.

Agrarian reform and food sovereignty commit us to a larger struggle to change the dominant neoliberal model. We must build alliances with other sectors of society, a citizens' power that can guarantee deep agrarian reforms. We commit ourselves to promote joint actions, articulations, exchanges, and all the forms of pressure that are underway, especially through the international campaigns that our organizations and networks are carrying out or developing. We are convinced that only the power of organized peoples and mobilization can achieve the needed changes, thus our principal task is to inform, raise awareness, debate, organize and mobilize with the people. We call on all the actors and forces present here to keep building our unity, and we will carry these conclusions back to debate with our social bases, and will use these ideas to confront the policies of international bodies like the FAO, and our governments. We ask that the International Planning Committee for Food Sovereignty (IPC) give priority in its work to the follow-up of these conclusions.

Land, sea, and territory to affirm our dignity.
Land, sea, and territory for dreams.
Land, sea, and territory for LIFE.

http://www.foodsovereignty.org/new/documents.php

Appendix 3

ROPPA—Pan-African Farmers' Platform

FINAL DECLARATION

Faced with the alarming situation that has struck the African populations, the networks of farmer and agricultural producer organizations of Southern Africa (SACAU), Central Africa (PROPAC), Eastern Africa (EAFF) and West Africa (ROPPA) met in Addis-Ababa, Ethiopia, from 21st to 23rd of May 2008, to share information and exchange ideas on the current state of African agriculture and possible solutions.

Considering that networks of African farmer organizations all have the same mission, i.e. to defend and promote the interests of agricultural producers;

Noting that these African agricultural producers share the same geographical space and natural resources: land, water, forests;

Noting also that, although they represent the demographic majority of the African population, these family farm households and agricultural producers still suffer the consequences of agricultural and rural policies that do not reflect the realities they live and the preoccupations they continually proclaim;

Noting also that, thanks to the sweat of their labor, which is badly remunerated thanks to constantly decreasing agricultural prices, the States—on the contrary—have been able to harvest significant wealth which has very often been invested elsewhere than in the rural areas;

Noting finally that, today—as yesterday—these agricultural producers are the main victims of conflicts, disasters and crises such as the current one on food;

The networks of African farmer and agricultural producer organizations reviewed the different factors that are at the origin of the food and agricultural crisis in Africa.

It must be recognized that, despite efforts to promote regional integration, most of the actions and initiatives are seriously behind schedule. On the contrary, despite the aspirations of NEPAD, Africa continues to be oriented more towards the outside than inwardly.

African agriculture has thus encountered a failure in which all of us have participated: we Africans in the first instance, African political leaders and farmers' organizations, as well as our partners and the bilateral and multilateral cooperation programs.

The farmer organization networks consider that the present situation of African agriculture is bad. However, they judge that this is not a fatality and that the situation of food price increases is not necessarily an unfavorable factor.

Seizing the current opportunity for African farmers to obtain a better remuneration for their products, however, requires that our States, our Regional Economic Communities and the AU urgently engage in a dialogue involving all of us, here in Africa and not elsewhere.

The farmer organization networks also noted that over more than five years they have strengthened their mutual knowledge and have built up a real spirit of solidarity through concerted action, in particular while working together to improve the feasibility of the NEPAD and to warn the world of the threats which the EPAs might pose for the future of African agriculture.

These challenges have convinced them that the progress of African agriculture can only be lasting if the farmers' organizations can act at continental level [sic]. The four networks of farmer organizations affirm, through this declaration, their total engagement to assume this historic necessity by deciding, here in Addis Ababa, to establish a "Pan African Platform for the Farmer of Africa".

The farmer organization networks have established a steering committee composed of the 4 presidents of the 4 sub-regional farmer organization networks and have designated Mr. Mamadou Cissokho as facilitator. This new instrument, in our eyes, brings a strong value added to the pursuit of the mandates and the activities of our local, national and sub-regional organizations. It also constitutes a powerful lever to promote a resurgence of African agriculture so that it can fulfill the functions of any agriculture worthy of its name.

Conclusion

Convinced that there are no alternatives to the mobilization of our own human resources and our own financial resources, however modest they may be, and conscious of the fact that our continent—despite the negative image of the outstretched hand, of suffering, of misery that is projected to us every day—possesses natural resources, high quality human resources, and positive values that are applicable to all of humanity, we commit ourselves, in the context of the Pan-African platform of farmers organizations, to save our lives, our families, our nations and Africa, our continent.

We the undersigned
Mrs Fanny Makina Vice President SACAU
Mr Philip Kiriro President EAFF
Mrs Elizabeth Atangana President PROPAC
Mr Ndiogou Fall President ROPPA
This date: 23rd May, 2008, Addis Ababa, Ethiopia

Appendix 4

Declarations of the African Organizations—Planet Diversity, May 12–16, 2008

We, the African civil society organizations meeting under the umbrella of Planet Diversity and the Meeting of Parties (MOP 4) in Bonn, Germany from 12–16 May 2008, United in the idea of Food Sovereignty in Africa, have shared and exchanged experiences and views with other civil society groups from Latin and North America, Europe and Asia,

Having analysed the state of African agriculture in the face of several threats: strong pressure from seed manufacturers to introduce GMOs into African agriculture under the guise of modern biotechnology, the effects of climate change, agrofuels, along with initiatives such as the Alliance for a Green Revolution in Africa (AGRA), all of which are aimed at commercializing agriculture at the expense of sustainable development.

Reaffirming that food sovereignty is an inalienable right, as enshrined in the Universal Declaration of Human Rights (UN, 1969). We therefore call upon our governments to reassert their sovereignty and their duty to set in place policies and safeguards to protect the genetic heritage of the continent and the rights of Africa's farmers,

We hereby declare:

1. That GMOs pose a risk to the environment, to health, to the genetic resources and the agrarian systems that produce them, and also threaten the social and cultural systems that manage them. Consequently, **We are in total opposition to any experimentation with, and development of GMOs on our continent**

2. That modern conventional agricultural methods have thus far failed to feed the population, or preserve the ecological balance. We have witnessed the introduction of inefficient, destructive and unethical technologies in an attempt to mitigate this failure of modern agriculture. Based on our conviction that the full

potential of ecological and biological agriculture has not been achieved, **We implore our governments and decision makers to promote sustainable agrarian systems, based on agro-ecological methods and the protection of the rights of peasant farmers and of traditional seed production**

3. That GMOs cannot feed the world. This is a fallacy, a commercial response that trivialises the real problems of agriculture on the continent. Furthermore, Africa should not be used as the Petri dish for privatization and the irreversible poisoning of the environment. Africa is poor and has no means to mitigate the damage. **We demand a general moratorium on behalf of the entire continent**

4. That we are opposed to the idea of a global seed and gene bank. This kind of centralisation will open the door to genetic piracy and theft of the continent's genetic resources. **We advocate for community and national management of seed/ gene banks**

5. That we vociferously condemn the establishment of AGRA in Africa as the driving force of a green revolution and **demand that this alliance dedicate itself to the promotion of sustainable agriculture and food sovereignty for the continent**

We, Africa civil society organizations celebrate our diversity with our peers from all over the world, and commit ourselves to work together to protect our agricultural and cultural diversity. We will develop the synergies necessary to build a strong and lasting network to protect this diversity. Whenever necessary, we shall avail balanced information, we will propose viable alternatives, and we will continue to pressurize those responsible for the planet's future to protect our heritage for future generations.

Signed this 15th Day of May, 2008
By the Networks:
COPAGEN
AREA-ED
Africa Biosafety Center (ABC)
ABN
PELUM
Les Amis de la terre (Friends of the Earth)

Appendix 5

Africa: 25th FAO Africa Conference—African Women's Statement

2008-06-19

Mr. Chairman, Honourable Delegates;

We are women's representatives from different organisations in Africa, representing farmers, Community Based Organisations, Landless Peoples Movements, Pastoralists and Youth, from Western, Southern and Eastern Africa, meeting in Nairobi from June 16–18, 2008, to share our diverse experiences on women's access, control and ownership of land/natural and productive resources in Africa and governments' extent of implementation of the International Conference on Agrarian Reform and Rural Development (ICARRD) Declaration in Africa and the current food crisis.

It is widely acknowledged that improved women's access, control and ownership of land/natural and productive resources, is a key factor in eradicating hunger and rural poverty. This has been restated in the framework of international commitments at the World Food Summit 1996 and its Plan of Action; in the Voluntary Guidelines on the Implementation of the Right to Food unanimously adopted by FAO Council; and most recently at the FAO's 32nd Committee on Food Security in October 2006. However there has not been concerted international action to address the question of women's access, control and ownership of land/natural and productive resources in Africa.

"The overall situation is that in the face of increased competition and conflict over land rights for mining, development, logging and other economic activities and as a result of trends towards market-based land reforms, and environmental and health disasters, African women are fast losing their already precarious access to land and resources. HIV-positive women or widows and children orphaned by HIV and AIDS risk losing all claims to family land and natural resources," notes Annette Mukiga from Rwanda Women's Network.

We note that the world is in a food crisis that is linked to a record increase in prices of 83%—a situation not seen in the last fifty years. For years, African governments, advised by international financial institutions and donors, have dismantled public support to agriculture and neglected the small farmers, particularly women farmers, who feed their people.

As Isabella Wandati of Butere Focus on Women's Development, Kenya, notes:

> The targets and goals to eradicate hunger and achieve food security will not be attained unless governments and international organisations take specific action to end the persistent discrimination against women in matters of access to, ownership and control over land and natural resources in Africa. Because women produce up to 80% of the food in developing countries, yet now comprise 60% of those suffering from hunger.

We are cognisant of the fact that the ICARRD Declaration in Africa will be implemented through the African Union's (AU), United Nation's Economic Commission for Africa (UNECA) and the Africa Development Bank (ADB)-led Africa Land Policy and Land Reform Framework and Guidelines currently being developed to: ensure secure land rights; increase productivity; improve livelihoods; enhance natural resource management; and contribute to a broad-based economic growth.

As Fatou Bah from the National Youth Association for Food Security in The Gambia points out:

> Improved women's access, control and ownership of land/natural and productive resources are key to the achievements of these aims. The process and content of the above Africa Framework and Guidelines must fully adhere to African governments commitments in the ICARRD Declaration 2006 and the African Union's Protocol on the Rights of Women in Africa 2003 on women's rights to land and natural resources to realize its aims.

Recommendations

1. To FAO and African Governments on implementation of ICARRD

To implement existing commitments as part of the follow up to the ICARRD Declaration March 2006 at continental, regional and national levels through concrete measures:

- Uphold equal citizenship rights for both women and men by eliminating all discriminatory cultural, religious and traditional laws on succession and inheritance included in statutory law at national level that exclude African women from citizenship on an equal footing with African men, as a first step to ensuring women's access, control and ownership of land/natural and productive resources in Africa;
- Support the establishment of a reporting, monitoring and evaluation mechanism for member states managed collaboratively by FAO, the African Union and regional economic communities regarding the implementation of ICARRD follow up;
- Fund agrarian reform and agricultural development through the development of long-term strategies linking all concerned ministries at national level-Agriculture, Land, Environment, Livestock and Natural Resources;
- Support establishment of gender disaggregated data-base, at national, regional and continental levels, to measure the ICARRD Declaration's implementation progress in order to inform policies, programmes and processes for women's access, control and ownership of land/natural and productive resources in Africa.

2. To FAO and African Governments to implement the measures below in the implementation of ICARRD in Africa through the African Land Policy and Land Reform Framework and Guidelines:

- Convene a continental round table on women's access, control and ownership of land/natural and productive resources in Africa in 2008 to develop indicators and benchmarks for the AU Land Framework and Guidelines before their adoption by the AU Heads of States Summit in 2009. Problems of women's access, control and ownership of land/natural and productive resources in

Africa are in many national contexts complex and sensitive issues. There is a need for policy makers and governments and civil society (particularly organisations of rural women farmers) in Africa to come together to assess the extent of the challenges and share possible ways forward at the sub-regional level and resolve collective action;

• Mainstream women's rights in the Draft AU Land Framework and Guidelines. Women's access, control and ownership over land/natural and productive resources need to be treated comprehensively in each of the aspects of the land question in line with government commitments on women's rights including the ICARRD Declaration 2006 and the African Union's Protocol on the Rights of Women in Africa 2003.

Conclusion

Women's access, control and ownership of land/natural and productive resources in Africa intersect with other problems such as discriminatory inheritance patterns, agriculture and food insecurity, violence against women, the appropriation and privatization of communal and indigenous lands and other natural resources, as well as gendered control over economic resources and the right to work. This inter-sectionality highlights the need for governments to secure women's rights to access, control and own land/natural and productive resources, in order to lessen the threat of discrimination, different forms of violence and HIV/AIDS, denial of political participation, and other violations of their economic and human rights. There is also need to ensure gender responsive land and environmental law to facilitate women's access to resources. The measures we have recommended above will be key to securing those rights.

Coast Women's Rights (COWER), Kenya
Rwanda Women's Network(RWN), Rwanda
Plateforme Sous Regionale Des Organisations Paysannes D'Afrique Central (PROPAC), Cameroon
National Youth Association for Food Security (NYAFS)/IFSN, The Gambia
Kenya Food Security Network (KEFOSPAN), Kenya
Kenya Land Alliance (KLA)
Eastern African Farmers Federation(EAFF), Tanzania

National Women's Farmers Association (NAWFA), The Gambia
Network of Ethiopian Women's Associations (NEWA), Ethiopia
Uganda Land Alliance (ULA), Uganda
Community Land and Development Foundation (COLANDEF), Ghana
La Via Campesina, South Africa
Network of Organisations Working on Food Sovereignty (ROSA), Mozambique
Eastern and Southern Africa Small Scale Farmers Forum(ESAFF), Zambia
Shelter Forum, Kenya
Food Rights Alliance-Uganda
Volunteer Efforts for Development Concerns, Uganda
ACORD International
ActionAid International

Appendix 6

High-Level Meeting on Food Security, Madrid, January 26–27, 2009

Final declaration of farmers and civil society organisations

SURPRISE ENDING IN MADRID!

NO CONSENSUS ON A G-8 DRIVEN PARTNERSHIP AGAINST HUNGER ... FOR NOW

As representatives of peasant farmers and other small scale food producers, together with organisations that support them,* we want to express the following:

We gathered in Madrid with low expectations. We were extremely unhappy with the process and the contents of this conference. Although WE are the ones who produce most of the world's food, we had not been offered a serious space to give our opinion on what should be done, either in the preparatory process or in the conference programme itself.

As a consequence, the meeting was not focussed on the crucial question of how to solve the dramatic food crisis that we are facing, but rather on a discussion by donors about how to spend their money. Without serious questioning the real structural causes behind the food crisis, any discussion about more or less aid money targets symptoms rather than addressing the real issues.

This explains the simplistic 'more of the same' recipes to solve the crisis presented in Madrid: more fertilizer, more hybrid seeds and more agrochemicals for small farmers. This approach has already been a total failure in the past, and has been the source of elimination and suffering of millions of small producers, environmental destruction and climate change.

It is also clear that none of the actors here were prepared to deal with the crucial and conflictual issue of how local food producers are being denied access to land and territories, which constitutes the single most important threat to local food production. Many of the communally held land territories are now under threat from privatisation and land grabbing by transnational corporations to plant agrofuels or other commodities for the international markets. We need fundamental agrarian and aquatic reforms to keep land in the hands of local communities to be able to produce food.

But several factors combined to squash the organizers' hope of ending the conference with the triumphal proclamation of an ethereal Global Partnership for Agricultural and Food Security crafted by the G8 with agribusiness corporations panting to take up residence. One factor was the fact that many developing country governments rejected a proposal on which no one had bothered to consult them. Another was the strong stand taken by FAO to keep global governance of food and agriculture centred in the Rome-based UN agencies. And our participation—both within the conference and in actions outside—helped to remind delegates that there can be no successful approach to the food crisis that does not build on the alternatives that millions of small food producers are developing day by day.

The solution to the food crisis exists, and is being fought for in many communities. It is called food sovereignty. An approach oriented towards peasant-based agriculture and artisanal fisheries, prioritizing local markets and sustainable production methods and based on the right to food and the right of peoples to define their own agricultural policies. To be able to achieve this, we need to:

- Reinstate the right of governments to intervene and regulate in the food and agricultural sector. The right to food, as already accepted by the UN, should be the central cornerstone on the basis of which the solutions to the food crisis are to be constructed.
- Dominate the disastrous volatility of food prices in domestic markets. National governments should take full control over the import and export of food in order to stabilize local markets.
- Reject Green Revolution models. Industrialized agriculture and fisheries are no solution.
- Set up policies to actively support peasant-based food production

and artisanal fishing, local markets and the implementation of agrarian and aquatic reform.
• Stop corporate land grabbing for industrial agrofuels and commodity production.

We need one single space in the UN system that acts in total independence of the international financial and trade institutions, with a clear mandate from governments, decisive participation by peasant, fisher-folk and other small scale food producers, and a transparent and democratic process of decision making. This has to be the unique space where food and agriculture issues are discussed, where policies and rules are set.

We see the proposed Global Partnership as just another move to give the big corporations and their foundations a formal place at the table, despite all the rhetoric about the 'inclusiveness' of this initiative. Furthermore it legitimates the participation of WTO, World Bank and IFM and other neoliberalism-promoting institutions in the solution of the very problems they have caused. This undermines any possibility for civil society or governments from the Global South to play any significant role. We do not need this Global Partnership or any other structure outside the UN system.

The battle was won in Madrid, but we have no illusions that the promoters of the Global Partnership have given up the fight, and we will continue to engage them.

* These include Via Campesina, COAG, and many NGOs. The organisations present at the Madrid meeting presented a detailed statement with our assessment and proposals "Accelerating into disaster—When banks manage the food crisis." It can be downloaded from the website of the IPC, which has facilitated our participation in this conference: www.foodsovereignty.org

Appendix 7

US Call to Action

As a result of decades of misguided policies and the recent sharp rise in food prices, a billion people around the world face hunger and food insecurity. Dangerous volatility in the financial system puts these people at even greater risk. We, the undersigned, call on people across the United States to use our political power and actions to fight for food system changes that:

1. Stabilize prices for farmers and consumers globally:
    - Regulate the finance sector's investment in food and energy commodities.
    - Establish and strengthen publicly-owned domestic, regional, and international strategic food reserves.
    - Suspend international trade and investments in industrial-scale biofuels (a.k.a. agrofuels).
    - Reform food aid.
    - Expand fair trade, not so-called free trade.
2. Rebalance power in the food system:
    - Reduce the political influence of agribusiness corporations on public policy.
    - Strengthen antitrust enforcement in agribusiness.
    - Convene multi-stakeholder, representative food policy councils at state and local levels.
3. Make agriculture environmentally sustainable:
    - Support family farming with agroecological practices through purchasing and procurement.
    - Halt expansion of government supported biofuels programs, mandates, and tax incentives and other subsidies unless they only support sustainable, domestic production.
    - Direct state and national farm policy, research and education, and investment toward biodiverse, agroecological farming and sustainable food businesses.
    - Guarantee the right to healthy food by building local and regional food systems and fostering social, ecological and economic justice.

- Call on the US to join the community of nations supporting the human right to food.
- Support domestic food production and independent community-based food businesses in the United States and around the world.
- Establish living wages, so that everyone can afford healthy food.
- Implement full workers' rights for farmworkers and other food system workers.
- Strengthen the social safety net for low-income people across the US.
- Create a solidarity economy that puts people before profit in the United States and around the world.

You can take action in many ways, in your community or across the country:

- Contact your elected officials to demand policies that support a fair food system.
- Write op-eds and letters to the editor of your newspaper.
- Host an event to educate and mobilize your community between World Food Day (October 16) and Thanksgiving.
- Join local or national organizations working for a fair food system.
- Get involved with the US Working Group on the Food Crisis.

http://www.usfoodcrisisgroup.org/

Appendix 8

Declaration for Healthy Food and Agriculture

We, the undersigned, believe that a healthy food system is necessary to meet the urgent challenges of our time. Behind us stands a half-century of industrial food production, underwritten by cheap fossil fuels, abundant land and water resources, and a drive to maximize the global harvest of cheap calories. Ahead lie rising energy and food costs, a changing climate, declining water supplies, a growing population, and the paradox of widespread hunger and obesity.

These realities call for a radically different approach to food and agriculture. We believe that the food system must be reorganized on a foundation of health: for our communities, for people, for animals, and for the natural world. The quality of food, and not just its quantity, ought to guide our agriculture. The ways we grow, distribute, and prepare food should celebrate our various cultures and our shared humanity, providing not only sustenance, but justice, beauty and pleasure.

Governments have a duty to protect people from malnutrition, unsafe food, and exploitation, and to protect the land and water on which we depend from degradation. Individuals, producers, and organizations have a duty to create regional systems that can provide healthy food for their communities. We all have a duty to respect and honor the laborers of the land without whom we could not survive. The changes we call for here have begun, but the time has come to accelerate the transformation of our food and agriculture and make its benefits available to all.

We believe that the following twelve principles should frame food and agriculture policy, to ensure that it will contribute to the health and wealth of the nation and the world. A healthy food and agriculture policy:

1. Forms the foundation of secure and prosperous societies, healthy communities, and healthy people.
2. Provides access to affordable, nutritious food to everyone.

3. Prevents the exploitation of farmers, workers, and natural resources; the domination of genomes and markets; and the cruel treatment of animals, by any nation, corporation or individual.
4. Upholds the dignity, safety, and quality of life for all who work to feed us.
5. Commits resources to teach children the skills and knowledge essential to food production, preparation, nutrition, and enjoyment.
6. Protects the finite resources of productive soils, fresh water, and biological diversity.
7. Strives to remove fossil fuel from every link in the food chain and replace it with renewable resources and energy.
8. Originates from a biological rather than an industrial framework.
9. Fosters diversity in all its relevant forms: diversity of domestic and wild species; diversity of foods, flavors and traditions; diversity of ownership.
10. Requires a national dialog concerning technologies used in production, and allows regions to adopt their own respective guidelines on such matters.
11. Enforces transparency so that citizens know how their food is produced, where it comes from, and what it contains.
12. Promotes economic structures and supports programs to nurture the development of just and sustainable regional farm and food networks.

Our pursuit of healthy food and agriculture unites us as people and as communities, across geographic boundaries, and social and economic lines. We pledge our votes, our purchases, our creativity, and our energies to this urgent cause.

http://fooddeclaration.org/

Acknowledgements

This book was made possible by the contributions and hard work of many friends and colleagues. Specific sections were written by Miguel Altieri, Walden Bello, Roland Bunch, George Naylor, Dori Stone, Marcia Ishii-Eiteman, Molly Anderson, Ivette Perfecto, Brahm Ahmadi, Anim Steel, Esther Vivas, Priscilla Claeys, José Maria Tardin, Isabella Kenfield, Alex Perrotti and Tanya Kerssen. Food First associates Rick Jonasse, Karla Pena, Ellen Parry Tyler, Amanda El-Khoury, Jasmine Tilly, Mihir Mankad, Tamara Wattnem, Kurt Eulau, Ashley Elles, Ingrid Budrovich, Heidi Conner, Juliana Mandell, Meera Velu and Alethea Harper all contributed to background research and writing. Many thanks to Marilyn Borchardt, William Wroblewski and Martha Katigbak-Fernandez, who provided essential review and editing.

Notes

1. Further, the FAO estimates that while cereal consumption by India will increase 2.17% this year to 197.3 million tons, in the US cereal consumption will increase five times as much (11.8%), from 277.6 million tons to 310.4 million tons, bringing its global share to a record high of nearly 15% (Financial Express 2008). In regards to grain-fed meat, China feeds 17% of its grain to animals, while 70% of US grain goes to feed livestock (Delgado et al. 1999).

2. Per capita meat consumption in India and China in 1993 was 4 and 33 kg/year, respectively. In the US it was 118 kg/yr — compared to 76 kg/yr in the developed world and 11 kg/yr in the developing world. The rate of meat consumption, however, was higher in the global South, doubling in ten years, compared to flat growth in the North. However, per capita meat production doubled in China, increased by 25% in India and over 30% in the developing world overall. Increase of meat production in the developed world rose only 1.1%. Grain fed livestock grew at 4% a year in developing countries and only 0.7% in developed countries (Delgado et al. 1999).

3. According to the FAO, "The global cost of imported foodstuffs in 2008 is forecast at US$1,035 billion, 26% higher than 2007's peak. This figure is still provisional as FAO's food import bill forecasts are conditional on developments in international prices and freight rates, which remain highly uncertain. Among economic groups, the most economically vulnerable countries are set to bear the highest burden in the cost of importing food, with total expenditures by lesser developed countries and low-income food dependent counties anticipated to climb by 37–40% from 2007, after already rising 30% and 37%, respectively, in 2007. The sustained rise in imported food expenditures for both vulnerable country groups is a worrisome development because by the end of 2008, their annual food import basket could cost four times as much as in 2000. This is in stark contrast to the trend prevailing for developed countries, where year-to-year import costs have risen far less" (FAO 2008d).

4. The term "Green Revolution" comes from a meeting of the Society for International Development in Washington DC in 1968.

Referring to record yields in Pakistan, India, the Philippines and Turkey, William Gaud, director of USAID announced, "These and other developments in the field of agriculture contain the makings of a new revolution. It is not a violent Red Revolution like that of the Soviets, nor is it a White Revolution like that of the Shah of Iran. I call it the Green Revolution." A perfect Cold War sound bite, the term quickly spread worldwide (see http://www.agbioworld. org/biotech-info/topics/borlaug/borlaug-green.html).

5. Globalization, Development, and Democracy: Lessons from the Global Food Crisis, by Walden Bello, (Keynote speech at the 2008 CASID annual conference, Vancouver, June 6, 2008).

6. Adapted from Esther Vivas, The CAP, Alternatives and Resistance: Something is Moving in Europe, email message, January 27, 2009.

7. HLTF participation has included: Food and Agriculture Organization (FAO), International Fund for Agricultural Development (IFAD); International Monetary Fund (IMF); United Nations Office of the High Representative for the Least Developed Countries, Landlocked Developing Countries and Small Island Developing States (OHRLLS); United Nations Conference on Trade and Development (UNCTAD); United Nations Development Program (UNDP); United Nations Environment Program (UNEP); Office of the United Nations High Commissioner for Refugees (UNHCR); United Nations Children's Emergency Fund (UNICEF); World Food Program (WFP); World Health Organization (WHO); World Bank; World Trade Organization (WTO); Department of Economic and Social Affairs (DESA); Department of Political Affairs (DPA); Department of Public Information (DPI); Department of Peacekeeping Operations (DPKO); the Special Adviser on Millennium Development Goals (MDGs); and the Organisation for Economic Cooperation and Development (OECD).

8. Adapted from M. Jahi Chappell, Shattering Myths: Can Sustainable Agriculture Feed the World?, *Food First Backgrounder*, vol. 13, no. 3, fall, 2007.

9. Adapted from Miguel Altieri, "Small farms as a planetary ecological asset: Five key reasons why we should support the revitalization of small farms in the Global South," http://www. foodfirst.org/en/node/2115.

10. "The most notable and problematic (effect) is the tendency of drought-tolerant GM lines to not perform as well under favorable conditions. This appears to be the case for CIMMYT's GM wheat and Monsanto's GM corn. The flaw is a profound one. It amounts to shifting the yield losses experienced in dry seasons onto the good years." From the Australian government's Grains Research and Development Corporation (GRDC 2008).

11. Adapted from Marcia Ishii-Iteman, Ivette Perfecto, and Molly Anderson with Phana Nakkharach, New Era for Agriculture?, *Food First Backgrounder*, vol. 14, no. 2, summer, 2008.

12. Unfortunately, thus far only six of the 53 countries are presently spending 10% of their national budgets on agriculture. This may decrease rather than increase as a result of the global financial crisis.

13. Sections adapted from Holt-Giménez, Out of AGRA: The Green Revolution Returns to Africa, *Development* 51(4): 464–71, 2008.

14. See http://www.pelum.net/.

15. See http://www.leisa.info/.

16. The projected expansion of Gates' funding has been put on hold—the foundation will increase its giving only slightly (from $3.3 to $3.8 billion) and is not likely to be expanding in the immediate future (Gates 2009).

17. The different interpretations of "agroecology" and "biodiversity" are good examples of this problem. For AGRA the former means producing hybrid seeds that fit local agroecosystems and the latter means diversity of single crop varieties. These interpretations are not likely to meet the needs or demands of ecological farmers who depend on a rich mix of flora and fauna on and around the farm to ensure healthy agroecosystem functioning. In AGRA's "integrated soil management" program, fertilizers purchased with "smart subsidies" come first. Cover cropping, composting and other soil building practices will supposedly follow, but it is not clear what means will be used (like fertilizer's subsidized credit) for farmers to undertake this hard work. For ecological farmers, soil building and conservation comes first— often making fertilizers unnecessary. Past experiences world-wide indicate that as long as subsidies for fertilizers are available, most

farmers avoid the hard work of soil building. This often leads to the total destruction of the soil—often to the point that even fertilizers cease to function (Gliessman 1998).

18. Adapted from Esther Vivas, The CAP, Alternatives and Resistance: Something is Moving in Europe, email message, January 27, 2009.

19. "...Convergence with diversity [recognizes] the diversity, not only of movements which are fragmented but of political forces which are operating with them, of ideologies and even visions of the future of those political forces; and that this has to be accepted and respected" (Kothari and Kuruvilla 2008).

Acronyms

AATF	African Agricultural Technology Foundation
AGRA	Alliance for a Green Revolution in Africa
AoA	Agreement on Agriculture
CAFTA–DR	Central American Free Trade Agreement (including the Dominican Republic)
CAP	Common Agricultural Policy (European Union)
CFA	Comprehensive Framework for Action
CGIAR	Consultative Group on International Agricultural Research
CIMMYT	International Maize and Wheat Improvement Center
CIW	Coalition of Immokalee Workers
CSA	community supported agriculture
DFID	British Department for International Development
EU	European Union
FAO	Food and Agriculture Organization of the United Nations
FTA	free trade agreement
GATT	General Agreement on Tariffs and Trade
GDP	gross domestic product
GMO	genetically modified organism
HYV	high-yielding hybrid varieties
IAASTD	International Assessment of Agricultural Knowledge, Science and Technology for Development
IFC	International Finance Corporation
IFPRI	International Food Policy Research Institute
IISD	International Institute for Sustainable Development
IMF	International Monetary Fund
IPCC	United Nations Intergovernmental Panel on Climate Change
IRDP	integrated rural development projects
IRRI	International Rice Research Institute
LDCs	less developed countries
NAFTA	North American Free Trade Agreement
NASA	National Aeronautics and Space Administration
NGOs	non-governmental organizations

OECD	Organization for Economic Cooperation and Development
OPEC	Organization of the Petroleum Exporting Countries
PRSC	Poverty Reduction Social Credit
RFA	Renewable Fuels Association
RFS	Renewable Fuels Standard
SAP	structural adjustment program
UNDP	United Nations Development Program
USDA	US Department of Agriculture
WTO	World Trade Organization

Glossary

agrofuels—biologically-based fuels produced on a centralized, industrial scale, mostly for use as a liquid vehicle fuel. Agrofuels can be made from corn, soy, sugarcane, canola, jatropha, palm oil, or so-called "second generation" crops such as swtichgrass, Miscanthus (canary grass), trees, and corn stover. The term contrasts with "biofuels," which refers to local, decentralized, farmer-owned, and small-scale fuels of a similar nature.

agroecology—the science of sustainable agriculture; a scientific discipline that uses ecological theory to study, design, manage and evaluate agricultural systems that are productive but also resource conserving. Agroecology links ecology, culture, economics, traditional knowledge and integrated management to sustain agricultural production and healthy food and farming systems.

agroforestry—a dynamic, ecologically based, natural resource management system that, through the integration of trees in farm and rangeland, diversifies and sustains production for increased social, economic and environmental benefits.[i]

Archer Daniels Midland—ADM is the second largest grain trader in the world, a major food processor, and the second largest ethanol producer in the US. ADM has been called the "largest recipient of corporate welfare in U.S. history" by the conservative Cato Institute.

Blair Commission for Africa—an initiative of the British government to spur development in Africa.

bushel—the unit of measurement in which corn and other commodities are most often traded. One bushel of corn = 56 pounds or 25.4 kg.

Cargill—the world's largest grain trader and the largest privately held company in the US.

community food security—a condition in which all community residents obtain a safe, culturally acceptable, nutritionally adequate diet through a sustainable food system that maximizes community self-reliance and social justice.[ii]

conditionality—in reference to loans from international financial institutions, this is a set of stipulations a nation must meet in order to qualify for financial assistance. Often loans are conditioned on structural adjustment and market liberalization.

crop board—an independent government body that markets and regulates the price of crops.

Doha round —the current round of WTO negotiations, which began in 2001 in Doha, Qatar. The negotiations have stalled over disagreements on agricultural import rules.

dumping – export of overproduced and/or subsidized commodities, often from industrial Northern countries, distributed below the cost of production, most often in the global South.

emerging economy—used to describe a nation in the process of rapid industrial growth, such as China, India and Brazil.

food justice—a movement that attempts to address hunger by addressing the underlining issues of racial and class disparity and the inequities in the food system that correlate to inequities in economic and political power.

food policy councils—a group of stakeholders that examine how the local food system is working and develop ways to fix it.

food security—according to the FAO, "food security exists when all people, at all times, have physical and economic access to sufficient, safe and nutritious food to meet their dietary needs and food preferences for an active and healthy life."[iii]

food sovereignty—people's right to healthy and culturally appropriate food produced through ecologically sound and sustainable methods, and their right to define their own food and agriculture systems; the democratization of the food system in favor of the poor.

futures—standardized legal agreements to transact in a physical commodity at some designated future time.

genetic engineering—experimental or industrial technologies used to alter the genome of a living cell so that it can produce more or different molecules than it is already programmed to make.[iv]

global South—formerly referred to as the "third world," the nations of Africa, Central and South America, and much of Asia with comparatively little economic power.

GMO—an acronym for genetically modified organism, a plant or animal with permanently, artificially modified genetic material derived across species boundaries. In reference to agriculture, this refers to proprietary, modified crop varieties.

Green Revolution—largely funded by the Ford and Rockefeller

Foundations, the Green Revolution refers to the process of industrialization in agriculture initiated in the 1950s and 60s, from the development and widespread adoption of high-yielding varieties, synthetic fertilizers, chemical herbicides and pesticides.

grain reserves—a stock of grain maintained in years of good harvest to buffer against shortage and regulate price volatility.

hedging—a mechanism to offset the risk of an asset's changing price.

hypermarket—a large retailer that combines a supermarket and a department or general merchandise store under one roof. Hypermarkets like WalMart, Carrefour, Target, K-mart, and Costco, often covering 14,000m^2 (150,000ft^2), survive on high-volume, low margin sales, and often put local retailers out of business.

industrial agrifood complex—describes the skewed power structure of the global food system, currently dominated by large grain traders, chemical and biotechnology companies, transnational food processors, and global supermarket chains, at the expense of small farmers who produce most of the world's food.

index investors—type of speculator that seeks long-term investments by hoarding commodities futures contracts for extended periods and betting on the continued rise of commodities prices.

industrial feedlot—a type of a confined animal feeding operation, where animals are fattened on grains and soy before slaughter for meat.

informal sector—economic activity that is neither taxed nor monitored by the government.

intercrop—a technique employed in traditional and ecological agriculture that involves the planting of multiple varieties and crop species in one agricultural area.

landraces—a population of plants, typically genetically heterogeneous, commonly developed in traditional agriculture from many years, even centuries, of farmer-directed selection, and specifically adapted to local conditions.[v] Local landraces are a reservoir of genetic diversity in agriculture.

marketing board—an independent government body that markets and regulates the price of crops.

Maseca—the largest producer of tortillas and corn flour in Mexico and the US.

Millennium Development Goals—a set of eight goals elaborated at the United Nations Millennium Summit in 2000 and to be completed by 2015: end poverty and hunger, universal education, gender equality, child health, maternal heath, combat HIV/AIDS, environmental sustainability, and global partnership.

millennium villages—villages in Africa that receive targeted investments in agriculture, health, education, and infrastructure to display possible ways of meeting the Millennium Development Goals.

monocrop or monoculture—the practice of cultivating a single variety of genetically uniform plants over a large agricultural area.

National Labor Relations Act—also known as the Wagner Act. This 1935 US federal law protects the rights of workers in the private sector to organize into labor unions, engage in collective bargaining, strike, and advocate for themselves. The act established the National Labor Relations Board.

participatory crop breeding—programs for crop varietal improvement wherein farmers have a level of involvement in selecting traits.

pastoralist—a farmer who primarily engages in the raising of livestock on pasture.

peasant land invasions—a form of non-violent direct action employed by farmers' groups wherein land owned by elites or corporations is peacefully taken over as a form of protest.

polyculture—the practice of growing many different species or different varieties of crops in a single space, modeling the diversity of natural ecosystems.

public–private partnerships—a government service or business venture funded and managed jointly by government agencies and business.

smallholder—a farmer with relatively few planted acres that relies primarily on family labor.

sovereign wealth fund—a state-owned investment fund composed of financial assets such as stocks, bonds, real estate, or other financial instruments funded by foreign exchange assets. SWFs tend to have a higher tolerance for risk than traditional foreign exchange reserves.

structural violence—a constraint on human potential due to political or economic forces.[vi] Sources of structural violence can include unequal access to resources, political power, education, food, and health care, as well as racism, sexism, religious discrimination, and other forms of oppression. Structural violence often leads to physical acts of violence.

supplemental food assistance programs—subsided food benefits from the government, such as food stamps in the United States.

transgenic—an organism that contains genes that have been moved across species lines into the germ line of a host.[vii]

Via Campesina—an international movement of peasant farmers' organizations that advocates for food sovereignty.

World Bank's Independent Evaluation Group—the internal assessment and accountability organization within the World Bank.

World Development Report—an annual report on development economics put out by the World Bank.

Notes

i. Definition by Dr Robert Leakey in Leaky, R. 1996. Definition of Agroforestry Revisited. *Agroforestry Today* 8(1).

ii. Definition by Mike Hamm and Anne Bellows. www.foodsecurity.org.

iii. http://www.fao.org/spfs/en/.

iv. Definition taken from Altieri, Miguel. 2004. *Genetic Engineering in Agriculture*. Oakland: Food First Books.

v. Definition taken from Altieri, Miguel. 2004. *Genetic Engineering in Agriculture*. Oakland: Food First Books.

vi. Adapted from Johan Galtung's original definition in Galtung, J. 1969. Violence, Peace and Peace Research. *Journal of Peace Research* 6(3): 167–91.

vii. Definition taken from Altieri, Miguel. 2004. *Genetic Engineering in Agriculture*. Oakland: Food First Books.

Annotated bibliography

Altieri, Miguel. 1987. *Agroecology: The Scientific Basis of Sustainable Agriculture*. Boulder CO: Westview Press.

Agroecology explains the key principles of sustainable agriculture and gives examples of management practices that really work. Drawing case studies from sustainable rural development, Altieri gives a vision for how a truly ecological agriculture can sustain us.

Altieri, M. 2004. *Genetic Engineering in Agriculture*. Oakland: Food First Books.

In *Genetic Engineering In Agriculture*, acclaimed agroecologist Miguel Altieri answers the big questions surrounding genetically modified crops, explaining exactly what GM crops are, who they benefit, and what we stand to lose from their widespread adoption.

Altieri, M., Peter Rosset and Lori Ann Thrupp. 1998. *The Potential of Agroecology to Combat Hunger in the Developing World*. Oakland: Food First Books.

Agroecology—the study of agricultural systems using ecological principles—is presented as a way to resolve hunger, inequality and sustainable development in the developing world.

Bello, Walden. 2001. *The Future in the Balance: Essays on Globalization and Resistance*. Oakland: Food First Books.

A collection of essays by third world activist and scholar Walden Bello on the myths of development as prescribed by the World Trade Organization and other institutions, and the possibility of another world based on fairness and justice.

Borras Jr., Saturnino M. 2004. *La Vía Campesina; An Evolving Transnational Social Movement*. Amsterdam: The Transnational Institute.

Focusing on the global campaign for agrarian reform, Borras looks at the development of Via Campesina, their agendas, alliances, strategies, and accountability to people on the ground.

Bunch, Roland. 1985. *Two Ears of Corn: A Guide to People-Centered Agricultural Improvement*. Oklahoma City: World Neighbors.

The classic manual for sustainable agricultural development.

Cook, Christopher. 2004. *Diet for a Dead Planet*. New York: The New Press.

In what *Mother Jones* magazine called a "far-reaching take-down of the American food industry," Christopher Cook outlines how deregulation, corporate control, and misplaced subsidies are destroying the American food system.

Daño, Elenita. 2007. *Unmasking the Green Revolution in Africa: Motives, Players and Dynamics*. Penang, Malaysia: Third World Network.

Asking whether the African Green Revolution is actually a cover for corporate interests, Daño explores the forces behind the African Green Revolution, and presents alternative solutions to food-security and rural development needs in Africa.

De Schutter, Olivier. 2008. *Building Resilience: A Human Rights Framework for World Food and Nutrition Security. Promotion and Protection of All Human Rights, Civil, Political, Economic, Social and Cultural Rights, Including the Right to Development*. Geneva: Human Rights Council, United Nations.

De Schutter analyses the current food crisis from a human rights perspective. Exploring the risks and opportunities of the food crisis, he presents why a human rights framework should be adopted to respond to food security.

Desmarais, Annette. 2006. *Via Campesina: Globalization and the Power of Peasants*. Halifax: Fernwood Publishing.

Desmarais, a former grain farmer and long time participant in Via Campesina, explains the development of the revolutionary peasant movement to maintain one's land, culture and food community.

Edwards, Michael. 2008. *Just Another Emperor? The Myths and Realities of Philanthrocapitalism*. London: Demos and the Young Foundation.

The non-profit world is increasingly utilizing business methods and models. Edwards analyses this new phenomenon, and questions the motives and outcomes behind the American philanthropy sector.

Evans, A. 2009. *The Feeding of the Nine Billion: Global Food Security for the 21st Century*. London: Royal Institute of International Affairs at Chatham House. http://www.chathamhouse.org.uk/files/13179_r0109food.pdf (accessed 5 May 2009).

Evans presents ten steps he deems necessary to prevent even higher global food prices, and pushes for putting the global food crisis at the forefront of the international political agenda.

Funes, Fernando, Luis García, Martin Bourque, Nilda Pérez, Peter Rosset. 2002. *Sustainable Agriculture and Resistance: Transforming Food Production in Cuba*. Oakland: Food First Books.

After the fall of the Soviet Union, fertilizers, farm machinery, pesticides and fuel disappeared from the Cuban countryside nearly overnight. In this book Cuban authors, for the first time in English, tell the story of the transformation of Cuban agriculture from industrial agriculture to the world's leader in sustainable farming.

Goldman, Michael. 2005. *Imperial Nature: The World Bank and Struggles for Social Justice in the Age of Globalization*. New Haven: Yale University Press.

Goldman looks into the "green neoliberalism" grounding the World Bank's environmental projects.

Halweil, Brian. 2004. *Eat Here: Reclaiming Homegrown Pleasures in a Global Supermarket*. New York and London: Norton and Worldwatch.

Brian Halweil discusses the growing local food movement that is "rediscovering homegrown pleasures" and changing the way we eat.

Harvey, David. 2003. *The New Imperialism*. New York: Oxford University Press.

Harvey looks at the modes and mechanisms through which industrial nations dominate the global South. *The New Imperialism* takes on the US imperial tradition, militarism, domestic policies, the sagging economy, the war in Iraq, and the logic of power.

Havnevik, K., Deborah Bryceson, Lars-Erik Biregard, Proper Matondi and Atakilte Beyene (eds) 2007. *African Agriculture and the World Bank: Development or Impoverishment?* Uppsala: Nordic Africa Institute.

An exploration of the impact of the World Bank's combination of structural adjustment policies and development projects on Africa's agriculture.

Holt-Giménez, E. 2006. *Campesino a Campesino: Voices from Latin America's Farmer to Farmer Movement*. Oakland: Food First Books.

In 1978 Eric Holt-Giménez, then a volunteer teaching sustainable agriculture in Mexico, invited a group of visiting Guatemalan farmers to teach a course in his village—this and other efforts marked the beginning of a broad-based farmer's movement. Written with dozens of farm leaders, this book chronicle 25 years of the continent's farmer-to-farmer movement for sustainable agriculture.

Holt-Giménez, Eric. 2008. The World Food Crisis—What's Behind It and What We Can Do About It. *Food First Policy Brief* No. 16. Oakland: Institute for Food and Development Policy.

Spurred by the current food crisis, this article covers the many factors—from the Green Revolution to agrofuels—that have created an unjust and broken food system. The report delves into the political and economic causes of the current global food crisis, and offers suggestions for reforming the international food system to permanently resolve the food crisis.

Holt-Giménez, Eric, Miguel Altieri and Peter Rosset. 2006. Ten Reasons Why the Rockefeller and the Bill and Melinda Gates Foundations' Alliance for Another Green Revolution Will Not Solve the Problems of Poverty and Hunger in Sub-Saharan Africa. *Food First Policy Brief* No. 12. Oakland: Institute for Food and Development Policy.

A report on the potential effects of the Alliance for a Green Revolution in Africa, "Ten Reasons" argues that, in addition to the long-term consequences of the Green Revolution, there remain specific issues of hunger and poverty in Africa that cannot be solved with another Green Revolution. The ten reasons illustrate the ongoing Green Revolution's negative impacts on local farming communities as well as its rejection of viable alternatives to decrease hunger and poverty in Africa.

Ishii-Eiteman, M., Molly Anderson with Phana Nakkharach and Ivette Perfecto. 2008. 'New Era for Agriculture.' *Food First Backgrounder* 14(2).

New Era for Agriculture presents the findings of reports from the International Assessment of Agricultural Knowledge, Science and Technology for Development (IAASTD), which suggests the need for many drastic changes in the global food system, including a move towards food sovereignty and sustainable agriculture.

Kimbrell, A. (ed). 2002. *The Fatal Harvest Reader: the Tragedy of Industrial Agriculture*. Washington DC: Island Press.

Fatal Harvest gives a view of our current destructive agricultural system and a vision for a healthier way of producing our food in a collection of essays from writers and scholars such as Wes Jackson, Wendell Berry, Vandana Shiva, Jim Hightower and Gary Nabhan.

Lappé, Frances Moore, Joseph Collins and Peter Rosset. 1998. *World Hunger: Twelve Myths*. New York: Grove Press.

World Hunger exposes the myths around the root causes of hunger, poverty and injustice, and calls for a renewed sense of public and political will to bring an end to hunger in a world of plenty.

Mousseau, F. 2005. *Food Aid or Food Sovereignty? Ending World Hunger in our Time*. Oakland: The Oakland Institute.

Analysing the current international food aid system, this report offers suggestions for reforming the system towards food sovereignty, rather than aid, to more effectively combat world hunger.

Patel, Raj. 2007. *Stuffed and Starved*. London: Portobello Books.

Tracing the global food chain, Patel exposes the unjust irony of our modern food system: we now have massive health epidemics of both starvation and obesity. Patel uncovers the truth behind corporate control over our food, and offers solutions to regain a more equitable and healthy food system.

Perfecto, Ivette and John Vandermeer. 2005. *Breakfast of Biodiversity: The Political Ecology of Rainforest Destruction*. Oakland: Food First Books.

Vandermeer and Perfecto expose the political, international, and economic forces driving rainforest destruction, and present democracy, sustainable agriculture, and land security as solutions to deforestation.

Pollan, Michael. 2006. *The Omnivore's Dilemma*. New York: Penguin Press.

Pollan's best-selling personal account of four very different meals uncovers surprising facts about growing, creating, and eating food.

Pretty, Jules. 1995. *Regenerating Agriculture; Policies and Practice for Sustainability and Self-Reliance*. London: Earthscan Publications.

Pretty provides a thorough account of alternative, sustainable agricultural practices as means for economic, environmental and social improvements.

Rapley, J. 1996. *Understanding Development: Theory and Practice in the Third World*. Boulder and London: Lynne Rienner.

Understanding Development chronicles the history of thought and practice in third world development over the past 50 years.

Richards, Paul. 1985. *Indigenous Agricultural Revolution: Ecology and Food Production in West Africa*. London: Hutchison.

Richards critiques the top–down model of agricultural research and highlights case studies of complex, ecologically sustainable peasant agricultural systems in Africa.

Rosset, Peter. 2007. *Food Is Different: Why We Must Get The WTO Out of Agriculture*. Halifax and London: Fernwood and Zed Books.

Food Is Different exposes the ways in which the World Trade Organization (WTO), in promoting the globalization and free trade of food, destroys farmers and local communities by introducing cheaper foreign food into local markets and eliminating local food production and livelihoods. Through intimate examples and detailed economic explanations, Peter Rosset illustrates the need for a return to food sovereignty in order to combat the destruction of local and sustainable farm systems caused by the principles and practices of the WTO.

Shiva, Vandana. 1991. *The Violence of the Green Revolution*. London: Zed Books.

Vandana Shiva shows how the long-term negative effects of the Green Revolution outweigh the short-term yield increases in the fertile region of India known as the Punjab. Shiva lays out the long-term impacts of the Green Revolution—from increased pests and diseases, to water scarcity, greater inequality, and social conflict—which embed a structural violence against the people and the land of Punjab.

Winnie, Mark. 2008. *Closing the Food Gap*. Boston: Beacon Press.

Closing the Food Gap outlines the food policy reform that is needed to achieve food security for all income levels, and offers suggestions for "projects, partners and policy" for the American food system.

Wright, Angus and Wendy Wolford. 2003. *To Inherit the Earth: The Landless Movement and the Struggle for a New Brazil*. Oakland: Food First Books.

Filled with personal stories from within Brazil's Landless Workers' Movement (MST), *To Inherit the Earth* provides the historical, political and environmental story of the struggle and success of an agrarian reform movement to secure over 20 million acres of farmland.

References

Abugre, Charles. 1993. *Behind Crowded Shelves: as Assessment of Ghana's Structural Adjustment Experiences, 1983–99*. Oakland: Food First.

Agra-Alliance. 2008. *Agricultural Education*. Alliance for a Green Revolution in Africa. http://www.agra-alliance.org/section/work/experts (accessed October 16, 2008).

Alexander, Nancy. 2005. The Value of Aid: A Critical Analysis of the UN Milliennium Project's Approach to the MDGs. New Delhi: ActionAid Asia.

Altieri, Miguel. 1999. Applying Agroecology to Enhance Productivity of Peasant Farming Systems in Latin America. *Environment, Development and Sustainability* 1:119–217.

Altieri, Miguel. 2000. *Ecological Impacts of Industrial Agriculture and the Possibilities for Truly Sustainable Farming*. College of Natural Resources University of California Berkeley. http://www.cnr.berkeley.edu/~christos/espm118/articles/modern_agriculture.html (accessed September 25, 2008).

Altieri, Miguel. 2004. Genetic Engineering in Agriculture: The Myths, Evironmental Risks, and Alternatives. 2 ed. Oakland: Food First Books.

Altieri, Miguel and Elizabeth Bravo. 2007. *The Ecological and Social Tragedy of Crop-Based Biofuel Production in the Americas*. Institute for Food and Development Policy. http://www.foodfirst.org/en/node/1662 (accessed October 20, 2008).

Asenso-Okyere, W.K. 1997. *Sustainable Food Security in West Africa*. Edited by Asenso-Okyere, W.K., E.Y Benneh and W. Tims. Dordrecht: Kluwer Academic Publishers.

Aslow, Mark. 2007. Biofuels: Fact and Fiction. *The Ecologist*, February 2.

Bacon, David. 2008. *Uprooted and Criminalized: The Impact of Free Markets on Migrants*. Oakland Institute. http://www.oaklandinstitute.org/pdfs/backgrounder_uprooted.pdf (accessed October 7, 2008).

Badgley, C., J.K. Moghtader, E. Quintero, E. Zakem, M.J. Chappell, K.R. Avilés Vázquez, A. Samulon, and I. Perfecto. 2007. Organic Agriculture and the Global Food Supply. *Renewable Agriculture and Food Systems* 22 (2):86–108.

Baker, Mindy L., Hayes J. Dermot, and Bruce A. Babcock. 2008. *Crop Based Biofuel Production Under Acreage Restraints and Uncertainty*. Center for Agricultural and Rural Development, Iowa State University.

Balassa, Bela A. 1971. *The Structure of Protection in Developing Countries*. Baltimore: Johns Hopkins Press for the International Bank for Reconstruction and Development and the Inter-American Development Bank.

Banker, David E., Robert A. Hoppe, Korb Penni, and Erik J. O'Donoghue. 2007. *Structure and Finances of U.S. Farms. Family Farm Report*. http://www.ers.usda.gov/publications/eib24/eib24fm.pdf (accessed September 23, 2008).

Bauer, P.T. 1981. *Equality, the Third World, and Economic Delusion*. Cambridge MA: Harvard University Press.

BBC. 2006. *Africa's Hunger — A Systemic Crisis*. British Broadcasting Corporation. http://news.bbc.co.uk/2/hi/afria/462232.stm (accessed January 21, 2006).

BBC. 2008. The Cost of Food: Facts and Figures: Explore the Facts and Figures Behind the Rising Price of Food Across the Globe. BBC News. http://news.bbc.co.uk/2/hi/7284196.stm (accessed April 8, 2008).

Beets, W.C. 1982. *Multiple Cropping and Farming Systems*. Boulder: Westview Press.

Bello, Walden. 2008. How the World Bank, IMF and WTO Destroyed African Agriculture. In *Hunger Notes*. Washington DC: World Hunger Education Service. http://www.worldhunger.org/articles/08/editorials/bello_afag.htm (accessed April 8, 2009).

Blaikie, P., T. Cannon, I. Davis and B. Wisner. 1994. *At Risk: Natural Hazards, People's Vulnerability, and Disasters*. London and New York: Routledge.

Blas, Javier and William Walls. 2009. U.S. Investor Buys Sudanese Warlord's Land. *Financial Times* January 9.

Brown, Garrett D. 2004. *NAFTA's 10 Year Failure to Protect Mexican Workers' Health and Safety*. Maquiladora Health and Safety Support Network September 20, 2008. http://mhssn.igc.org/NAFTA_2004.pdf (accessed May 6, 2009).

Brown, Lester R. 2007. *Distillery Demand For Grain To Fuel Cars Vastly Understated: World May Be Facing Highest Grain Prices in History*. Earth Policy Insitute. http://www.earth-policy.org/Updates/2007/

Update63_notes.htm (accessed January 4, 2007).

Bunch, Roland. 1982. *Two Ears of Corn*. Oklahoma City: World Neighbors.

Business World. 2003. Trade Talks Round Going Nowhere Sans Progress in Farm Reform. *Business World*, September 8, p. 15.

CBOT. 2008. *Products and Trading 2008*. http://www.cmegroup.com/trading/commodities/ (accessed October 27, 2008).

CCC. 2008. *CCC Net Outlays by Commodity and Function*. USDA FSA. http://www.fsa.usda.gov/Internet/FSA_File/msr09_tbl35a.pdf (accessed September 24, 2008).

Cha, Ariana Eunjung, and Stephanie McCrummen. 2008. *As Global Prices Soar, More People Go Hungry*. Washington Post Foreign Service. http://www.washingtonpost.com/wp-dyn/content/article/2008/10/25/ (accessed October 26, 2008).

Chang, Ha-Joon. 2007. *Bad Samaritans: Rich Nations, Poor Policies and the Threat to the Developing World*. London: Random House Business Books.

Cline, William R. 2007. *Global Warming and Agriculture Impact Estimates by Country in Brief*. http://bookstore.petersoninstitute.org/book-store/4037.html (accessed October 21, 2008).

CNBC. 2007. Venture Capital Investments in Biofuels, Including Ethanol and Biodiesel, Grew to $740 Million in 2006 from $110.5 Million in 2005. Green Technology Revs Up Venture Capitalists. CNBC. http://today.msnbc.msn.com/id/18204222 (accessed April 20, 2007).

Collins, B. 2008. Hot Commodities, Stuffed Markets, and Empty Bellies. *Dollars & Sense* 9:70.

Coordinadora Europa de la Via Campesina. 2008. *Creación de la Coordinadora Europea Via Campesina* July 1. http://www.viacampesina.org/main_sp/index.php?option=com_content&task=view&id=537&Itemid=1 (accessed January 30, 2009).

CropLife. 2008. Press Release: Science and Technology are Key to Growing More Food: CropLife Believes the IAASTD Report Falls Short of Goals by Overlooking the Potential of Modern Plant Science. Brussels, Belgium: CropLife International.

Crutzen, P.J., A.R. Mosier, K.A. Smith and W. Winiwarter. 2007. Nitrous Oxide Release from Agro-Biofuel Production Negates Global Warming Reduction by Replacing Fossil Fuels. *Atmospheric Chemistry and Physics* 7:11191–205.

Daño, Elinita C. 2007. Unmasking the Green Revolution in Africa:

Motives, Players and Dynamics. Penang, Malaysia: Third World Network.

De La Torre Ugarte, Daniel G. and Sophia Murphy. 2008. The Global Food Crisis: Creating an Opportunity for Fairer and More Sustainable Food and Agriculture Systems Worldwide. In *Eco-Fair Trade Dialogue* 11. Berlin: Heinrich Boell Foundation and MISEREOR. http://www.ecofair-trade.org/pics/de/EcoFair_Trade_Paper_No11_Ugarte__Murphy_1.pdf (accessed April 9, 2009).

De Schutter, Olivier. 2008. Building Resilience: A Human Rights Framework for World Food and Nutrition Security. Report of the Special Rapporteur on the Right to Food to the Human Rights Council. A/HRC/9/23. New York: United Nations.

Delgado, C., Mark Resegrant, Henning Steinfield, Simeon Ehui and Claude Courbois. 1999. *Livestock to 2020: The Next Food Revolution.* Washington DC: International Food Policy Research Institute.

DFID. 2007. *A Record Harvest in Malawi.* Department for International Development (DFID). http://www.dfid.gov.uk/casestudies/files/africa%5Cmalawi-harvest.asp (accessed May 8, 2007).

Ecologist, The. 1996. CGIAR Agricultural Research for Whom? *The Ecologist* 26:259–70.

Economist, The. 2008. The New Face of Hunger. April 17. http://www.economist.com/world/internatiional/PrinterFriendly.cfm?story_id=11049284 (accessed April 17, 2008).

Economist, The. 2009. U.S. Financial Bail-Outs. *The Economist.* January 15.

Energy Information Administration. 2008. *Diesel Fuel Prices—What Consumers Should Know.* Energy Information Administration. http://www.eia.doe.gov/bookshelf/brochures/diesel/ (accessed October 16, 2008).

Eunjung Cha, Ariana and Stephanie McCrummen. 2008. *As Global Prices Soar, More People Go Hungry.* Washington Post Foreign Service. http://www.washingtonpost.com/wp-dyn/content/article/2008/10/25/AR2008102502293.html (accessed November18, 2008).

Evanson, R.E. and D. Gollin. 2003. Assessing the Impact of the Green Revolution, 1960 to 2000. *Science* 300 (5620):78-82.

EWG. 2009. *Ethanol's Federal Subsidy Grab Leaves Little For Solar, Wind And Geothermal Energy.* Environmental Working Group. http://

www.ewg.org/node/27498 (accessed January 31, 2009).

FAO. 2003. *Some Trade Policy Issues Relating to Trends in Agricultural Imports in the Context of Food Security*. Rome: Committee on Commodity Problems, FAO.

FAO. 2004. *The State of Agricultural Commodity Markets 2004*. Food and Agriculture Organization. ftp://ftp.fao.org/docrep/fao/007/y5419e/y5419e00.pdf (accessed September 25, 2008).

FAO. 2006. *FAO Statistical Yearbook 2005–6*. Rome: Food and Agricultural Organization. http://www.fao.org/statistics/yearbook/vol_1_1/pdf/b01.pdf (accessed April 23, 2009).

FAO. 2008a. *Climate Change: Greenhouse Gas Emissions*. Food and Agriculture Organization. http://www.fao.org/climatechange/49369/en/ (accessed October 20, 2008).

FAO. 2008b. *Estimated World Water Use*. Food and Agriculture Organization. http://www.fao.org/nr/water/art/2008/wateruse.htm (accessed October 14, 2008).

FAO. 2008c. *Gender and Food Security Synthesis report of regional documents: Africa, Asia and Pacific, Europe*. Rome: Food and Agriculture Organization of the United Nations. http://www.fao.org/docrep/X0198E/X0198E00.htm (accessed January 15, 2009).

FAO. 2008d. *Market Summaries—Cereal*. Food and Agriculture Organization. http://www.fao.org/docrep/010/ai466e/ai466e01.htm (accessed October 14, 2008).

Fargione, Joseph, Jason Hill, David Tilman, Stephen Polasky and Peter Hawthorne. 2008. Land Clearing and the Biofuel Carbon Debt. *Science* 319. (5867).

Faurès, Jean-Marc and Guido Santini. 2008. *Water and the Rural Poor: Interventions for Improving Livelihoods in Sub-Saharan Africa*. Rome: FAO.

FIAN. 2008. *Time for a Human Right to Food Framework of Action FIAN Position on the Comprehensive Framework of Action of the High-Level Task Force on the Global Food Crisis*. Edited by FIAN. Heidelberg: FoodFirst Information and Action Network.

Financial Express. 2008. Developed State Should Take Responsibility to Solve Global Food Crisis. *Financial Express*. http://www.thefinancialexpress-bd.com/search_index.php?page=detail_news&news_id=33343 (accessed October 14, 2008).

Financial Times. 2008. Ethanol Boom and Bust. *Financial Times*. http://www.ft.com/cms/s/0/6ed47d6e-9f7a-11dd-a3fa-000077b07658.html (accessed October 28, 2008).

Food First. 2007. *Agroecological Alternatives to the New Green Revolution for Africa*. Institute for Food and Development Policy. December 12. http://www.foodfirst.org/en/node/1807 (accessed January 29, 2009).

Frankel, Francine R. 1973. Politics of the Green Revolution: Shifting Peasant Participation in India and Pakistan. In *Food, Population, Employment: The Impact of the Green Revolution* . Edited by Thomas T. Poleman and Donald K. Freebairn. New York: Praeger Publishers.

Freebairn, Donald K. 1995. Did the Green Revolution Concentrate Incomes? A Quantitative Study of Research Reports. *World Development* 23 (2):265–79.

Friedman, Milton. 1968. The Role of Monetary Policy. *American Economic Review* 58:1–17.

G8. 2008. G8 Leaders Statement on Global Food Security. G8 Hokkaido Toyako Summit.

Garten Rothkopf. 2007. *A Blueprint for Green Energy in the Americas: Strategic Analysis of Opportunities for Brazil and the Hemisphere. Featuring: The Global Biofuels Outlook 2007*. Washington DC: Inter American Development Bank.

Gates, Bill. 2008. From a speech given at the World Economic Forum in Davos, Switzerland. http://www.egovmonitor.com/node/16877 (accessed April 8, 2009).

Gates, Bill. 2009. *Annual Letter*. Bill and Melinda Gates Foundation. January. http://www.gatesfoundation.org/annual-letter/ Documents/2009-bill-gates-annual-letter.pdf (accessed April 8, 2009).

Gates Foundation. 2008. *Agricultural Development Strategy 2008-2011*. July 11. Seattle: Bill and Melinda Gates Foundation.

Gliessman, Stephen R. 1998. *Agroecology: Ecological Processes in Sustainable Agriculture*. Chelsea: Ann Arbor Press.

Goldschmidt, Walter. 1978. *As You Sow: Three Studies in the Social Consequences of Agribusiness*. New York: Allenheld, Osmun.

Gore, Charles. 2000. The Rise and Fall of the Washington Consensus as a Paradigm for Developing Countries. *World Development* 28 (5):789–804.

GRAIN. 2007. Corporate Power—Agrofuels and the Expansion of Agribusiness. *Seedling*. July. http://www.grain.org/ seedling/?id=478 (accessed April 30, 2009).

GRDC. 2008. *Scientists Share Keys to Drought Tolerance*. Australian

Government Grains Research and Development Corporation. http://www.grdc.com.au/director/events/groundcover.cfm?item_id=A931F5F99CBB129138C3554A201497DC&article_id=D224AACBA71FE327988ED49319CE6772 (accessed January 31, 2009).

Greenpeace España. 2004. *España es la puerta trasera de entrada de transgénicos a Europa*. April 19. http://www.greenpeace.org/espana/news/espa-a-es-la-puerta-trasera-de (accessed January 30, 2009).

Green Revolution. 2008. *The Development of African Agriculture*. http://www.africangreenrevolution.com/en/african_agriculture/development/index.html (accessed October 31, 2008).

Guttal, Shalmali. 2008. *The Four Fold Crisis: Food, Energy, Climate, and Finance Implications for Small-Hold Agriculture*. Presentation to the V International Conference of La Via Campesina, Maputo, Mozambique, October 20, 2008. Focus on the Global South.

Halweil, Brian. 2004. *Eat Here: Reclaiming Homegrown Pleasures in a Global Supermarket*. New York/London: Norton/Worldwatch.

Hansen-Kuhn, Karen. 2007. *Women and Food Crises: How US Food Aid Policies Can Better Support Their Struggles—a Discussion Paper*. Washington DC: ActionAid USA.

Hasan, Hamza. 2007. *The U.S. Ethanol Industry*. Food First. http://www.foodfirst.org/node/1723 (accessed October 14, 2008).

Havnevik, Kjell, Deborah Bryceson, Lars-Erik Birgegard, Prosper Matandi, and Atakilte Beyene. 2007. *African Agriculture and the World Bank: Development or Impoverishment?* Uppsala: Nordic Africa Institute.

Hewitt de Alcántara, Cynthia. 1976. *Modernizing Mexican Agriculture: Socioeconomic Implications of Technological Change 1940–1970*. Geneva: United Nations Research Institute for Social Development.

Ho, Mae-Wan, Sam Burcher, Lim Li Ching et al. 2007. *Food Futures Now *Organic *Sustainable *Fossil Fuel Free*. Institute of Science in Society. http://www.i-sis.org.uk/foodFutures.php (accessed October 23, 2008).

Holt-Giménez, Eric. 2001. *Measuring Farmers' Agroecological Resistance to Hurricane Mitch in Central America*. London: International Institute for Environment and Development.

Holt-Giménez, Eric. 2002. Measuring Farmers' Agroecological Resistance after Hurricane Mitch in Nicaragua: a Case Study in Participatory, Sustainable Land Management Impact Monitoring.

Agriculture, Ecosystems & Environment 93:87–105.

Holt-Giménez, Eric. 2006. *Campesino a Campesino: Voices from Latin America's Farmer to Farmer Movement for Sustainable Agriculture.* Oakland: Food First Books.

Holt-Giménez, Eric. 2007. *Biofuels: Myths of the Agrofuels Transition.* Food First. http://www.foodfirst.org/node/1711 (accessed October 14, 2008).

Holt-Giménez, Eric and Isabella Kenfield. 2008. When Renewable Isn't Sustainable: Agrofuels and the Inconvenient Truths Behind the 2007 U.S. Energy Independence and Security Act. *Food First Policy Brief* 13.

IAASTD. 2008. *IAASTD Reports*. International Assessment of Agricultural Knowledge, Science and Technology for Development. http://www.agassessment.org/index. cfm?Page=IAASTD%20Reports&ItemID=2713 (October 16, 2008).

IDA. 2006a. International Development Association Program Document for a Proposed Credit In the Amount of SDR 16.83 Million (U.S.$25 Million Equivalent) to the Republic of Nicaragua for a Second Poverty Reduction Support Credit. World Bank. http://www-wds.worldbank.org/servlet/WDSContentServer/ IW3P/IB/2006/10/18//000090341_20061018085549/Rendered/ INDEX/37404.txt (accessed October 14, 2008).

IDA. 2006b. Program Document for Proposed Poverty Reduction Support Credit in the Amount of SDR 6.8 Million (U.S.$10 Million Equivalent) to the Republic of Moldova. Washington DC: World Bank Group.

IDA. 2007a. Program Document for a Proposed Credit in the Amount of Sdr 127.6 Million (U.S.$190 Million Equivalent) to United Republic of Tanzania for a Fifth Poverty Reduction Support Credit (PRSC-5). Washington DC: World Bank Group.

IDA. 2007b. Program Document Regarding a Proposed Fourth Poverty Reduction Support Credit (PRSC-4) to the Republic of Benin (Ida/R2007-0138). Washington DC: World Bank Group.

IFAD. 2008. *Food Prices: Smallholder Farmers Can Be Part of the Solution*. IFAD. http://www.ifad.org/operations/food/factsheet/ food_e.pdf (accessed November 11, 2008).

IFDC. 2008. High Fertilizer Prices, Shortages Cause Worldwide Social Unrest: An International Center for Soil Fertility & Agricultural Development. http://www.ifdc.org/focusonfertlizer7. html (accessed October 16, 2008).

IFPRI. 2000. *Women: The Key to Food Security. 8 Findings.*
International Food Policy Research Institute. www.ifpri.org/pubs/
ib/ib3.pdf (accessed January 15, 2009).

IISD. 2006. *Biofuels: At What Cost? Government Support for Ethanol
and Biodiesel in the United States.* Geneva: International Institute
for Sustainable Development (Global Subsidies Initiative). http://
www.globalsubsidies.org/files/assets/Brochure_-_US_Update.pdf
(accessed April 8, 2009).

Intermón Oxfam. 2005. *Goliat contra David. Quién gana y quién
pierde con la PAC en España y en los países pobres.* March.
http://www.intermonoxfam.org/UnidadesInformacion/
anexos/2970/0_2970_170305_Goliat_contra_David.pdf (accessed
January 30, 2009).

International Trade Administration. 2008. *Free Trade Agreements.*
http://www.trade.gov/fta/ (accessed October 29, 2008).

IPCC. 2007. *Climate Change 2007 Synthesis Report. adopted Valencia
Spain November 2007.* http://www.ipcc.ch/ipccreports/ar4-syr.htm
(accessed October 21, 2008).

Jarvis, Devra et al. 2008. A Global Perspective of the Richness and
Evenness of Traditional Crop-Variety Diversity Maintained by
Farming Communities. *Proceedings of the National Academy of
Sciences* 105 (14):5326–31.

Jennings, Bruce H. 1988. *Foundations of International Agricultural
Research: Sciences and Politics in Mexican Agriculture.* Boulder:
Westview Press.

Jung-a, Song and Christian Oliver. 2008. Daewoo to Cultivate
Madagascar Land for Free. *Financial Times.* November 19.

Kapur, Devesh, John P. Lewis and Richard Webb. 2007. *The
World Bank: Its First Half Century.* Washington DC: Brookings
Institution.

Koont, Sinan. 2009. The Urban Agriculture of Havana. *Monthly
Review* 60 (8).

Kothari, Smitu and Benny Kuruvilla. 2008."*There is no alternative to
socialism.*" *An Interview with Egyptian Economist Samir Amin.* Focus
on the Global South. http://focusweb.org/there-is-no-alternative-
to-socialism.html?Itemid=1 (accessed December 29, 2008).

La Via Campesina. 2008 *La Via Campesina Release Regarding the WTO
Bilateral and Mini Ministerial Meeting.* Via Campesina. http://
www.viacampesina.org/main_en/index.php?option=com_content
&task=view&id=586&Itemid=35 (accessed August 24, 2008).

Lamy, Pascal. 2008. No One is Throwing in the Towel: Audio Statement by Pascal Lamy. World Trade Organization. http://www.wto.org/audio/2008_07_31_gc_dgstat.mp3 (accessed May 4, 2009).

Lappé, Frances Moore, Joseph Collins and Peter Rosset. 1998. *World Hunger: Twelve Myths*. 2nd ed. New York: Food First.

Lappé, Frances Moore, Joseph Collins, Peter Rosset, and Luis Esparza. 1986. *World Hunger: 12 Myths*. Oakland: Institute for Food and Development Policy.

LaSalle, Tim and Paul Hepperly. 2008. *Regenerative Organic Farming: A Solution to Global Warming*. Rodale Institute. http://www.rodaleinstitute.org/files/Rodale_Research_Paper-07_30_08.pdf (accessed April 8, 2009).

Lean, Geoffrey. 2008a. Rising Prices Threaten Millions with Starvation, Despite Bumper Crops. *The Independent*. http://www.independent.co.uk/environment/green-living/rising-prices-threaten-millions-with-starvation-despite-bumper-crops-790319.html (accessed March 2, 2008).

Lean, Geoffrey. 2008b. Multinationals Make Billions in Profit out of Growing Global Food Crisis. *The Independent*. http://www.independent.co.uk/environment/green-living/multinationals-make-billions-in-profit-out-of-growing-global-food-crisis-820855.html (accessed October 14, 2008).

Masters, M.W. and A.K. White. 2008. *How Institutional Investors Are Driving Up Food And Energy Prices*. The Accidental Hunt Brothers Special Report. Living on Earth Radio. http://www.loe.org/images/080919/Act1.pdf (accessed May 4, 2009).

Matthews, Christopher 2008. The World Only Needs 30 Billion Dollars a Year to Eradicate the Scourge of Hunger. Time for Talk Over—Action Needed. Review of Reviewed Item. *FAO Newsroom*. http://www.fao.org/newsroom/en/news/2008/1000853/index.html (accessed April 8, 2009).

McMichael, Philip. 2004. Global Development and the Corporate Food Regime - Symposium on New Directions in the Sociology of Global Development. *XI World Congress of Rural Sociology* (Trondheim).

Miller, Morris. 1991. *Debt and the Environment: Converging Crisis*. New York: United Nations.

Mitchell, Paul D. 2008. *The New Farm Bill: New Programs and New Requirements*. University of Wisconsin, Madison Extension.

September 10. www.aae.wisc.edu/mitchell/CropInsurance/ NewFarmBillRequirements.ppt (accessed April 9, 2009).

Monbiot, George. 2007. If We Want to Save the Planet, We Need A Five-Year Freeze on Biofuels. *The Guardian*. March 27.

Moore, Melissa. 2005. *CAFTA—The Central American Free Trade Agreement*. Food First. http://www.foodfirst.org/en/node/183 (accessed September 19, 2008).

Mortimore, M.J. and W.M. Adams. 2001. Farmer Adaptation, Change and Crisis in the Sahel. *Global Environmental Change*.1 (11):49–57.

Nagayets, Oksana. 2005. Small Farms: Current Status and Key Trends. In *Information Brief Prepared for the Future of Small Farms Research Workshop Wye College, June 26–29*. Washington DC: International Food Policy Research Institute.

National Farmers Union. 2008. *Farmers Share*. National Farmers Union. http://nfu.org/issues/agriculture-programs/resources/ farmers-share (acessed October 14, 2008).

NFFC. 2008. *Press Release: U.S. Family Farmers Applaud Demise of Doha Negotiations*. National Family Farm Coalition. http://www. foodfirst.org/en/node/2208 (accessed August 14, 2008).

Ng, Francis and M. Ataman Aksoy. 2008. *Who are the Net Food Importing Countries?* Edited by Development Research Group Trade Team. Washington DC: World Bank.

Nierenberg, Danielle. 2004. The Commercialization of Farming: Producing Meat for a Hungry World. *USA Today*. January 22.

O'Keefe, Phil, Ken Westgate and Ben Wisner. 1976. Taking the Naturalness Out of Natural Disasters. *Nature*. 15:566–77.

OECD. 2007. *Aid Effectiveness: 2006 Survey on Monitoring the Paris Declaration: Overview of the Results*. Paris: OECD.

Ortega, E. 1986. *Peasant Agriculture in Latin America*. Santiago: Joint ECLAC/FAO Agriculture Division.

Oxfam. 2006. *Causing Hunger: An Overview of the Food Crisis in Africa*. Oxford: Oxfam International.

Oxfam. 2007. Climate Alarm: Disasters Increase as Climate Change Bites. *Oxfam International Briefing Paper* 108.

Paasch, Armin, F. Garbers and Thomas Hirsch. 2007. *Trade Policies and Hunger: The Impact of Trade Liberalisation on the Right to Food of Rice Farming Communities in Ghana, Honduras and Indonesia*. Geneva: Ecumenical Advocacy Alliance (EAA) and FoodFirst Information and Action Network (FIAN).

Pacific Institute. 2008. *Water Data and The World's Water*. World Water. http://www.worldwater.org/data.html (accessed October 14, 2008).

Patel, Raj. 2007. *Stuffed and Starved*. London: Portobello Books.

Pearse, A. 1980. *Seeds of Plenty, Seeds of Want: Social and Economic Implications of the Green Revolution*. Oxford: Clarendon Press.

Pieterse, Jan Nederveen. 1998. My Paradigm or Yours? Alternative Development, Post-Development, Reflexive Development. *Development and Change* 29:343–73.

Pimentel, D. and Marcia Pimentel. 1990. Comment: Adverse Environmental Consequences of the Green Revolution. *Population and Development Review* 329–32.

Posey, Lee. 2008. *Agriculture, Environment & Energy Federal Update: 2008 Farm Bill Report*. National Conference on State Legislators. http://www.ncsl.org/standcomm/scagee/AEEFederalUpdate2008FarmBillReport.htm (accessed September 25, 2008).

Preston, P.W. 1996. *Development Theory*. Oxford: Blackwell.

Pretty, J. N., J. I. L. Morison and R.E. Hine. 2003. Reducing Food Poverty by Increasing Agricultural Sustainability in Developing Countries. *Agriculture, Ecosystems & Environment* 87–105.

Pretty, Jules, and Rachel Hine, and Sophia Twarog. 2008. *Organic Agriculture and Food Security in Africa*. UNEP-UNCTAD Capacity-building Task Force on Trade. New York and Geneva: United Nations Conference on Trade and Development/ United Nations Environment Programme.

Quist, David and Ignacio Chapela. 2001. Transgenic DNA Introgressed into Traditional Maize Landraces in Oaxaca, Mexico. *Nature* 414:541–3.

Rapley, J. 1996. *Understanding Development: Theory and Practice in the Third World*. Boulder and London: Lynne Rienner Publishers.

Reij, C., I. Scoones and C. Toulmin. 1996. Sustaining the Soil: Indigenous Soil and Water Conservation in Africa. London: Earthscan.

RFA. 2009. *Industry Statistics*. Renewable Fuels Association. http://www.ethanolrfa.org/industry/locations/ (accessed April 13, 2009).

Roberts, Michael and Nigel Key. 2008. Agricultural Payments and Land Concentration: A Semiparametric Spatial Regression Analysis. *American Journal of Agricultural Economics* 90 (3):627–43.

Rockefeller Foundation. 2007. *Africa's Turn: A New Green Revolution for the Twenty-first Century*. The Rockefeller Foundation. http://www.rockfound.org/library/africas_turn.pdf (accessed August 15, 2008).

Rosegrant, M. W. and Prabhu L. Pingali. 1994. *Confronting the Environmental Consequences of the Green Revolution in Asia "Urban Development in the Philippines."* Washington DC and Philippines: World Bank and IFPRI.

Rosset, P.M., R. Patel and M. Courville. 2006. *Promised Land: Competing Visions of Agrarian Reform*. Oakland: Food First Books.

Rosset, Peter M. 1999. The Multiple Functions and Benefits of Small Farm Agriculture In the Context of Global Trade Negotiations. *Policy Brief* 4. Food First/Institute for Food and Development Policy, http://www.foodfirst.org/en/node/246 (accessed April 8, 2009).

Rosset, Peter M. 2006. *Food is Different: Why We Must Get the WTO Out of Agriculture*. New York: Zed Books.

Rosset, Peter. 2007. *Food Is Different: Why We Must Get the WTO Out of Agriculture*. Halifax and London: Fernwood and Zed Books.

Rossi, Andrea and Yianna Lambrou. 2008. *Gender and Equity Issues in Liquid Biofuels Production: Minimizing the Risks to Maximize the Opportunities*. Rome: Food and Agricultural Organization of the United Nations.

Rostow, W. W. 1960. *The Stages of Economic Growth: A Non-Communist Manifesto*. Cambridge: Cambridge University Press.

Runge, C. Ford and Benjamin Senauer. 2007. How Biofuels Could Starve the Poor. *Foreign Affairs* May/June.

Sayre, Laura. 2003. Organic Farming Combats Global Warming… Big Time. In *New Farm Field Trials*. Rodale Institute. http://newfarm.rodaleinstitute.org/depts/NFfield_trials/1003/carbonsequest_print.shtml (accessed April 8, 2009).

Scott, Robert E. 2003. *The High Price of "Free" Trade: NAFTA's Failure has Cost the United States Jobs Across the Nation*. Economic Policy Institute. http://www.epi.org/content.cfm/briefingpapers_bp147 (accessed July 20, 2008).

Searchinger, Timothy and Ralph Heimlich, R. A. Houghton, Fengxia Dong, Amani Elobeid, Jacinto Fabiosa, Simla Tokgoz, Dermot Hayes, Tun-Hsiang Yu. 2008. Use of U.S. Croplands for Biofuels Increases Greenhouse Gases Through Emissions from Land-Use Change. *Science* 319 (5867):1238–40.

Shiva, Vandana. 1991. *The Violence of the Green Revolution*. London: Zed Books.

Shiva, Vandana. 2008. *The Food Emergency and Food Myths: Why Bush is Wrong to Blame Indians for the Rise in Food Prices*. GRAIN. http://www.grain.org/seedling/?id=552 (October 29, 2008).

Singh, R.B. 2000. Environmental Consequences of Agricultural Development: A Case Study from the Green Revolution State of Haryana, India. *Agriculture, Ecosystems and Environment* 82:97–103.

Smithfield Foods. 2008. Smithfield Foods Announces the Sale of 4.95 Percent of Shares to China's Largest National Agricultural Trading and Processing Company COFCO Limited. Smithfield Foods. http://investors.smithfieldfoods.com/releasedetail.cfm?ReleaseID=319052 (acessed October 14, 2008).

Soil Association. 2005. *Cultivating Communities: Farming at Your Fingertips*. Bristol: Soil Association.

Soler, M. 2007. OMC, PAC y globalización alimentaria. *Viento Sur* 94:37–43.

Sonntag, H. et.al. 2000. Modernism, Development and Modernization. *Pensamiento Propio* 11 (Jan–Jun):3–30.

Spencer, D. 2002. The Future of Agriculture in Sub-Saharan Africa and South Asia: W(h)ither the Small Farm? In *Sustainable Food Security for All by 2020*. Proceedings of an International Conference, September 4–6, 2001, Bonn, Germany. International Food Policy Research Institute.

Steinfeld, Henning, Pierre Gerber, Tom Wassenaar, Vincent Castel, Mauricio Rosales and Cees de Haan. 2006. *Livestock's Long Shadow; Environmental Issues and Options*. Edited by LEAD. Rome: Food and Agriculture Organization.

Stern Review. 2007. *The Economics of Climate Change*. London and Cambridge: HM Treasury and Cambridge University Press.

Thompson, Herb. 2007. Grains in China: Foodgrain, Feedgrain and World Trade. *Journal of Contemporary Asia* 37 (4):524.

Thorpe, Kenneth E., Curtis S. Florence, David H. Howard and Peter Joski. 2004. Trends: The Impact Of Obesity On Rising Medical Spending. *Health Affairs* 10.

Tillman, David and Jason Hill. 2007. Corn Ethanol Can't Solve Our Climate and Energy Problems. *Washington Post*. March 25.

Tyson Foods Inc. 2008. *Tyson Enters Third Poultry Joint Venture in China ; Venture Involves Vertically-Integrated Operations in Eastern*

China. Tyson. http://www.tyson.com/Corporate/PressRoom/
ViewArticle.aspx?id=3035 (accessed October 14, 2008).

UNIFEM. 2005. *Investing in Women—Solving the Poverty Puzzle Facts
and Figures*. United Nations Development Fund for Women and
Women's Funding Network. http://www.wfnet.org/resource/fact-
sheet/poverty-fact-sheet (accessed January 15, 2008).

University of Georgia College of Agriculture and Environmental
Sciences. 2008. *Changes in U.S. Agriculture; From the 1950's to
the 1990's*. The University of Georgia. http://www.ces.uga.edu/
Agriculture/agecon/pubs/agric50-90.htm (accessed October 14,
2008).

Uphoff, N. 1999. Agroecological Implications of the System of Rice
Intensification (SRI) in Madagascar. *Environment, Development and
Sustainability* 1 (Netherlands):297–313.

USDA. 2002. *Census of Agriculture*. Washington DC: National
Agricultural Statistics Service, US Department of Agriculture.

USDA. 2008a. *Food Security Assessment, 2007*. Washington DC:
Agriculture and Trade Reports United States Depeartment of
Agriculture. http://www.ers.usda.gov/Publications/GFA19/
GFA19fm.pdf (Accessed April 8, 2009).

USDA. 2008b. *USDA Agricultural Projections to 2017*. Washington
DC: Office of the Chief Economist, World Agricultural Outlook
Board, United States Department of Agriculture.

USDA. 2008c. *Adoption of Genetically Engineered Crops in the U.S.*
USDA Economic Research Service. http://www.ers.usda.gov/
Data/BiotechCrops/alltables.xls (accessed April 8, 2009).

USDA. 2008d. *Farmer's Market Growth 1994-2008. Wholesale and
Farmers Markets*. Washington DC: Agricultural Marketing Service.
US Department of Agriculture. http://www.ams.usda.gov/
AMSv1.0/ams.fetchTemplateData.do?template=TemplateS&navI
D=WholesaleandFarmersMarkets&leftNav=WholesaleandFarme
rsMarkets&page=WFMFarmersMarketGrowth&description=Far
mers%20Market%20Growth&acct=frmrdirmkt (accessed April 8,
2009).

von Braun, Joachim. 2007. *Rising Food Prices Threaten the World's
Poor People*. Washington DC: International Food Policy Research
Institute. http://www.ifpri.org/pressrel/2007/20071204.asp
(accessed December 4, 2008).

Vorley, Billy. 2003. *Food Inc.: Corporate Concentration From Farm to
Consumer*. United Kingdom Food Group. http://www.ukfg.org.

uk/docs/UKFG-Foodinc-Nov03.pdf (accessed July 15, 2008).

Watkins, K. 2003. Northern Agricultural Policies and World Poverty: Will the Doha 'Development Round' Make a Difference? Paper read at the Annual World Bank Conference on Development Economics, Paris.

Weitzman, Hal. 2008. Ill Wind Bends Corn-Belt to Obama. *Financial Times* October 15.

WFP. 2008. *Overview of Operations 2008*. World Food Program. http://www.wfp.org/appeals/projected_needs/documents/2008/Overview.pdf (accessed October 29, 2008).

Wiggins, Steve and Stephanie Levy. 2008. *Rising Food Prices: A Global Crisis*. London: Overseas Development Institute.

Williams-Walsh, Mary. 2008. A Question for A.I.G.: Where Did the Cash Go? *The New York Times* November 3.

Woods, Ngaire. 2006. *The Globalizers: the IMF, the World Bank, and their Borrowers*. Ithaca: Cornell University Press.

World Bank. 2003. *The CGIAR at 31: An Independent Meta-Evaluation of the Consultative Group on International Agricultural Research*. Washington DC: The World Bank.

World Bank. 2007. *World Bank Assistance to Agriculture in Sub Saharan Africa: An Independent Evaluation Group Review*. Washington DC: World Bank.

World Bank. 2008a. *Rising Food Prices: Policy Options and World Bank Response*. World Bank. http://siteresources.worldbank.org/NEWS/Resources/risingfoodprices_backgroundnote_apr08.pdf (accessed September 25, 2008).

World Bank. 2008b. *World Development Report 2008: Agriculture for Development*. Washington DC: The World Bank Group.

World Bank. 2008c. *World Bank Launches $1.2 Billion Fast-Track Facility for Food Crisis*. World Bank. http://web.worldbank.org/WBSITE/EXTERNAL/NEWS/0,,contentMDK:21783685~pagePK:64257043~piPK:437376~theSitePK:4607,00.html (accessed November 11 2008).

Zhu, Y., H. Fen, Y. Wang, Y. Li, J. Chen, L. Hu and C.C. Mundt. 2000. Genetic Diversity and Disease Control in Rice. *Nature* 406:718–72.

Ziegler, Jean. 2007. *The Right to Food, Report of the Special Rapporteur on the Right to Food*. United Nations General Assembly, A/62/289. http://www.righttofood.org/A62289.pdf (accessed August 22, 2008).

Zigomo, Muchena. 2008. *Stakes High For South African Land*

Reform. Reuters. http://www.reuters.com/article/worldNews/ idUSTRE49804T20081009 (accessed February 2, 2009).

Zimbalist, Zach. 2007. Colombia Palm Oil Biodiesel Plantations: A "Lose-Lose" Development Strategy? *Food First Backgrounder* 13 (4).

Zoellick, Robert B. 2008 *A Challenge of Economic Statecraft*. Center for Global Development. April 2, 2008. http://web.worldbank.org/ WBSITE/EXTERNAL/NEWS/0,,contentMDK:21711307~pagePK:3 4370~piPK:42770~theSitePK:4607,00.html>> (accessed January 30, 2009).

Index

About the authors

Eric Holt-Giménez is executive director of Food First/Institute for Food and Development Policy. He is the author of *Campesino a Campesino: Voices from Latin America's Farmer to Farmer Movement for Sustainable Agriculture*, which chronicles two and a half decades of farmers' movements in Mexico and Central America. Trained in political economy and agroecology, Eric has worked as a rural organizer, trainer, researcher, and professor of development studies in countries of Latin America, Asia, Africa and the United States for over 30 years.

Raj Patel is an activist, academic, and author of the critically acclaimed *Stuffed and Starved: Markets, Power and the Hidden Battle for the World Food System*. He is an honorary research fellow at the University of KwaZulu-Natal and works with the South African Shackdwellers' movement, Abahlali baseMjondolo. He is also a fellow at Food First and a visiting scholar at the Center for African Studies at the University of California, Berkeley. He has degrees from Cornell, the London School of Economics, and Oxford University.

More books from Pambazuka Press

Available at www.pambazukapress.org

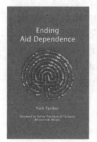

Ending Aid Dependence

Yash Tandon

'The message of this book needs to be seriously considered and debated by all those that are interested in the development of the countries of the South. If this means the rethinking of old concepts and methods of work, then let it be so'
Benjamin W. Mkapa, former President of Tanzania (1995–2005)

Developing countries reliant on aid want to escape this dependence, and yet they appear unable to do so. This book shows how they may liberate themselves from the aid that pretends to be developmental but is not.

ISBN: 978-1-906387-31-0

September 2008   £9.95   158pp

Where is Uhuru?

Reflections on the Struggle for Democracy in Africa

Issa G. Shivji

Edited by Godwin R. Murunga

The neoliberal project promised to engender development and prosperity and expand democratic space in Africa. However, several decades on its reforms have delivered on few of its promises. Whether one is examining the rewards of multiparty politics, the dividends from a new constitutional dispensation, the processes of land reform, women's rights to property or the pan-Africanist project for emancipation, Issa G. Shivji, Mwalimu Nyerere Professor of African Studies at the University of Dar es Salaam, illustrates how these have all suffered severe body blows. Where, indeed, is Uhuru?

ISBN: 978-1-906387-46-4

April 2009   £16.95   257pp

Aid to Africa: Redeemer or Coloniser?

Edited by Hakima Abbas and Yves Niyiragira

This book offers a critical analysis of aid to Africa. The authors examine the framework of aid from 'traditional' Western donors while investigating how the emergence of new donors to Africa has changed the international aid discourse. The uniquely African perspectives in this book provide both a framework for reshaping aid and an alternative development paradigm rooted in Africa's self-determination. Contributing authors to this volume include Samir Amin, Patrick Bond and Demba Moussa Dembele.

ISBN: 978-1-906387-38-9   July 2009   £12.95

The Crash of International Finance Capital and its Implications for the Third World

Dani Wadada Nabudere

This book first appeared in 1987 following the Black Monday crash. With new material on contemporary conditions in the global economy, this re-issue argues that capitalism exists in a permanent state of crisis, a crisis which will ultimately escalate into a megacrisis for which world leaders will have little in the way of a solution. Are we in that crisis now?

ISBN: 978-1-906387-43-3   September 2009   £16.95

SMS Uprising: Mobile Activism in Africa

Edited by Sokari Ekine

Activists in Africa are using mobile technology to organise and document their experiences so the phones' capabilities are having a dynamic influence on their aims and strategies. This book's authors – activists, academics and technology specialists – look at inequalities in access to technology based on gender and rural and urban usage, and consider how mobile phones' increasing integration with the internet helps activists internationalise their struggles.

ISBN: 978-1-906387-35-8   October 2009   £9.95

More books from Food First

Beyond the Fence
A Journey to the Roots of the Migration Crisis
Dori Stone

This book examines how U.S./Mexico policy affects families, farmers, and businesses on both sides of the border, exposing irretrievable losses, but also hopeful advances. Companion DVD, *Caminos: The Immigrant's Trail*, with study guide.

Paperback, $16.95

Agrofuels in the Americas
Edited by Rick Jonasse

This book takes a critical look at the recent expansion of the agrofuels industry in the U.S. and Latin America and its effect on hunger, labor rights, trade and the environment.

Paperback, $18.95

Alternatives to the Peace Corps
A Guide to Global Volunteer Opportunities, Twelfth Edition
Edited by Caitlin Hachmyer

Newly expaned and updated, this easy-to-use guidebook is the original resource for finding community-based, grassroots volunteer work—the kind of work that changes the world, one person at a time.

Paperback, $11.95

Campesino a Campesino
Voices from Latin America's Farmer to Farmer Movement for Sustainable Agriculture
Eric Holt-Giménez

The voices and stories of dozens of farmers are captured in this first written history of the farmer-to-farmer movement, which describes the social, political, economic and environmental circumstances that shape it.

Paperback, $19.95

Promised Land
Competing Visions of Agrarian Reform
Edited by Peter Rosset, Raj Patel and Michael Courville

Agrarian reform is back at the center of the national and rural development debate. The essays in this volume critically analyze a wide range of competing visions of land reform.

Paperback, $21.95

Sustainable Agriculture and Resistance
Transforming Food Production in Cuba
Edited by Fernando Funes, Luis García, Martin Bourque, Nilda Pérez and Peter Rosset

Unable to import food or farm chemicals and machines in the wake of the Soviet bloc's collapse and a tightening U.S. embargo, Cuba turned toward sustainable agriculture, organic farming, urban gardens and other techniques to secure its food supply. This book gives details of that remarkable achievement.

Paperback, $18.95

The Future in the Balance
Essays on Globalization and Resistance
Walden Bello. Edited with a preface by Anuradha Mittal

A collection of essays by global south activist and scholar Walden Bello on the myths of development as prescribed by the World Trade Organization and other institutions, and the possibility of another world based on fairness and justice.

Paperback, $13.95

Views from the South
The Effects of Globalization and the WTO on Third World Countries
Edited by Sarah Anderson
Foreword by Jerry Mander. Afterword by Anuradha Mittal

This rare collection of essays by activists and scholars from the global south describes, in pointed detail, the effects of the WTO and other Bretton Woods institutions.

Paperback, $12.95

Basta!
Land and the Zapatista Rebellion in Chiapas, Third Edition
George A. Collier with Elizabeth Lowery-Quaratiello
Foreword by Peter Rosset

> The classic on the Zapatistas in its third edition, including a preface by Rodolfo Stavenhagen.

> Paperback, $16.95

America Needs Human Rights
Edited by Anuradha Mittal and Peter Rosset

> This anthology includes writings on understanding human rights, poverty and welfare reform in America.

> Paperback, $13.95

The Paradox of Plenty
Hunger in a Bountiful World
Edited by Douglas H. Boucher

> Excerpts from Food First's best writings on world hunger and what we can do to change it.

> Paperback, $18.95

Education for Action
Undergraduate and Graduate Programs that Focus on Social Change
Fourth Edition
Edited by Joan Powell

> An updated authoritative and easy-to-use guidebook that provides information on progressive programs in a wide variety of fields.

> Paperback, $12.95

We encourage you to buy Food First Books from your local independent bookseller; if they don't have them in stock, they can usually order them for you fast. To find an independent bookseller in your area, go to www.booksense.com.

Food First books are also available through major online booksellers

(Powell's, Amazon, and Barnes and Noble), and through the Food First website, www.foodfirst.org. You can also order direct from our distributor, Perseus Distribution, at (800) 343-4499. If you have trouble locating a Food First title, write, call, or e-mail us:

Food First
398 60th Street
Oakland, CA 94618-1212 USA
Tel: (510) 654-4400
Fax: (510) 654-4551
E-mail: foodfirst@foodfirst.org
Web: www.foodfirst.org

If you are a bookseller or other reseller, contact our distributor, Perseus Distribution, at (800) 343-4499, to order.

Films from Food First

The Greening of Cuba
Jaime Kibben

A profiling of Cuban farmers and scientists working to reinvent a sustainable agriculture based on ecological principles and local knowledge.
DVD (In Spanish with English subtitles), $35.00

America Needs Human Rights

A film told in the voices of welfare mothers, homeless men and women, low-wage workers, seniors, veterans and health care workers.
DVD, $19.95

Caminos: The Immigrant's Trail
Juan Carlos Zaldivar

Stories of Mexican farmers who were driven off their land, forced to leave their families and risk their lives to seek work in the U.S.
DVD and Study Guide, $20.00

How to Become a Member or Intern of Food First

Join Food First

Private contributions and membership gifts fund the core of Food First/Institute for Food and Development Policy's work. Each member strengthens Food First's efforts to change a hungry world. We invite you to join Food First. As a member you will receive a 20 percent discount on all Food First books. You will also receive our quarterly publications, Food First News and Views and Backgrounders, providing information for action on current food and hunger issues in the United States and around the world. If you want to subscribe to our Internet newsletter, People Putting Food First, send us an e-mail at foodfirst@foodfirst.org. All contributions are tax deductible.

You are also invited to give a gift membership to others interested in the fight to end hunger. www.foodfirst.org

Become an Intern for Food First

There are opportunities for interns in research, advocacy, campaigning, publishing, computers, media and publicity at Food First. Our interns come from around the world. They are a vital part of the organization and make our work possible.

To become a member or apply to become an intern, just call or visit our website: www.foodfirst.org.